THE ORATION IN SHAKESPEARE

The Oration
IN
Shakespeare

MILTON BOONE KENNEDY

CHAPEL HILL

The University of North Carolina Press

1942

Copyright, 1942, by
THE UNIVERSITY OF NORTH CAROLINA PRESS

To

LANCELOT MINOR HARRIS

and

JOHN CALVIN METCALF

Preface

THE PRESENT VOLUME has grown out of a master's essay on "The Oration in the Early Elizabethan Drama," written at the suggestion of Professor L. M. Harris at the College of Charleston. This essay led later to a master's thesis written at Columbia University on "The Oration in Shakespeare." The Columbia thesis developed into a doctoral dissertation at the University of Virginia, which has been revised and is here presented in book form.

The line of investigation—definition, classification, structure, and dramatic integration—is that suggested originally by Mr. Harris, who suggested also that the practice of writing orations in Elizabethan plays might be traced to the study of the classics in the schools. A reference to Ebisch and Schucking's *Shakespearean Bibliography* reveals that work has been done on the Monologue, Dialogue, and Chorus (German monographs), and on the *Soliloquies of Shakespeare* in the monograph by Arnold; but nothing has been recorded on the oration.

In a field so carefully worked over for years by specialists as is the field of Elizabethan literature, I am, of course, following where many, many others have led. I have attempted, in my bibliography and notes, to give credit to others for assistance in writing this book. Particularly here would I name, in Elizabethan Drama, Ashley Horace Thorndike; in rhetoric and poetic, Charles Sears Baldwin and Donald L. Clark; in Aristotle's *Poetics*, Lane Cooper and Marvin Herrick.

Preface

It is a source of great pleasure to make acknowledgment here of the courtesies and help extended me by the libraries in which I have worked: The Charleston Library, The Libraries of Columbia University, The Library of the University of Virginia, Charlottesville Library, Washington Public Libraries, The Folger Shakespeare Library, The Library of Congress.

There remains the peculiar pleasure to acknowledge my indebtedness and express my appreciation to the members of the English faculty at the University of Virginia, who so generously assisted me while a graduate student there. The writing of the dissertation was done under the direction of John Calvin Metcalf—Dean, teacher, friend. His faith, encouragement, inspiration, and guidance were always mine; and his criticism and guidance in the matter of revision pointed me in the direction of presenting the study in its final form. Professors James Southall Wilson and Atcheson Laughlin Hench read, with Dr. Metcalf, the first draft of my dissertation and worked out with me its final form. I wish here to express my gratitude to these of my committee for their interest and criticism in the writing of the monograph.

MILTON B. KENNEDY

Kentucky Wesleyan College
Winchester, Kentucky
April 23, 1941

Contents

Preface	vii
I. Rhetoric in Poetic	3
II. The Oration in the Drama	26
III. Sophistic Rhetoric in Shakespeare	37
IV. Classification and Sources	63
V. Structure of Orations	103
VI. Dramatic Integration	148
VII. Elizabethan Oratory	166
VIII. Elizabethan Education	198
IX. Literary Criticism	217
X. Shakespeare and Rhetoric in Poetic	247
Bibliography	250
Index	261

THE ORATION IN SHAKESPEARE

CHAPTER I

Rhetoric in Poetic

AFTER DWELLING AT LENGTH upon what he emphasized as the primary element in tragedy, the element of plot action, Aristotle, in his *Poetics*, devotes a small section to what he calls the subsidiary element of thought, the rhetorical element:

"It remains to speak of the Diction and Thought, the other parts of Tragedy having been already discussed. Concerning the Thought, we may assume what is said in the Rhetoric; to which inquiry the subject more strictly belongs. Under Thought is included every effect which has to be produced by speech; in particular,—proof and refutation; the excitation of the feelings, such as pity, fear, and anger, and the like; the heightening or extenuating of facts. Further, it is evident that the dramatic incidents must be treated from the same points of view as the dramatic speeches, when the object is to evoke the sense of pity, fear, grandeur, or probability. The only difference is that the incidents should speak for themselves without verbal exposition; while the effects aimed at in a speech should be produced by the speaker, and as a result of the speech. For what were the need of a speaker, if the proper impression were at once conveyed, quite apart from what he says."[1]

From this it can be clearly seen that, for Aristotle, rhetoric in poetic meant the introduction of a minor movement in the course of a major movement; and too much cannot be made at the outset of the fact that, for Aristotle, rhetoric in this connection is a subsidiary and not a primary movement. In the

1. Chapter XIX; translation by Butcher.

next place, it is important to note that, when this rhetorical element is introduced into tragedy, the movement is one of thought expressed in speech rather than one of action brought about by character and circumstance. Then, for Aristotle, this kind of rhetorical speech was persuasive speech, speech designed to further the interests of the plot by swaying an audience, as distinct from other kinds of speech which helped to further the plot action through reciprocal exchange of ideas as in conversation. Thus, the introduction of rhetoric in poetic for Aristotle was a point of focusing,[2] which consisted in persuasive thinking.

Moreover, such a conception of the use of rhetoric in poetic points to a clear-cut distinction between the two movements: at the point of focusing, one kind of movement is for the moment suspended and is replaced by another kind. Aristotle regarded the movement of rhetoric as distinct from the movement of poetic; certain characteristics of the one differentiated it from the other. Both the fact that Aristotle treated each primarily as a movement and not a method of construction[3] and the fact that he perceived the two movements as distinct are fundamental ideas about this early ancient conception of rhetoric that are supremely essential to an appreciation and evaluation of the subsequent developments of both in the history of literary criticism.

Separating the two thus in his mind, rhetoric was consid-

2. As will appear through illustrative material in Chapter VI, the idea suggested by Aristotle may be figuratively represented; that is, with the word *focusing*.

3. Professor C. S. Baldwin, in both of his books, *Ancient Rhetoric and Poetic* (hereafter cited *ARP*), and *Medieval Rhetoric and Poetic* (hereafter cited *MRP*), lays stress on the understanding of rhetoric and poetic as movements as a means of keeping the two distinct from one another. I quote some significant sentences from his *Ancient Rhetoric and Poetic:* "We are to think of poetic composition, not as a structure, but as a movement." p. 144.—"From Aristotle's introductory grouping of drama with music and dance, throughout his long discussion of plot, runs the idea of movement." p. 158.—"That the distinction between the *habitual composition*, or *movement*, of rhetoric and that of poetic is not oftener made explicitly by ancient critics need cause little surprise." p. 3.

ered by him as the movement of what we call today, in textbooks on rhetoric, exposition and argument; what we term today narration and description, he considered the movement of poetic. We include, then, as the four forms of prose discourse what Aristotle separated as the movements of prose and poetry. But we must remember that, for Aristotle, prose covered hardly more than oratory or public speaking: what we know as prose fiction, prose narrative, did not exist for him; narrative and description suggested to him epic with its kindred forms and drama. In understanding, then, Aristotle's distinction between rhetoric and poetic, one needs to think not in terms of types of literature so much as in terms of characteristic movements of expression with distinctive appeals. For him the movement of rhetoric makes its appeal primarily to the intellect through logical reasoning; the movement of poetic makes its appeal primarily to the emotions through exercise of the imagination.[4] The line of demarcation

4. It is very important to realize that no hard and fast rules of definition can ever be laid down for literary types, and much depends on the words "characteristic movements" and "primarily." Moreover, it is equally important to distinguish between the rhetoric of oratory, the kind of rhetoric with which this study is chiefly concerned, and emotional rhetoric, which is discussed in Chapter III. Then, too, there is what has been called the "Rhetoric of Verse." For a discussion of this kind of rhetoric see Wightman Fletcher Melton, *The Rhetoric of John Donne's Verse*. Two passages will indicate the point of view. The title is suggested by Professor Bright, who gives this definition:

"By the rhetoric of verse, or the rhetoric of poetry, is meant the emphasis elicited by verse-stress, when it is at variance with the usual (prose) emphasis." p. 103. "The rule by which Donne seems to have worked, was: When a word, a syllable, or a sound, appears in arsis, get it into thesis as quickly as possible, and *vice versa:* having twisted, pressed, or screwed (Coleridge uses all three of these words in his quatrain) all the meaning out of that word, take up another and carry it through the same process. Better still, instead of pressing one word at a time, whenever convenient, take a whole handful of words and twist them so that men will not find out for centuries what it all means." p. 148. Compare the kind of rhetoric Melton is speaking of with the rhetoric of oratory in the drama of which Aristotle is thinking when he says:

"Third in order (after plot and character) is thought, that is, the faculty of saying what is possible and pertinent in given circumstances. In the case of oratory, this is the function of the political wit and of

is thus clearly drawn between the *rhetoric* of the orations of Demosthenes on the one hand and the *poetic* of the epics of Homer and of the tragedies of Aeschylus, Sophocles, and Euripides on the other: the dominant movement of the one is a logical appeal to one's reason; that of the other, an emotional appeal to one's feelings. However, while Aristotle clearly perceived the distinction between the two movements, he none the less realized the inevitableness and desirability of the blending of the two. His section on rhetoric included in his treatise on poetic has already been mentioned. He likewise recognized the part played by the element of poetic in rhetoric by devoting the greatest part of the third book of his treatise on rhetoric to a discussion of style—prose rhythm and prose diction, and the use of figures in prose—and by pointing out that stylistic appeal is peculiarly characteristic of poetry. Rhetoric, then, makes use of the poetic appeal; but Aristotle is careful to make it plain that the element of style is, for the purposes of rhetoric, a subsidiary element, and even goes so far as to differentiate between prose style, the style of public address, and the style of poetry, that of tragedy and epic. The blending of the two movements is thus recognized by Aristotelian criticism; the proportions of the blending give dominant tone to the movements and differentiate rhetorical movement from poetical.

In literary composition, the two movements have always been freely woven together. The movement of rhetoric emerges in the course of the movement of poetic when exposition and argument halt, for the moment, narrative and de-

---

the art of rhetoric; and so indeed the older poets make their characters speak the language of civic life; the poets of our time, the language of the rhetoricians. Character is that which reveals moral purpose, showing what kind of things a man chooses or avoids. Speeches, therefore, which do not make this manifest, or in which the speaker does not choose or avoid anything whatever, are not expressive of character. Thought, on the other hand, is found where something is proved to be or not to be, or a general maxim is enunciated."—*Poetics*, VI, Translation by S. H. Butcher, p. 29.

scription; the movement of poetic appears in the course of the movement of rhetoric when description and narrative are interwoven with exposition and argument. The frequency with which the ornately developed set speech is introduced in epic is recalled at once from *The Iliad, The Odyssey, The Aeneid, Beowulf,* and *Paradise Lost*. One example to illustrate both of the literary processes which are being considered is *The Iliad*, which Aristotle had in mind in formulating his treatises of criticism. Into the poetic movement of the epic, rhetoric emerges in the great speech of Andromache,[5] in which she tries to persuade Hector not to return to the field of battle. The dominant tone is argumentative. She argues that his death, which is practically certain, will take away from her, bereft of parents, him who has stood in the place of parents to her, and thus add another grief for her to bear. In view of this and of the fact that others can take the field while he can help to defend Troy, she implores him to stay with her and her child. For the moment, the movement of action is abandoned for the movement of thought. But within this speech of thought there appears the movement of poetic when the speaker recalls in picturesque narrative how both father and mother were taken from her. Applied to the drama, rhetoric is found in poetic when oratory emerges in the course of the development of dramatic action, and poetic is found in rhetoric when lively narrative and picturesque description are interwoven in the fabric of an oration to adorn and set off the plainer tapestry of exposition and argument. In Sophocles,[6] the moving speech of Oedipus delivered at the moment of discovery of the imminent fulfilment of the prophecy furnishes an example of Aristotle's rhetorical element in tragedy; the long picturesque narrative of his life is an instance of the blending of the movement of poetic with the movement of rhetoric. In

5. Book VI. Pope's translation.
6. Translation by E. H. Plumptre.

Shakespeare, the emergence of the speeches of Antony, of Othello, of Coriolanus[7] at moments of tension in the development of plot illustrates the introduction of rhetoric in poetic; the imagery of these speeches furnishes an illustration of poetic in rhetoric.

Upon the clear distinction between these two movements and a respect for proportion in blending the two depends the purity of poetical and rhetorical art; the blurring of the distinction makes for contamination and confusion. When the imagery of poetic is introduced into an oration merely as a means of adornment and illustration to the end of persuasion based on an appeal to reason, the art of rhetoric has been kept pure in the fine, stringent, and Aristotelian sense of that term; but when the imagery takes possession of the oration and transforms it into an appeal made primarily to the emotions, the oration loses in convincingness as a piece of argument and therefore can no longer be regarded as true rhetoric in the Aristotelian sense. On the other hand, when a play becomes a mere mass of long speeches, and dialogue a mere mass of debate, drama ceases to represent true poetic and assumes the function of rhetoric. The poetic of drama is kept pure through emphasis on unity of plot action, the persuasiveness of rhetoric being used only at moments of tension and crisis. A large part of the history of literary criticism has to do with the varying attitudes of criticism toward the Aristotelian tradition.

In beginning a brief review of the history of rhetoric and poetic down to Shakespeare's time, the fact must be recalled that Aristotle's poetic came as a reaction to what is known as the "first sophistic." This "first sophistic" was dominated by style.[8] The effect of this was to make sophistic rhetoric primarily a matter of style and that style designedly ornate for the purpose, not of persuasion but display. Moreover,

---

7. J C, III, ii; O, I, iii; C, III, i.
8. From the "Gorgian figures" of this "first sophistic" are descended the medieval "colors of rhetoric" and the modern "mechanical tricks of style."

sophistic rhetoric, the rhetoric of Gorgias and Protagoras, had, as rhetoric always has, a large part to play in education; and, through education, sophistic rhetoric gave color to Greek life and thus influenced tremendously Greek morality. It produced at its best the orations of Isocrates. Plato, among the philosophers, first challenged the mechanical methods and the shallow aims of the sophists;[9] Aristotle, in his *Rhetoric*, presented a concrete rejection of their methods and aims by championing an informing spirit to rhetorical movement and calling rhetoric to a distinctive mission as the art of persuasion.[10] Aristotle thus established philosophically the theory of classical rhetoric, and this theory has always been the one that has found expression in the best and most vital of rhetorical practice.

But sophistic rhetoric has persisted in practice right on from the days of Gorgias and Protagoras to our own time; and ancient rhetoric, instead of following Aristotle, even in theory, became more and more sophistic in theory as well as in practice. To be sure, Cicero and Quintilian are found among the Romans standing for the finer traditions of ancient rhetoric and furnishing individual survivals of the Aristotelian theory, and, in the case of Cicero, practice as well as theory. But Roman education of the late republic and the empire, reflecting as it did the rhetoric of the times, became more and more schematic, mechanical, and florid in its methods as the rhetors and professional orators formulated rhetorical projects for the schools, exhibited their own ability in declamation of the showy, high-sounding kind, and drilled their pupils in exercises which were to furnish them with rules of rhetorical etiquette and opportunities for rhetorical practice.[11] The finer traditions of ancient rhetoric which

9. See *Gorgias, Protagoras*, and *Phaedrus*.
10. See the opening of the *Rhetoric*.
11. See G. Saintsbury's *History of Criticism*, Vol. I, Book II, especially, Chapters I and IV and Interchapter II; also, Baldwin's Chapter IV in *ARP* and the two works by Henri Bornecque, *Sénèque Le rheteur, contro-*

made rhetoric a means of training men for the exigencies of life were crowded out by those theories of sophistic rhetoric which made it an end in itself. It is Seneca who typifies the rhetoric of the late classical period and he has given his name to that kind of rhetoric which exhibits primarily declamation and display.[12] This is the kind of rhetoric which held sway during the early Christian centuries among both Greeks and Romans and, to this period, the term "second sophistic" has been generally applied.

To sum up, then, the history of ancient rhetoric. In the beginning, rhetoric was practically synonymous with public speaking. Among the early Greeks, public speaking assumed a highly utilitarian function in life as a means of swaying assemblies and as a part of the procedure of the law courts. The teaching of rhetoric in the schools as the art of argument and persuasion served, under such conditions, a very practical purpose of preparing youths to take and maintain their places in later life. Early, however, the teaching of rhetoric as the art of display and personal triumph in speaking tended to pervert the true conception of rhetoric and to rob rhetoric of its high moral value by laying the primary emphasis, not on argument and persuasion, but on declamation and style. As the opportunities for the use of rhetoric in swaying assemblies became fewer and fewer and the use of rhetoric in the courts became more and more relegated to minor cases, the way was made wider and all the more open for the triumphs of the pretentious rhetoric of the sophists. And during the late classical period, the finer ancient rhetoric became contaminated and deprived of its convincingness through subordination of reasoning to declamation and through the emphasis on stylistic appeal to the emotions rather than upon logical appeal to the intellect. As we shall

---

verses et suasoires; and *Les déclamations et les déclamateurs d'après Sénèque le père.*

12. See Seneca's tragedies and J. W. Cunliffe's *Influence of Seneca on Elizabethan Tragedy.*

see later, the net result was a wholesale confusion of rhetoric and poetic.

Meanwhile, the theory of poetic was faring even worse at the hands of the ancients. The ancient theory of poetic as a distinctive literary movement had begun in Aristotle with plot action as the matter of primary concern.[13] In epic, Homer had given concrete exemplification of the effectiveness of this principle, both in the more nearly drama-like construction of *The Iliad* in its concentration of plot action and in the more characteristically epic-like construction of *The Odyssey* with its character-unity binding together the unified single stories. In tragedy, the plays of Aeschylus, Sophocles, and Euripides gave Aristotle evidence of the effectiveness of the principle in drama. For the great Greek dramatists, unity of plot action was primary. Drama consisted in the depiction of a series of events so progressively, intensely, and inevitably related as to produce a totality of impression at the end. Where epic could link together a series of stories, drama concentrated about one single character in one single dramatic situation. Everything—character, speech, song—contributed to the working out of this concentrated picture of life.[14]

This ancient poetic, which was conceived as imitation—that is, as representation of life—and which appealed through imagination to the feelings, was the art of imagery growing out of the use of the imagination.[15] This art of imagery naturally divided in practice into the imagery of plot action and the imagery of style. For the great Greek dramatists, im-

13. Aristotle's *Poetics*, Chapter VI ff.
14. This Aristotelian conception is essentially that of the theory of the composition of the nineteenth-century short story, notably expressed in Poe's essay on the philosophy of composition and worked out with supreme technical finish in stories of Poe and Maupassant. It determined in part, too, the theory and practice of the great French drama of the seventeenth century and the Restoration drama in England. It has determined, also, in large measure, the movement of the modern drama of the late nineteenth and early twentieth centuries.
15. See the opening chapters of the *Poetics*, I-VI.

agery of plot action meant unified imitation of life; imagery of style meant clearness and aptness in word and figure and sentence. For them, unity and harmony of action and style combined with character to produce the totality of effect culminating in the catharsis at the end. But while style harmonized with plot to produce a pure poetic whole, plot was distinctly primary, style secondary. And it is this conception of dramatic structure which determines poetic movement as conceived by Aristotle.

The Aristotelian conception of poetic, like the Aristotelian conception of rhetoric, continued to claim its supporters, of course, throughout the classical period. But two things must be borne in mind. First, rhetoric and not poetic gave direction to literary criticism after Aristotle throughout the ancient period, and indeed, on to the Renaissance; in fact, it is only with the Renaissance that any new body of criticism of poetic is found to be taking form. Second, the poetic which was typical of the later classical period was not the poetic of Aristotle, but the poetic of the rhetoricians who had learned their literary criticism in the declamation schools. The result was that ancient poetic became colored by rhetoric, the sophistic rhetoric of the *rheteurs* and *déclamateurs*. Emphasis was shifted, as in rhetoric, to style. The weight of the poetic of epic, as in Ovid, was shifted from narrative to description; of drama, as in Seneca, from plot action to declamation. Criticism of poetic, as in Horace, discussed poetic in terms of rhetoric, and, like the rhetoric of the times, laid greatest stress on matters of style. Thus both late classical rhetoric and late classical poetic lost for practical purposes their original distinctions of function and laid emphasis on style. Mere ornateness and picturesqueness of description and narrative, which were subsidiary in the Aristotelian conceptions of both rhetoric and poetic, became the main consideration of both and the means of confusing both by blurring the identity of each.

This confusion of the two movements was passed on to the Middle Ages. What was passed on was primarily, of course, rhetoric. Horace, the critical authority on poetic who reigned throughout the Middle Ages, was in large measure rhetorical in his treatment of the art of poetry.[16] Boethius, indeed, preserved the older traditions of poetic[17] to a great extent, but his critical work, like all criticism, took its direction from rhetoric.[18] Even grammar, which included the study of literature in general and thus provided an approach to the study of poetry, was rhetorical in its method, approaching the study of poetry purely from the linguistic standpoint—from the angle of etymology and metrics and textual criticism.[19] So far as furnishing the Middle Ages with a basis for literary criticism is concerned, then, the ancients passed on to them only the formal rhetoric which had prevailed during the closing years of the Roman Empire. And this formal rhetoric maintained its hold on education and its authority in the prescription of the purely mechanical tricks of style for centuries to come.

Meanwhile, medieval poetic developed, in the main, without any inheritance of poetic as such from the classics. Naturally emphasizing style from the inherited rhetoric, medieval poetic lost in dramatic power in proportion as it

16. The *Ars Poetica* not only does not clearly distinguish poetic from rhetoric, but, in the treatment of poetry, makes use of the characteristic approach of the rhetoricians; and much of what Horace says of poetry is equally applicable to rhetoric, and to that sophistic rhetoric which prevailed in his time.

17. See the *Consolatio Philosophiae*, the Lyrics of Philosophy. But even these stress the dialectic mission of poetry; and, in Book V, discussing Divine foreknowledge and man's free will and the nature of God, Boethius strikingly anticipates the later medieval scholasticism in his method and habit of thought.

18. See the translations and commentaries.

19. Grammar stressed figures of decoration, effective tricks of style, and meters and rhythm; in the exposition and interpretation of poetry, the purely mechanical matters of diction and metrics received the weight of the study of the grammarian. Professor Baldwin gives a comprehensive exposition of the methods of medieval education in *Medieval Rhetoric and Poetic*. See also E. P. Cubberley's *History of Education*.

neglected plot structure and emphasized extensive narrative and expansive description. But medieval poetic, left thus unrestrained by the bonds of an inherited tradition, was free to develop as it pleased. This it did along many lines and gave to literature new forms and a new basis for criticism. While the medieval romance was like the epic in some respects, it was in most respects distinctly different; the medieval lyric was not the same kind as the classical lyric; medieval allegory made use of symbolism as it had never been used before; and medieval drama, when it did arise and take form in the later Middle Ages, was quite a different sort of thing from classical drama.[20]

Medieval rhetoric, on the other hand, did have a direct classical inheritance; it inherited the contaminated rhetoric of the declamation schools. And with this contaminated rhetoric went also the inheritance of the sensational orator, dispensing the wares of sophistic art and holding the attention of audiences with his "colors of rhetoric" and neatly systematized working out of his set piece of pyrotechnic oratorical display.[21] Clearly, this kind of rhetoric is not the kind

[20] I have opened up here a very extensive side issue. Edward Kennard Rand, in *Founders of the Middle Ages*, discusses, in Chapter VII, "The New Poetry," the differences which the Christian Church wrought into literary forms: the "Apologetic" poetry, didactic poetry, the "Christian Romance," saint's legend, adaptation of Biblical subjects to Greek and Roman literary forms, the Biblical epic, the allegorical epic, the Christian hymn. For further reading, see W. P. Ker's *Epic and Romance* and *The Flourishing of Romance and the Rise of Allegory* by George Saintsbury.

[21] The sophistic orator has always been with us. In *Quo Vadis*, there are references to rhetors and professional orators who entertained at public baths and in the Forum Romanum, and to poets who entertained on the street corners by declaiming their poetry. In Book VIII of Fielding's *Amelia*, at the time when Col. James enters during the conversation between Booth and the author at the house of Bailiff Bondum, Fielding writes of the author's "Florid oration, which the reader, when he recollects that he was a speechmaker by profession, will not be surprised at." In an earlier chapter, Fielding had referred to his "parliament speeches for your magazines." In the Middle Ages, this sophistic oratory dominated in the preaching of the church—from the very first in the Eastern Church and, in the later Middle Ages, in the Western Church also. Guy Carleton Lee

employed in purposeful logical argument and debate; this kind seeks to entertain, primarily, not persuade. When this kind of rhetoric is used for debate, debate is more than likely to become a contest in stunts of language and meticulous quibbling over small points rather than an orderly, logical, and ample discussion of two sides of a question. In fact, so inadequate was medieval rhetoric for serious purposeful debate that the study of logic became entirely divorced from rhetoric; and in time dialectic assumed the function of the Aristotelian rhetoric and occupied first place, from the eleventh century on, as the dominant study in the trivium of the medieval schools. Moreover, medieval rhetoric was inadequate for instruction in the art of medieval preaching when that preaching sought to make the sermon an effective speech of persuasion; and a new division of public speaking, homiletic, what we call today pulpit oratory in the better sense of that term, came into being. And the significant thing to remember about this medieval homiletic is that it records the survival of the Aristotelian conception of rhetoric. It was based upon the pulpit rhetoric of St. Augustine, who upheld the Aristotelian ideal.

So far as any corpus of medieval criticism goes, the Middle Ages have very little to offer by way of advance in the history of criticism: as a whole, the Middle Ages were a time of creative and imitative effort rather than one of critical acumen and interpretation. The one great work which the Middle Ages contributed to the advance of literary criticism was Dante's *De Vulgari Eloquio*.[22] Like the ancient treatise usually referred to as "Longinus on the Sublime,"[23] Dante's work concerned itself with the attainment of the heights of style; but, whereas the ancient rhetorician undertook a criti-

---

gives an excellent discussion of this church oratory in the opening pages of his *Orators of the Early and Medieval Church*.

22. Saintsbury gives an outline of this critical work in *History of Criticism*, I, Chapter II, 419-431.

23. Baldwin gives a digest in *ARP*, pp. 123-125.

cism of poetic style with reference to its use in rhetoric to heighten the effects of persuasive thinking, the medieval poet undertook a criticism of poetic style with reference to its function in the writing of poetry alone. Aside from Dante's work of criticism, nothing from the Middle Ages has laid claim to anything like the importance enjoyed by the great contributions of the ancients to the advancement of literary criticism.

When one begins to take stock, on the eve of the Renaissance, of the state of rhetoric and poetic as literary movements, it is necessary at once to make a distinction between old and new.[24] In general, throughout the Middle Ages, the old rhetoric and old poetic were in a state of confusion; except for hints here and glimpses there in the compends and manuals,[25] the Aristotelian conception of rhetoric as distinct in movement from poetic influences was but negligible medieval theory and hardly at all medieval practice. So far as criticism went, there was no sustained allegiance to the Aristotelian conception; and, though writers of textbooks started out sometimes in the Aristotelian vein, they soon found themselves unable to keep rhetoric and poetic distinct and concluded regularly by leveling them under style. In time, rhetoric ceased to function as composition and lost ground as a vital part of the educational process, and dialectic came to function in its stead and to assume first place among the studies of the trivium.[26] Poetic, as a part of the system of education, began by being a part of grammar. In the late Middle Ages, however, it broke away from grammar as *poetria;*[27] but this new poetic recorded no advance in criti-

24. *Old* and *new* seem convenient words to distinguish the older classical traditions from what are characteristically medieval traditions.

25. See especially Baldwin's discussion of Martianus Capella's *Marriage of Philology and Mercury,* Isidore's *Etymologiae or Origines,* and John of Salisbury's *Metalogicus, MRP,* pp. 91-98; 156-172.

26. See Baldwin on Hugh of St. Victor, *Lore of Teaching,* John of Salisbury's *Metalogicus,* Alain's *Anticlaudianus,* St. Bonaventure's *de Reductione Artium ad Theologiam, MRP,* pp. 153-155; 172-174; 176-178.

27. Vincent of Beauvais, in his compend *Speculum Doctrinale,* Book IV,

Rhetoric in Poetic

cism because it was the same old rhetoricated poetic of style. At the end of the Middle Ages, then, the old rhetoric and the old poetic were, for purposes of criticism, in practically the same state of confusion as at their beginning. In addition, rhetoric, as this confused body of criticism was called, was perverted by the misunderstanding and misapplication of some of the terms of the older rhetoric.[28] No advance at all was made in the history of rhetoric, and Dante's treatise alone marked a permanent advance in the history of poetic.

The old rhetoric appeared, however, as dialectic and homiletic; the former functioning as the older rhetoric had done in the fields of logical argument and debate; the latter appropriating the older principles to make secure the art of preaching. The new rhetoric—and by *new* is meant medieval as represented by the medieval sophists—perpetuated the confusion with poetic and, in the late Middle Ages, was completely overshadowed as an educational force by dialectic and served merely as a sort of adjunct to rhetoricated poetic. The new poetic—that is, medieval poetic as represented by medieval poetry—made ample use of this medieval rhetoric as it branched out into various new forms of literary expression. The new poetic was widespread; and only in such dis-

---

gave *poetica* a place independent of grammar; Geoffroi de Vinsauf devoted an entire work to *Poetria Nova*. Both are discussed in *MRP*, pp. 174-176; 187-189.

28. The steps in the preparation of a speech were: *inventio* (collecting of material), *dispositio* (arrangement for purposes of progressive movement), *elocutio* (diction), *pronuntiatio* (delivery), and *memoria* (memory). Sophistic rhetoric tends to pervert *inventio* to make it merely the discovery of the characteristic, striking, or bizarre for stylistic effects; *dispositio*, to make it merely static pattern; *memoria*, to make it merely parrot-like repetition; *elocutio* and *pronuntiatio*, to make them the main supports of the speech. All these perversions were recorded in ancient times during the periods of the first and second sophistic. They persisted on through the Middle Ages. Moreover, in the Middle Ages, *narratio*, the part of a speech devoted to a statement of facts, was made to mean narrative as a whole and thus confused with *dispositio*; and in Johannes de Garlandia's *Poetria*, the parts of a discourse, after being defined traditionally, are illustrated by poetry. See Baldwin, *MRP*, pp. 191-193 for a concise discussion of these perversions in this work.

tinguished achievements as Dante's *Divina Commedia*, Chaucer's *Troilus and Criseyde* and the *Franklin's Tale* do we see the old poetic of Aristotle, with its insistence on progressive, intense, culminating movement, making its appearance in medieval poetic art.

There were, though, unmistakable signs during the Middle Ages of a growing sense of the need for a new body of literary criticism. The hints and glimpses of Aristotelian criticism in compends and manuals to which we have already referred seemed to grow out of a feeling that there was a need for a new start. In rhetoric, no one was able to make the start; in poetic, Dante made a notable beginning not only as a creative artist but as a critic as well. Chaucer did not undertake any criticism in addition to his achievements as a poet; but he has given us what can easily be taken as evidences of a recognition of the weaknesses of both medieval rhetoric and medieval poetic.[29] By 1400, there seems every reason to feel that the medieval experience in rhetoric and poetic has already ended and the Renaissance experience has already begun. A review of this experience is a valuable approach to the state of rhetoric and poetic in the time of Shakespeare.

---

29. *The Rhyme of Sir Thopas*; *The Nun's Priest's Tale* 521-534 (B 4531-4544); 386-393 (B 4396-4403); *Franklin's Prologue* F 709-728; *Clerk's Prologue* E 17-20, E 31-55; *Squire's Tale* 24-33 (F 32-41), 393-400 (F 401-408). The line in the last passage noted, "For fulsomnesse of his prolixitee," reminds us of another reference to "Prolixitee" in the "House of Fame," when the eagle, very likely in a satirical vein, thus refers to the "heigh style"—the Ovidian descriptive style:

> Have I not proved thus simply,
> Withouten any subtiltee
> Of Speche, or gret prolixitee
> Of termes of philosophye,
> Of figures of poetrye,
> Or colours of rhetoryke?
> Pardee, hit oghte thee to lyke:
> For hard language and hard matere
> Is encombrous for to here
> At ones; wost thou not wel this?

See Florence E. Teager, "Chaucer's Eagle and the Rhetorical Colors," *PMLA*, XLVII (June, 1932), 410-418.

In beginning this review, there is need to recall that Renaissance criticism registered the birth of something new which had been gradually taking form before it came forth as a body of new literary expression.[30] The new thing was *criticism* in the modern understanding of that term. It was no longer just rhetoric. Criticism began now to be independent of rhetoric as a new department of knowledge; the critic was more than just a rhetorician.

This new criticism was inevitable. Medieval rhetoric was concerned with codification, with mere schematic exposition of traditional form. The Renaissance situation called for comparison, argument, the establishment of opinion, defense. The revival and concentration of interest in direct and extensive study of the classics furnished criticism with a body of material, creative as well as critical. This material served as a basis of comparison with the literature of the Middle Ages. The medieval body of creative literature had about spent itself; the older body of literature, critical as well as creative, was being revived. What direction was to be given to the literature of the future? It could attempt to revive the medieval conceptions; it could become a revival of the classical conceptions translated into the vernaculars; it could become an entirely new kind of literature which would represent the vigor and romanticism of the medieval chastened and disciplined by the strength and classicism of the ancient. The criticism of the Renaissance was faced with the problem of taking stock of the two kinds of material of the past, weighing the one against the other, presenting an evaluation of the two, and taking a position with reference to the future.

Naturally three schools of critics are conceivable under these circumstances. One, composed essentially of medievalists, would attempt to square medieval literature with the

---

30. For the Italian and French criticism I have leaned heavily on the studies of Saintsbury and upon D. L. Clark, *Rhetoric and Poetry in the Renaissance*, and also J. E. Spingarn, *A History of Literary Criticism in the Renaissance*.

older classical theories or frankly contend for the maintenance of those post-classical theories that had already been appropriated by the Middle Ages. Another, the champions of the revived classics, would turn their backs on medieval theory and practice, which were, in many ways, difficult to square with the revived classical theories, and contend for simon-pure classicizing of the modern literatures. The third school would attempt to preserve the strong elements in medieval practice and, by tempering them with classical theory, produce new native modern literatures.

It is very significant to note what actually happened. The earliest Renaissance criticism was turned in the direction of putting a new life into the study of the classics. Indeed, the medieval methods of rhetoric—schematic, sometimes meticulous, analytical, and panegyrical—still survived, as in Vida's *Poetics*, for example, which suggested slavish imitation and thus lacked the vigor of Dante's criticism. But while Vida and Trissino[31] marked out a technique for a classicized poetry by following the lines of the poetic of Horace and by imitating Vergil and were thus *still* medieval in their approach, these early critics made an advance in basing their criticism more directly upon the classics than upon medieval versions. And Erasmus, while still rhetorical in his approach, took a step forward in emphasizing the value of the classics for their thought and content as well as for their stylistic form.[32] The later Renaissance critics in Italy, however, writing in the sixteenth century, carried the criticism of poetic a long way forward by abandoning, in the main, the medieval method of rhetorical approach and adopting what was, in the main, the Aristotelian approach to poetic. Many tried their hand at formulating this new poetic. In Italy, Daniello, Cinthio,

---

31. The Poeticas of Vida and Trissino mark the beginning of that line of criticism based on Horace which later extended into France and England, culminating in England in the criticism of the Neo-Classicists. It is interesting thus to connect Pope with the Middle Ages.

32. *Ciceronianus, Colloquies, Letters.*

Rhetoric in Poetic

Scaliger, Minturno, Castelvetro, Francastoro and Patrizzi are names that stand out for distinct achievement among the early efforts to organize the new poetic. In France, Du Bellay and Ronsard among the Pleiade made the start. In England, Gascoigne, Ascham, Wilson, Puttenham,[33] Sidney, Jonson undertook the pioneering. By the time Shakespeare had ceased to write, Renaissance criticism had become definitely established in a sort of literary creed.

All liberal Renaissance critics, it seems fairly certain, realized that Aristotle's *Poetics* could not be expected to cover any more types of poetry than those with which the ancients of his time were familiar, and, therefore, could not be expected to cover romance and the medieval drama, particularly comedy. Consequently, in their works on poetic, after following Aristotle's *Poetics* as a guide as far as the ancient work could serve them, these Renaissance critics did not hesitate to recognize the possibility of the extension of the classical rules to cover romance and comedy. Their recognition of these medieval forms, however, was in most cases by way of a concession.[34] For, at best, these medieval forms seem to have been generally regarded as inferior, and the classical forms held up as the models worthy of imitation.[35] The general tendency of Renaissance criticism, except in the case of the most rabid classicists, seemed to be to try to strike a compromise between medieval and classical practice by accounting critically for the medieval extensions, but still championing the older classical traditions. The medieval in-

---

33. *The Arte of English Poesie* has been ascribed to both Richard and George Puttenham (in one edition, Webster alias George Puttenham). Percy Allen, in *The Life Story of Edward de Vere as William Shakespeare*, p. 261, suggests that the author of *The Arte of English Poesie* was probably Oxford's cousin, Lord Lumley. In this book the author shall be referred to as Puttenham.

34. Renaissance criticism, as a rule, was criticism that concerned itself with the ancient literature to the neglect of contemporary literature. By way of exception, we may note Cinthio's *Romanzi*, Webbe's praise of Spenser in the *Discourse of English Poesie*, and Daniel's *Defence of Rime*.

35. See Scaliger, Sidney, and Jonson.

terest in the merely linguistic criticism of literature still survived, however, in the large place still accorded to diction and style.

But Renaissance criticism had to take into account not only the nature of medieval literature, but religious prejudice as well; it had to defend itself against attacks from what is most comprehensively called the Puritan position.[36] Poetry had to be defended as a means of philosophical enlightenment and thus an ally of truth as well as a means of affording pleasure. In Italy, Savonarola stated the attitude of the church reformer in his *De Scientiis* when he fired away at the abuses of poetry; and Minturno was constrained to open his second book of *De Poeta* by pointing out the instructive power of poetry. In England, Stephen Gosson challenged the Renaissance poetic in his *School of Abuse;* and Sidney made a notable effort to come to the rescue in his *Apology for Poetry*.

The most ardent among the classicists frankly distrusted medievalism and urged the claims of the new classicism. They distrusted medievalism for several reasons. On purely technical grounds, the medieval romance, with its loose and often illogical structure, seemed impossible for a permanent cultured poetic. For them, the classics, without any extension of forms, seemed the only solution. Again, in the matter of content, the medieval literature seemed equally impossible. Medieval literature was saturated with the religious philosophy of the Catholic Church and with the ethereal imagery of fairyland and magic. These strict classicists felt as if both of these medieval elements ought to go: the one, on the grounds that medieval church corruption had been successfully discredited by the Protestant revolt; the other, on the

---

36. The word *Puritan* is here used in a rather broad sense to cover the reform movement in general: the early reform movement within the Catholic Church itself; the later reform movement away from the Church and against it, which we know as the Protestant movement.

grounds that poetry should give an imitation of life—and by their own restriction of Aristotle, life as it is.[37]

Such were the conflicting tendencies that Renaissance critics recorded in the direction of a Renaissance theory of poetic; but, in the hands of these critics, criticism of poetic made a distinct advance. So far as rhetoric went, however, criticism seemed to make very little, if any, advance. In fact, rhetoric continued to be the formal rhetoric that had prevailed throughout the Middle Ages. There was a recognition of the authority of Cicero, and, through Cicero, a sort of second-hand glimpse of Aristotle; but, like the rhetoric of the Middle Ages, Renaissance rhetoric was concerned primarily with style. Few attempts were made to advance the criticism of rhetoric; and Wilson in England seems to have been the only one to mark any signal advance in achieving the correction of medieval extravagance through classical discipline.

In the matter of criticism, then, Renaissance rhetoric marked in the main no advance in the history of criticism; Renaissance poetic, on the other hand, marked a distinct advance in reviving the classical point of view of poetic as distinct from rhetoric. To be sure, the experience in poetic was one of conflict, and the conflict was still on when Shakespeare came up to London. But in the midst of the conflict, there were some critics who were able to recognize, even though apologetically, that the medieval experience in poetic had not been all for naught, but contained results of experimentation that might be disciplined by the classics to form a vital and permanent poetic.

For the present, the review of criticism of rhetoric and poetic will be left at this point.[38] The rapid survey has led up

37. Jonson and the later Elizabethans. See also Pope and the Neo-Classicists. Later, I shall have occasion to return to this Elizabethan and Neo-Classical criticism of poetic in discussing the poetic of Shakespeare.
38. Many matters have been hastily referred to; others have been en-

to and established a point of view as to *rhetoric in poetic* in the time of Shakespeare. First, Elizabethan rhetoric in poetic was mainly medieval rhetoric, which, in turn, was Senecan rhetoric, itself sophistic rhetoric; and Elizabethan criticism had made but a small advance toward correcting this sophistic rhetoric by the application of Aristotle's theory of rhetoric in poetic as the art of explanation and persuasion. However, the classical theory of rhetoric as the art of persuasion, in which matters of style are purely secondary, was the theory of rhetoric Aristotle had in mind when he provided, in his treatise on poetic, for the introduction of rhetoric in poetic. There is a conflict here, therefore, between distinctly Elizabethan rhetoric in poetic and Aristotelian rhetoric in poetic: that is, rhetoric in poetic was mere decoration in the minds of some and speeches full of explanation and persuasion in the minds of others. Second, in ancient times, rhetoric determined the direction of criticism and finally obscured poetic by confusing rhetoric and poetic, and the sophistic rhetoric resulting from the confusion dominated criticism throughout the Middle Ages. During the Middle Ages, a new poetic developed which gave form to various new types of poetic unknown to the ancients, but appropriated, in large measure for style, the sophistic inheritance in rhetoric. For the medievalists, then, *rhetoric in poetic* meant merely rhetoricated poetic. With the Renaissance, the revival of the older classical poetic theory and the influence of classical drama tended to revive the classical conception of *rhetoric in poetic*. But Senecan tragedy, which influenced early Elizabethan drama, was essentially rhetorical drama—"declamation" drama; so that in such drama *rhetoric in poetic* still meant for the most part rhetoricated poetic. Even in that type of Elizabethan drama then which represented the revival of the older clas-

---

tirely left out. Comprehensive and detailed studies have been made by Saintsbury, Baldwin, and Clark. The history of criticism will be further discussed from time to time.

sical tragedy, *rhetoric in poetic* did not have the same signification it had in Aristotle's time.[39]

Thus, in approaching the study of rhetoric in Shakespeare there is need always to distinguish between the sophistic or Senecan rhetoric found in his plays and the older classical rhetoric in them. There is need to distinguish, too, between rhetorical drama as represented by the Senecan type of play and the drama developed according to the Aristotelian conception of poetic. Then there must be kept in mind the distinction between the declamation as the kind of speech typical of sophistic rhetoric, the art of decoration and display, and the oration as the kind of speech typical of Aristotelian rhetoric, the art of argument and persuasion. Finally, it cannot be too strongly emphasized that the Aristotelian conception of rhetoric in poetic was that of a point of focusing at which the onward movement of epic narrative was halted for the moment by circular movement about a central thought, or a point at which the interest in plot movement as determined by dramatic action was changed for the moment into interest in plot movement as determined by logical thought —the rhetoric in both instances being movement of persuasion.

39. Compare classical tragedy and early Elizabethan revivals of the classical tragedy; also, see Sidney's attack on Elizabethan classical tragedy, specifically *Gorboduc*, generally considered the best revival.

CHAPTER II

The Oration in the Drama

IN UNDERTAKING A definition of the oration in the drama, it is necessary, first, to relate the oration to other types of set speech: declamation, soliloquy, and rhetorical conversation. All set speeches stand out from their context in that they are passages of sustained, more or less centralized speaking which halt the onward movement of dramatic narrative; they represent a conscious effort to center attention upon themselves. With declamation, soliloquy, and passages of rhetorical conversation, the oration shares this general "set" quality. Its distinctive "set" quality will appear by a comparison with the other types.

A declamation is a set speech which is an end in itself. It is a speech which centers attention primarily on its style and delivery. In the drama, the declamation is a detachable speech, of interest particularly as the performance of a skilful speaker. While principally narrative or descriptive, the declamation may be expository or argumentative; but, if argumentative, it will be unrelated as a vital part of plot structure.[1] A declamation may be entirely detached from plot action, as in prologues and epilogues,[2] or it may be re-

1. As shall be seen more clearly in Chapter VI, a set speech, to be related as a vital part of plot structure, must come at a critical moment in plot development and grow directly out of antecedent action and influence subsequent action. A speech that is mere declamation is an end in itself as an exercise in rhetorical expression.

2. See Shakespeare's *Troilus and Cressida*, Chapman's *Bussy D'Ambois*, Jonson's *Volpone* and *Epicoene*, and some of Middleton's plays. The prologue and epilogue are also characteristic of the Restoration Drama. Shakespeare's *Henry V* makes a special use of the prologue before each act, with an epilogue at the end of the play.

lated to plot action, not in a dynamic way to further plot action through intellectual persuasion, but merely by way of explanation or characterization, recalling, in a way, chorus parts of the ancient classical drama.[3] As a speech of explanation, the declamation may serve the purpose of exposition in the dramatic sense. In the rhetorical drama in which a sense for dramatic action is undeveloped, we are likely to get a host of such expository speeches.[4] In plays, too, where a sense for dramatic action is developed, the declamation is a convenient vehicle for exposition near the opening of the play to acquaint us with the situation; and sometimes speeches of this type which start out in the expository vein take a turn and end in an appeal for action in some particular direction.[5]

The declamation, being an end in itself, lends itself easily to the sophistic rhetoric of display and may easily become the vehicle for a mere exercise in rhetorical stunts. As has been said before, this type of speech[6] in the hands of the ancient rhetoricians became the type of speech of the professional rhetor, in classroom or abroad, and is the quality of speech which characterizes the rhetorical drama of Seneca. It was the principal kind of speech handed on by tradition to the Middle Ages and shows up in profusion in the Senecan revival of the Renaissance. In England, the profusion of declamatory speeches is a characteristic feature of Elizabethan drama. Chronicle-history plays abound in declamations; Shakespeare's history plays come immediately to mind.

3. Recalls the classical chorus merely in the kind of thing used, not in the use of it. An interesting study is provided by comparing the use of the ancient classic chorus and that of Elizabethan "chorus" speeches: see *Henry V*, Greene's *Alphonsus of Aragon, Misfortunes of Arthur, Jocasta,* and *Gismond of Salerne*, noting similarities and differences.

4. See *Sir Clyomon and Clamydes.*

5. The Ghost in *Hamlet.*

6. It is important not to confuse *declamation* and *declamatio*. The latter is the hypothetical exercise used in the declamation schools. These hypothetical exercises were called *suasoriae* when exercises in deliberative rhetoric, *controversiae* when exercises in forensic rhetoric. *Declamatio* of these two types is the subject of Bornecque's essay; and it is included in Quintilian's treatise, *Institutes of Oratory* (II, x).

Again, where the story is classical or where the play is based on some classical model, there is an abundance and variety of the set speech. For example, *Troilus and Cressida* furnishes a remarkably copious and brilliant display of rhetorical speeches of various kinds.[7] Such tragedies as *Gorboduc, Jocasta, Gismond of Salerne,* and the *Misfortunes of Arthur* are full of declamations reminding us of the speeches characteristic of the plays of Seneca. The revenge tragedy, marking the adaptation of the classics to the Elizabethan stage, gives the dramatist repeated opportunity for a great and various display of long declamatory speeches.[8]

When the set speech is used in a choral way and the speaker acts the part of speaking to himself alone, the set speech is called a soliloquy. The soliloquy is essentially declamation and is traceable to the declamation schools of the Roman Empire.[9] It may be narrative, descriptive, expository, or argumentative. When argumentative, it may conceivably be used to further plot action;[10] and, used in this way, it approaches near to the borders of the oration in the ancient classical sense, certainly satisfying, in principle, Aristotle's rhetoric in poetic. Shakespeare's *Hamlet*, of course, offers a classic example of the abundance and variety possible in the use of the soliloquy.

The third type of set speech is that of rhetorical conversa-

---

7. See also *Julius Caesar* and *Coriolanus*. Jonson's *Catiline* and *Sejanus* show intensive as well as extensive use of the set speech, and often abound in close translations of classical sources.

8. See Shakespeare's *Hamlet*, Kyd's *Spanish Tragedy*, Marston's *Antonio and Mellida*, Chapman's *Bussy D'Ambois*, and Tourneur's *Revenger's Tragedy*.

9. See Ovid's *Metamorphoses* and Baldwin's comment, *ARP*, p. 218; also, Arnold's *Soliloquies of Shakespeare*. The soliloquy as a dramatic device for conveying important mental workings, motives, etc., to the audience is discussed at length in Chapter III.

10. A splendid example is in Greene's *Selimus*, the soliloquy of Selimus, when he argues with himself in defense of his contemplated rebellion against his father—not only an example of the soliloquy of the argumentative type, but also a reminiscence of some of the typical arguments of the "schoolmen."

The Oration in the Drama

tion. This rhetorical conversation may be carried on between only two persons, as in the "private conference" which Henry IV holds with the Prince;[11] or in an informal group where there is, for the moment, the atmosphere of formality, as in Kate's speech in the closing scene of Shakespeare's *Taming of the Shrew*. In Henry's admonitions to the Prince and in Kate's speech before her husband and friends, it is easy to recognize the "set" quality of the conversation, but sometimes it is difficult to say just where the usual conversation ceases and the "set" speech begins, as is particularly true in romantic comedy. Whether the rhetorical movement emerges but slightly or distinctly, however, heightened style and sustained speech structure characterize the emergence of rhetorical conversation and serve to differentiate this kind of conversation from the usual kind.

The oration can now be defined. As generally regarded down to the present day, an oration is a formal public speech spoken before an audience.[12] In drama, it differs from the other types of set speech in being a speech which is spoken on an occasion where there is the atmosphere of formality and a speech which furnishes a point of focusing in plot development. As its name implies, it is a "prayer" speech, a speech of petition, a speech of persuasion. And, in defining and classifying orations in Shakespeare, the term shall be considered as meaning a speech delivered in public for the purpose of persuading an audience to adopt the speaker's view of the question in hand.[13] Specifically, there should be

---

11. *1 Henry IV*, III, ii.
12. See Aristotle's *Rhetoric*, Cicero's *De Oratore*, Quintilian's *Institutes of Oratory*, Wilson's *Arte of Rhetorique*, Shurter's *Rhetoric of Oratory*. See also Baldwin and Clark. See also note 14 below.
13. In this connection, the question as to the Elizabethan understanding of an oration arises sometimes. A discussion of this matter will be taken up in a later chapter. It is interesting to note here, however, a point arising in the distinction between rhetorical conversation and the oration. In North's translation of Plutarch's life of Coriolanus, the speech which Coriolanus makes to Aufidius in explanation of his appearance before Aufidius is called an oration. To include as an oration the speech in

kept in mind, in addition to the definition given the oration by the ancient classical writers on rhetoric,[14] the Elizabethan definition with which Wilson begins his *Arte of Rhetorique:* "Rhetorique is an Arte to set forth by utterance of words matter at large, or (as Cicero doth say)[15] it is a learned, or rather an artificial declaration of the mynd, in the handlyng of any cause called in contention, that may through reason largely be discussed." Rhetoric, in this fine and stringent sense, comes to be the art of logical expression through the medium of spoken words. Rhetoric thus comes to be synonymous with oratory, and the oration the vehicle through which the art is given expression.

An analysis of Wilson's definition sketches the outlines of the oration. "It is a learned or rather artificial declaration of the mynd" defines the nature of the structure. The oration is an elaborately worked out unit of composition: diction is elegant; phrasing is careful and exhibits plan in arrangement; the speech exhibits the work of an artist in that it is built up as a coherent work of conscious art. "In the handlyng of any cause called in contention" indicates the occasion of the speech. The occasion of the oration is one calling for exposition and argument: a brief for one of two sides of a question; an answer to a question raised; or even further, debate. "That may through reason largely be discussed" suggests the method of development. The oration, delivered upon a critical occasion, is a discourse directed by logical procedure.

Shakespeare derived from this speech in North's translation would necessitate the inclusion of the speech of Henry IV counseling the Prince, Prospero's narrative spoken to Miranda in Act I of *The Tempest*, and the narrative of the Ghost in *Hamlet*. But like all these speeches, the speech of Coriolanus to Aufidius is "private conference."

14. *Rhetoric*, I, i; *De Oratore*, I, xlix; *Institutes*, II, xi-xxi.

15. The treatise, *Rhetorica ad Herennium*, which seems to have been the one Wilson had in mind here, was ascribed throughout the Middle Ages to Cicero.

The Oration in the Drama

An oration in the drama, then, is a set speech spoken before an audience in a critical situation; a speech exhibiting painstaking, systematic structure and embellished with pleasing, precise, ornate diction. The speech of Othello before the Duke and Council of Venice[16] and the speech of Hermione before Leontes and his Court[17] furnish excellent examples of the oration in Shakespeare.

Rhetoricians, ancient and modern, agree upon three general classes of orations: orations of persuasion or dissuasion, delivered before an assembly; orations of accusation and defense, delivered in connection with a trial before a court of justice; orations of praise or blame, delivered on public occasions of a commemorative or circumstantial nature. Orations of the first class are called deliberative orations; of the second, judicial or forensic orations; of the third, epideictic, demonstrative, or occasional orations.[18]

Deliberative orations are delivered before an assembly for the purpose of weighing the subject in hand and of persuading the assembly to adopt the speaker's point of view and line of argument. To this class belong orations delivered in legislative halls or other places of public discussion on occasions where the main "cause called in contention" is one involving the adoption or rejection of a policy with reference to the future.[19] In ancient times, this type of oratory was

---

16. *O*, I, iii.   17. *W. T.*, III, ii.

18. *Rhetoric*, I, iii, ix, x; *De Oratore*, opening of Book II; *Institutes*, III, iv; *Arte of Rhetorique* (G. H. Mair's edition), pp. 11, 29, 86; *Rhetoric of Oratory*, Chapter II. Note, however, that Cicero speaks of the two kinds of oratory as deliberative and forensic, regarding Aristotle's third kind as rather a method of developing thought and making an appeal.

19. "The oration demonstrative standeth either in praise, or dispraise of some one man, or of some one thing, or of some one deed doen.

"An oration deliberative is a meane, whereby we doe perswade, or disswade, entreate, or rebuke, exhorte, or dehort, commend or comforte any man.

"Oration Judiciall, is an earnest debating in open assemblie, of some weightie matter before a Judge, where the complainaunt commenceth his action, and the defendant thereupon answereth at his perill, to all such

even more popular than today, though the practice fell off in the time of the late Republic and the Empire. Deliberative oratory flourishes under conditions of democracy.

In the drama, the deliberative oration is sometimes found directed to one person; for example, the speech of Katherine to King Henry (*Henry VIII*, I, ii). The ideal use, however, directs the oration to a group. The oration of Coriolanus before the patricians is a good example of this ideal use (*Coriolanus*, III, i). Other examples in the Elizabethan Drama are: Tamburlaine, to persuade Theridamus, envoy from the King of Persia, to desert the Persian monarch and swear allegiance to him (Marlowe's *Tamburlaine*, First Part, I, ii); Eubulus, to persuade the Lords to pursue a certain course after the death of Ferrex and Porrex (*Gorboduc*, V, i); Bishop of Durham, to dissuade King James from carrying out his intention of fighting against King Henry (Ford's *Perkin Warbeck*, III, iv); Eubulus, to dissuade Dionysius from killing Damon (Edward's *Damon and Pithias*, near beginning).

Judicial or forensic orations are orations of the bar, delivered before a judge and court of justice in connection with a trial or answer to an accusation. Forensic oratory was very frequently used in the early ancient courts when the custom of defending one's self in court was common among the ancients; and the custom continued common until the time of the Empire.[20] With the passing out of the custom of defending one's self in court and the substitution of the cus-

---

things as are laid to his charge." Wilson's definitions of the different types of orations reflect, in the main, of course, the definitions of these types by Aristotle, Cicero, and Quintilian. As this book progresses, the classifications will show a shifting of the line dividing deliberative from demonstrative; but this shifting seems to be both natural and convenient for a classification of orations.

20. The defense speeches of Paul in Jerusalem and Caesarea, recorded in Acts 22, 24, 26, not only recall the custom of defending one's self in court, but also reflect the Apostle's classical training in rhetoric of the forensic type.

The Oration in the Drama

tom of having an advocate present one's defense,[21] forensic oratory lost a considerable part of its original function.

The defendant's speech, spoken in defense of one's self, is illustrated in Shakespeare by the oration of Othello before the Council of Venice and by the oration of Hermione at the Court of Leontes. The advocate's speech, spoken in defense of someone else, is illustrated in Shakespeare by the speech of Isabella in defense of Claudio (*Measure for Measure*, II, ii) and that of Alcibiades in defense of his friend (*Timon of Athens*, III, v). Other examples of the use of the forensic in the Elizabethan Drama are: plea of Paris before the Council of the Gods (Peele's *Arraignment of Paris*, IV, iv); plea of Sforza before Charles and attendants (Massinger's *Duke of Milan*, III, i); plea of Byron before Henry IV of France and his court (Chapman's *Tragedy of Charles, Duke of Byron*, V, i); plea of David in behalf of his son Absalom (Peele's *David and Bethsabe*, II, vii); brief of an Advocate against the Admiral (Chapman's *Admiral of France*, III, ii).[22] The plea of Paris in defense of the stage (Massinger's *Roman Actor*, I, iii) is an interesting use of the forensic in defense of some cause.

The third class of orations is the class called by Aristotle "epideiktikos." This class of oration has always been popular from very earliest times. It is the class which furnishes the best vehicle for sophistic rhetoric; consequently, the epideictic oration was popular with the declamation schools of the Roman Empire and has been popular from that time until today. It furnishes opportunity for the exhibition of

21. Swift recalls the substitution in his reference to the surprise of the Houyhnym when Gulliver told him that Englishmen hired lawyers to defend them in court.

22. The play is assigned to Chapman and Shirley in the edition by R. H. Shepherd; see note to play. This speech of the Proctor-general is in prose as is also the speech of the advocate against the Chancellor in Act V, ii. The movement of rhetoric is thus made to stand out visually from the movement of poetic. The reply of the defendant in each case, however, is in poetry. Moreover, in both of these scenes it may be that Chapman is satirizing court procedure.

the "spread-eagle" type of oratory and gives the orator a fine opportunity to make a good show and win applause. But, while it is the favorite type of oration with the sophists, it has its part to play in the finer rhetoric as well; and Aristotle regarded it as capable of just as worthy a use as orations of the other types. The abuse lies in allowing it to degenerate from a speech with a serious purpose to one which is merely a spectacular performance to bring glory to the speaker.

This third class is designated by three terms; epideictic, demonstrative, occasional.[23] These terms represent attempts to convey the meaning of Aristotle's *epideiktikos* and to group the different kinds of orations that are included in this general class. *Epideictic* suggests fit for display, and refers to rhetorical style "suited to narrative, panegyric, and the declamations of the sophists, but not proper for the forum and deliberative assemblies.[24] *Demonstrative* suggests pointing out, showing forth, explaining, and the word is derived from the Latin word for the class of orations "containing praise or dispraise."[25] *Occasional* is the term used in modern times to suggest what the French call *discours de circonstance*. Of the three terms used, *demonstrative* or *occasional* (the

23. For a concise statement of the difficulties involved there is the following note from Baldwin, *ARP*, p. 15: "Of the various translations of Aristotle's epideiktikos, 'demonstrative' is flatly a mistranslation, 'oratory of display' is quite too narrow a translation, and 'epideictic' is not a translation at all. The nearest word in current use is 'panegyric,' which is right as far as it goes. But English use, though it lacks a single word, is none the less familiar with the thing. The kind of oratory that Aristotle means is the oratory of the Gettysburg Address, of most other commemorative addresses, and of many sermons. The French equivalent is *discours de circonstance*."

24. Harper's *Latin Dictionary: epidicticus.*

25. *Idem: demonstrativus* (Gr. *apodeiknumi, endeiknumi*). Cicero seems to represent the third class of Aristotle's rhetoric as a rhetorical manner and method of thinking that may be employed in deliberative and forensic oratory rather than as a distinct class; but the Aristotelian classification is certainly the one demanded by the distinctive character of this kind of oratory, and Cicero himself feels the need of providing, in *De Oratore* (II, lxxxii-lxxxv), a section on this type of speaking. Quintilian regards it as a distinct class (*Inst.* III, iv).

The Oration in the Drama

attempts to interpret *epideictic*) will be the ones used to designate orations of this class.

Demonstrative or occasional orations are orations principally of the expository and commemorative types, which grow out of the circumstances of the occasion. They are designed primarily to set forth, in an elaborate manner, matter commemorative of some person or event, or to make a special appeal to the emotions of the audience based upon the circumstances of the situation. In the drama, this class includes eulogies, denunciations, presentation speeches, speeches to soldiers, funeral orations, and narrative speeches with an oratorical setting. The funeral orations in *Julius Caesar* (III, ii), Margaret's denunciation speech in *3 Henry VI* (I, iv), the orations before the soldiers in *Richard III* (V, iii), Wolsey's presentation speech in *Henry VIII* (II, ii), the speech of the 3rd Messenger in *1 Henry VI* (I, i) are examples in Shakespeare of orations of this third general class. Other examples in Elizabethan drama are: Divine rebuking the Lawyer in Greene's *James IV* (V, iv); Sulpitius commending Marius to the Romans at the opening of Lodge's *Wounds of Civil War*; Mariner's narrative of the battle to King John in *The Raigne of King Edward the Third* (III, i).

Pulpit oratory is sometimes regarded as forming a division of occasional oratory, and sometimes as a fourth class by itself. As has been seen, the sophistic rhetoric inherited by the Middle Ages was found inadequate for purposes of effective didactic preaching, and homiletic arose to supply the need. Homiletic still survives as that branch of rhetoric which has to do with the preparation and delivery of sermons.

When preaching aims to entertain, or display a striking or spectacular interpretation of Scripture, it is essentially sophistic, and the term *epideictic* fitly applies. When the sermon is regarded as an expository oration growing out of the circumstances of the worship of the Church, it is rightly regarded as occasional oratory. But the greatest pulpit oratory goes beyond either of these types of sermon; it seeks to move men by persuading or dissuading, and thus takes on the function of deliberative oratory as well as occasional. It would seem best, then, to regard pulpit oratory as a distinct class and designate it by the name homiletic. The homiletic speech is inherent in the morality play; and speeches in *Everyman* furnish excellent examples of the use of homiletic in drama.

Such definition and classification of the oration in the drama mark it, first, as a speech of vital purpose—a speech with a dramatic mission; and, in this light, the oration is an integral part of dramatic action. Moreover, in varying dramatic situations, the oration is called upon to perform varying dramatic missions; and thus orations lend themselves to classification as deliberative, judicial, or demonstrative (occasional). Again, the definition of the oration as a speech with a dramatic mission makes it the vehicle of the Aristotelian rhetoric in poetic, not sophistic rhetoric. Furthermore, being an integral part of dramatic action, its use is controlled by the poetic of the drama.

In taking up in detail, then, the study of the oration in Shakespeare, there is need, by way of preparation, of distinguishing the oration from the sophistic rhetoric found in Shakespeare's plays; next, of analyzing it to determine its structure as a unit of composition; and then of relating it to Shakespeare's poetic by a study of its dramatic integration in Shakespeare's plays.

CHAPTER III

Sophistic Rhetoric in Shakespeare

IT HAS BEEN pointed out that sophistic rhetoric is essentially rhetoric of display and attracts more attention to the speaker than the speech. In its most sensational form it recalls Tennyson's indulgence in some fine satire on the sensational preacher in "Sea Dreams":

> Now seaward bound for health they gain'd a coast
> All sand and cliff and deep in-running cave,
> At close of day; slept, woke, and went next,
> The Sabbath, pious variers from the Church,
> To chapel, where a heated pulpiteer,
> Not preaching simple Christ to simple men,
> Announced the coming doom, and fulminated
> Against the Scarlet Woman and her creed.
> For sideways up he swung his arms, and shrieked
> "Thus, thus with violence," even as if he held
> The Apocalyptic millstone, and himself
> Were that great Angel; "Thus with violence
> Shall Babylon be cast into the sea;
> Then comes the close!" The gentle-hearted wife
> Sat shuddering at the ruin of a world,
> He at his own; but when the wordy storm
> Had ended, forth they came and paced the shore,
> Ran in and out the long sea-foaming caves,
> Drank the large air, and saw, but scarce believed—
> The soot-flake of so many a summer still
> Clung to their fancies—that they saw, the sea.

Conrad, in *Nostromo*,[1] has vividly described an orator indulging in the mannerisms of sophistic rhetoric when he pic-

1. Part III, Chapter V.

tures the scene in which Pedrito Montero is addressing the crowds of enthusiasts on the Plaza:

"The crowd stared literally open-mouthed, lost in eager stillness, as though they had expected the great guerillero, the famous Pedrito, to begin scattering at once some sort of visible largesse. What he began was a speech. He began it with the shouted word 'Citizens!' which reached even those in the middle of the Plaza. Afterwards the greater part of the citizens remained fascinated by the orator's action alone— his tiptoeing, the arms flung above his head with the fists clinched; a hand laid flat upon the heart; the silver gleam of rolling eyes; the sweeping, pointing, embracing gestures; a hand waved formally towards the little black-coated person of Señor Fuentes, advocate and politician and a true friend of the people. The *vivas* of those nearest the orator, bursting out suddenly, propagated themselves irregularly to the confines of the crowd, like flames running over dry grass, and expired in the opening of the streets. In the intervals, over the swarming Plaza brooded a heavy silence in which the mouth of the orator went on opening and shutting and detached phrases—'The happiness of the people,' 'Sons of the country,' 'The entire world' (el mundo enteiro)—reached even the packed steps of the cathedral with a feeble, clear ring, thin as the buzzing of a mosquito. It was the supreme effort of his peroration."

After Señor Fuentes and Montero had gone into Intendencia, Gamacho, making his oration "delectable to popular ears, went on in the heat and glare of the Plaza like the uncouth howlings of an inferior sort of devil cast into a white hot furnace. Every moment he had to wipe his streaming face with his bare forearm; he had flung off his coat and had turned up the sleeves of his shirt high above the elbows, but he kept on his head the large cocked hat with white plumes. This ingenuousness cherished this sign of his rank as Commandante of the National Guards. Approving and grave murmurs greeted his periods."

The type of speaking described by Tennyson and Conrad is oratory that satisfies in a way Aristotle's definition of rhetoric; in each case the purpose of the speaker is to persuade. But in each case the appeal is made primarily through an appeal to the emotions as affected by the use of voice and gesture, and thus departs from the standard of the better rhetoric which makes appeal primarily through reason.

Rhetoric of this sophistic kind has its legitimate place in the history of public speaking. Sophistic preaching wins converts that the more orderly intellectual type of sermon would never move. Political oratory of the sophistic kind appeals to a certain type of citizen and brings political considerations to the attention of those citizens who would not be reached by the more intellectual type of deliberative oratory. Commemorative occasions quite naturally stir the emotions, and sophistic rhetoric furnishes the means for making the emotional appeal. It would seem unfair, then, to disparage unreservedly all sophistic rhetoric, and also unfair to deny a sophistic speech the right to be called an oration.

It is imperative, however, in the discussion of the oration in the drama to restrict the term to a speech making its primary appeal to reason and functioning as an element of plot structure. It is also expedient to restrict the term to public address as much as possible, a restriction entirely in keeping with the general conception of what oratory is. Such restriction of the oration in the drama, however, makes necessary, by way of differentiation, a general consideration of sophistic rhetoric in Shakespeare's plays. The plays will be taken up in chronological order in the periods of development of Shakespeare's dramatic art.[2]

Naturally, sophistic rhetoric should first be looked for in

---

2. More detailed discussion follows the early rapid survey.

those plays in which the influence of the Senecan type of rhetoric is most pronounced; namely, the history plays. The *Henry VI* plays contain a great deal of spectacle, and much Marlowesque rhetoric contributes to the attainment of spectacular effects in all these plays. *1 Henry VI* opens in the declamatory vein, and Joan, Talbot, The Third Messenger, Mortimer, King Henry, the General, Sir Wm. Lucy, and Suffolk are all made the vehicles for declamatory speaking. Talbot plays the leading part in this speaking. From the time of his entrance in I, iv, his speeches, narrative in conversation or reflective and at times intensely emotional in soliloquy, are distinctly suggestive either of the hand of Marlowe as collaborator or of Shakespeare's writing with Marlowe's rhetoric as a model. Talbot's rhetoric is made particularly theatrical in his unknighting of Sir John Fastolfe and his lamentings on the field of battle just before his death. *2* and *3 Henry VI* contain much rhetorical dialogue and much sophistic rhetoric in soliloquies. Henry, York, Cardinal Beaufort, Gloucester, the Duchess and Margaret, Salisbury, Say, Clifford, Warwick, and Edward are made the vehicles for the speaking parts, the sophistic rhetoric in Shakespeare rising to some of its most emotional heights in the speeches of Margaret. The rhetoric becomes strikingly Marlowesque in Act III, of *2 Henry VI*. The sophistic vein is continued in *Richard III*, with Margaret, Anne, Queen Elizabeth, and Richard playing the leading parts. And there is plenty of sophistic rhetoric in *King John* in the speeches of Philip and Constance. There is this to be noted, however: in this play, the speaking parts are more in character, and distinctly more art is displayed in the use of sophistic rhetoric.[3] *Titus Andronicus*, assigned to this period, shows also a contemporary interest in the use of sophistic rhetoric. Titus, Aaron, Tamora, and Marcus are made the vehicles of a great deal of

---

3. There is good contrast in II, i, between the unrestrained outburst of Constance and the ordered speeches of the Kings.

rhetoric of the Senecan type, and Titus affords probably the best vehicle in Shakespeare, with the possible exception of Timon, for the use of sophistic rhetoric of the melodramatic kind.

A review of these plays generally assigned to Shakespeare's period of apprenticeship points to this conclusion: abundance of unrestrained sophistic rhetoric is coincident with uncertainty of authorship or certainty of revision of earlier plays. This conclusion becomes all the more pertinent when we compare these plays with Shakespeare's earliest independent ventures in the field of comedy. *Love's Labor's Lost*, with its interest in diction, contains rhetoric that might be denominated sophistic, but the sophistic rhetoric is distinctly more restrained here and seems partly burlesque or criticism. In *A Comedy of Errors*, there is also much speech-making but, with the main interest in incident, the speaking is free of the studied extravagances of rhetoric for its own sake. In *Two Gentlemen of Verona*, with the increased skill in plot and character, sophistic rhetoric of the traditional kind is conspicuous by its absence. In this period of apprenticeship, then, we see Shakespeare early breaking away from the influence of the Senecan rhetoric of the early Elizabethan drama and freeing his speeches from the inflated and mechanical rhetoric of his immediate predecessors.

This is to be noticed too in the history plays following *King John*. *Richard II*, with all of its abundance of speech-making, stands out as remarkable for the number of its great speeches that have freed themselves from the Marlowesque style. In the *Henry IV* plays, there is a good deal of declamatory rhetoric—the emotional rhetoric of Lady Percy, for example; but there is much less of the gaudy sophistic rhetoric which characterized the earlier history plays. *Henry V* is full of declamatory and poetic rhetoric, revealing character and depicting scene, but in this play Shakespeare seems to strike a happy balance between rhetoric of the purely declamatory and emotional sort and rhetoric of the Aristotelian kind.

When the comedies following the *Two Gentlemen* are considered, the need is felt for making a distinction between sophistic rhetoric of the purely mechanical type which shows off the speaker's cleverness in the use of words or becomes the method of expression of unbridled emotion, and the rhetorical poetry which uses the devices of rhetoric as merely the means of achieving pictorial art or of giving expression to genuine and more ordered emotion. The distinction can be made at once when the speeches of *Richard III* are compared with those of *Midsummer Night's Dream*. Those of the former have all the earmarks of the ranting, declaiming rhetoric of the schools—they are exercises in word display; those of the latter are freed from the bombast and mouthing of the former as they are colored by word painting or as they attain the heights of lyric poetry. The same point is to be made of the speeches in *As You Like It* and *Twelfth Night*. Shakespeare's sense for plot structure and character portrayal saves the speaking in the great comedies of the second period from degeneration into sophistic rhetoric of the Senecan type, and much of what sophistic rhetoric there is from now on needs, it would seem, to be differentiated as sophistic rhetoric of the Shakespeare kind. The speeches of the suitors in *Merchant of Venice*, for example, are mechanical in a way, but somehow Shakespeare's[4] art prevents their being obtrusively so. Again, the emotional rhetoric of Leonato in *Much Ado* is saved by a certain restraint and economy from being anything like the emotional rhetoric of Talbot, say, or even Constance.

The two tragedies of the second period are significant in the development of Shakespeare's rhetoric. In *Romeo and Juliet* many of the principal speeches are likely to impress

---

4. I suggest a thesis subject (in Chapter V, p. 140 n) on the "Colors of Rhetoric in Shakespeare" which would analyze the "somehow" and show Shakespeare's method in the use of mechanical tricks of style.

one as lyric or descriptive rather than sophistic. In *Julius Caesar,* however, Shakespeare evidences a growing sense for moderation and discrimination in the use of declamation, for the effective use of rhetorical conversation, and also for the proper use of the oration in the drama.

The third period comes in on a wave of sophistic rhetoric of the conventional kind. *Troilus and Cressida* contains a great deal of rhetoric, much of the florid kind; in fact, this play and the later *Pericles* seem to assume "grand opera" proportions in the use of rhetoric.[5] *Hamlet*, of course, abounds in emotional rhetoric and much declamatory speaking reminiscent of Senecan rhetoric. *Othello* reveals a matured sense for moderation and discrimination in the use of declamation, for the effective use of rhetorical conversation, and for the proper use of the oration. *Lear* employs much declamatory and emotional rhetoric, and what rhetoric there is in *Macbeth* is of the declamatory or emotional kind. *Timon* breaks out in much sophistic rhetoric in the title role. *Antony and Cleopatra* contains a good deal of the emotional or descriptive kind of rhetoric. *Coriolanus* strikes a splendid balance between sophistic rhetoric and the rhetoric of the oration; the play furnishes some of the best of both types of rhetoric. In *All's Well*, Helena is the vehicle for emotional rhetoric. *Measure for Measure* contains rhetoric of a high order—much good rhetorical conversation and good Aristotelian rhetoric in the speeches of Isabella. *Pericles* is extravagant, like *Troilus and Cressida,* in the use of sophistic rhetoric; Pericles indulges in much speaking.

As in the case of the earlier history plays, *Henry VIII* contains much spectacle and an abundance of speaking. The last comedies all contain an abundance of speaking parts. Imogen's emotional rhetoric, Iachimo's "grand opera" type of rhetoric, and a great deal of extended expository declamation make *Cymbeline* one of the longest of Shakespeare's

5. Note that these two plays present problems in authorship.

plays. In *A Winter's Tale*, the denunciatory outbursts of Leontes contrast with the calm, ordered rhetoric of Hermione's defense. In the *Tempest*, however, as in *Romeo and Juliet* and *Midsummer Night's Dream*, most of what we might be tempted to call sophistic rhetoric seems more justly called rhetorical poetry.

This running review of Shakespeare's plays reveals many significant things about Shakespeare's rhetoric. In the first place, thinking of the word "rhetorical" as suggesting bombastic theatrical speaking or extended, mechanically clever speaking, we discover that Shakespeare was conspicuously unrhetorical in the vast majority of his plays: the proportion of artificial, high-sounding rhetoric in his plays is exceedingly small in comparison with the whole amount of speaking to be found in them. Then, too, a large percentage of this typically sophistic rhetoric breaks out in those plays which offer a problem in authorship or in the matter of revision, the *Henry VI* plays, *Henry VIII*, *Titus Andronicus*, *Timon of Athens*, *Pericles*; and a large proportion of the remainder of this rhetoric is to be found in plays studiedly Senecan in development—abundant and unbridled in *Richard III*, abundant but more restrained in *Hamlet*. As shall be seen later,[6] Shakespeare the critic broke early with the spectacular melodrama that had become so popular when he began to write for the stage. And the fact that Shakespeare the dramatist, when he undertook drama independent of his predecessors, either struck a happy economy in the use of sophistic rhetoric or so toned it down by the use of his skill as a poet as to make us want to call much of his speaking rhetorical poetry rather than sophistic rhetoric, contributes in large measure to his superlative achievement as a dramatic artist. What makes earlier Elizabethan drama a tedious morass of reading today is the interminable speech-making through which one has to wade to get to the end—the sound of the actor's

---

6. In Chapter IX.

voice, the facial expressions, and the movements of gestures evidently made it less tiresome when acted on the stage. But Shakespeare's use of economy in speech-making and his sense of proportion in the development of the individual speech enabled him to write, not typically Elizabethan drama for the Elizabethan stage, but world-drama for all time. His plays make good reading as well as good acting today. And this is true because his drama is not the rhetorical drama that was popular in his own day.

Again, a consideration of the rhetoric in Shakespeare's plays calls to mind the kinship between rhetorical drama and grand opera. The history of the opera goes back to the sixteenth century.[7] The sixteenth-century Italians, Galilei and his companions, trying in vain to revive the style of musical declamation peculiar to Greek tragedy, invented the cantata —one voice and one musical instrument. In the same century, Palestrina, in his transformation of church music, had brought to perfection the "contrapuntal richness of the polyphonic school." This contrapuntal music, however, was not suited for dramatic purposes; and, for it, the Galilei group substituted the simplest melodies. Out of this cantata music developed the lyric drama: "pure, well-accented declamatory recitative."

In the seventeenth century (1637), the Venetian Cavalli marked a distinct advance in the history of opera. His "natural taste suggested the cultivation of a more flowing style of melody than that in which his contemporaries were wont to indulge; and he was not so bigoted a disciple of the Renaissance as to think it necessary to sacrifice that taste to the insane Hellenic prejudice which would have banished rhythmic melody from the opera for no better reason than that it was unknown in the time of Pericles. Galilei and his Florentine associates condemned such melody as puerile and de-

---

7. For a discussion of the history of the opera, see George Grove, *Dictionary of Music and Musicians*, III, 690-707. Quotations in text are from this summary.

graded to the last degree. But Cavalli not only employed it constantly, for the sake of relieving the monotony of continuous recitative, but even foreshadowed the form of the regular *aria*, by that return to the first part which was afterwards indicated by the term *da capo*." From 1637 on through the century there was the great "opera house" period in Venice when the opera was transferred from the nobility to the people. In the same century Scarlatti freed the opera in expression by using three distinct forms of dramatic expressions: recitativo secco, simple narrative; recitativo stromentato, pathos; aria, impassioned soliloquy. In 1672, Lully went from ballet to grand opera. Grand opera in France substituted for *recitativo secco* accompanied recitative "so well adapted to the spirit of the best French poetry that the declamatory portions of Lully's operas soon became even more attractive than the scenes which depended for their success upon more spectacular display."

Eighteenth-century high opera was bound by severely formal rules, allowing the composer no freedom. The rules laid restrictions upon the number of singers, the divisions of the opera, and the distribution of the movements. Emphasis was placed on the solo parts and the duet at the end. There was not much combination of voices.

Then Gluck appeared on the scene. An unsatisfactory performance of his own *Piramo et Tisbe* in London in 1746 seems to have made him question "the logical consistency" of the orthodox Italian opera. The opera had degenerated until it had become little more than a collection of songs; dramatic situation was neglected in favor of arias written to show off the singers. Gluck's own opera, in keeping with the conventions of the time, was made up of a collection of arias from his best and most popular works; dramatically, it was a failure. In 1762, his new opera, *Orfeo*, proclaimed his freedom from the fetters of the old. In *Orfeo*, "he made his music everywhere subservient to the action of the drama;

finished his airs without the stereotyped *da capo*; introduced appropriate choruses and other concerted pieces; and never sacrificed the true rendering of a dramatic situation for the sake of attracting attention to his own powers as a composer, or of affording a popular singer the opportunity of displaying the flexibility of his voice."[8] That his dramatic force was "irresistible" and the "flow of his melody excellent" was admitted even by his severest critics, Metastasio and Hasse, for example, who maintained that recitative was of more importance than melody. In 1774, *Iphigenie en Aulide* established the triumph of the new form.

The history of the opera has been reviewed because it suggests much that is applicable to Shakespeare and rhetorical drama.[9] Scarlatti's *recitativo secco*, *recitativo stromentato* and *aria* are certainly akin to declamatory narrative, dramatic lament, and impassioned soliloquy in drama. When one reads that the declamatory portions of Lully's operas soon became even more attractive than the scenes which depended for their success upon mere spectacular display, and that eighteenth-century opera placed emphasis on the solo parts and neglected dramatic situation in favor of arias written to show off the singers, there inevitably comes to mind the rhetorical drama of Seneca and the earlier Elizabethans with its mass of declamatory speeches and its sacrifice of plot action to show off histrionic actors or display the dramatist's skill in the manipulation of words.[10] And when one learns

---

8. A recent rendering of the Gilbert and Sullivan operas by the D'Oyly Carte Company has been laudably successful in recapturing the spirit of the artists by subordinating solo parts and choruses and melodies to the dramatic action as a whole. This rendering of the operas has been indeed refreshing, and the interpretation has been particularly gratifying in the case of "The Mikado." For press comments upon a week's performances in Washington (Feb. 18-23, 1935) see Nelson Bell's discussions in the *Washington Post*.

9. Baldwin (*ARP*, p. 187, note) calls attention to the fact that E. C. Chickering (*An Introduction to Octavia Praetexta*, which discusses Seneca and his tragedies) suggests a resemblance to grand opera.

10. Compare, too, the conventional formal nature of eighteenth-century grand opera and that of the heroic drama of the Restoration period. For

of Gluck's emancipating the opera from the older "grand opera" conventions and making his music everywhere subservient to the action of the drama, of his freeing the solo parts from the conventional *da capo* and never sacrificing the true rendering of a dramatic situation to his own powers as a composer or to affording a popular singer the opportunity of displaying the flexibility of his voice, one thinks immediately of the freedom which Shakespeare brought to the Elizabethan drama by making rhetoric subservient to plot action, toning down the speech-making through the exercise of economy and moderation in expression, and to such an extent developing individual character that the solo parts are kept, by being written in terms of character, from being mere displays of the dramatist's powers of expression or mere vehicles for showing off an histrionic actor's skill in the use of face and voice and gesture. Moreover, when one knows that Gluck's excellence in dramatic force and in the flow of his melody was admitted by even his severest critics, one cannot help recalling that Shakespeare's excellence was recognized and commended, though with reservation, by such classicists as Ben Jonson, Dryden, and Dr. Johnson. Indeed, Shakespeare did for Elizabethan drama—in fact, for drama of all time—what Gluck did for opera. Gluck gave the solo parts their right place in opera; Shakespeare gave declamation and emotional passages their proper place in drama.

The sophistic rhetoric in Shakespeare's plays suggests fur-

reading in the history of the opera, see Joseph Goddard, *Rise and Development of the Opera*, especially Section IV on "English Opera," pp. 142-170. See also, Richard Wagner, *Oper und Drama*, trans. by Edwin Evans, especially Part II, "The Stage Play and Dramatical Poetic Art in the Abstract" —references to Shakespeare. For a concise critical discussion of opera of the seventeenth and eighteenth centuries see Arthur Elson, *A Critical History of Opera*, Chapters I and II on the origin of opera and Gluck's reforms (pp. 11-61). For a concise critical discussion of Restoration drama, see A. H. Thorndike, *Tragedy*, Chapters VIII and IX on Restoration and eighteenth-century drama (pp. 243-324). For a more extended discussion, see C. V. Deane, *Dramatic Theory and the Rhymed Heroic Play*.

Sophistic Rhetoric in Shakespeare 49

ther the matter of the actors who played the parts when the plays were written. Our rapid review of the plays has shown the prominence of the histrionic parts in the earlier plays. Talbot, Margaret, Titus, Richard III, Philip, and Constance were all parts that called for histrionic acting, much of which might be made unduly melodramatic. Later, Hamlet, Lear, Othello, Coriolanus, and Timon called for superb histrionic skill tempered with faithful interpretation of character to save them from being merely melodramatic. Practical dramatist that Shakespeare was, he must have written parts with actors in mind. As to the assignment of individual parts in individual plays, we have no complete original records; we have to be content with references here and there. We do know, however, of the histrionic talent of Burbage and can well conceive his acting with distinction the parts of Talbot, Titus, Richard III, Philip, Hamlet, Lear, Othello, Coriolanus, and Timon.[11] None but experienced actors should at-

11. According to Collier, a manuscript epitaph upon Burbage (who died in 1619), records that he was the original Hamlet, Romeo, Prince Henry, Henry V, Richard III, Macbeth, Brutus, Coriolanus, Shylock, Lear, Pericles, and Othello. (Noted in Collier's Edition, I, xxii, in a footnote to Chapter VI, of "The Life of William Shakespeare.") See also, however, T. W. Baldwin, *The Organization and Personnel of the Shakespearean Company*, Chapter IX, "The Actors in Shakespeare's Plays," for the discussion of actors and their parts. The following quotations from Baldwin are significant:

1. "No guiding lists to any of the plays themselves, and but few assigned parts." p. 229.

2. "Burbage had by this time (1594) established incontestably his inalienable right to the leading role, having already created Hamlet and Richard III by 1594, others of his known later characters being Lear and Othello. These four are the only Shakespearean parts definitely assigned to Burbage by contemporary evidence." p. 237.

For further discussion of this point of controversy, see *The Shakespeare Allusion-Book*, I, 272-273; "A Funerall Ellegye on y[e] Death of the Famous Actor Richard Burbedge who dyed on Saturday in Lent the 13 of March, 1618. (ll. 12-16.)

"hee's gone & with him what A world are dead.
which he reviv'd, to be revived soe,
no more young Hamlett, ould Heironymoe,
Kind Leer, the Greved Moore, and more beside,
that lived in him;"

From MS 1.27, pp. 90-93, in the Folger Library, a transcript of the long

tempt such parts as these: in the hands of good actors, these parts become some of the best achievements of dramatic art; in the hands of poor ones, those that were not written in a melodramatic vein can be robbed of effectiveness by futile attempts to make them so and those that were intentionally melodramatic can be made excessively so. Particularly, in such emotional rhetoric as that of the great tragedies, good acting makes all the difference in the world between what Shakespeare must have intended in the writing and what melodramatic interpretation of his speeches makes of them.

The need for good acting of the speaking parts in Shakespeare becomes all the more pertinent when we consider the women parts. Shakespeare evidenced an intense interest in the portrayal of noble women, and his women characters are repeatedly made the vehicles for much of his emotional rhetoric. Margaret, Constance, Portia the heiress and Portia the wife of Brutus, Isabella, Imogen, Hermione, Lady Macbeth, Cleopatra, and Volumnia are characters that call for not only excellent memory in the great amount of speaking that they do, but judgment and understanding in the proper interpretation of their emotional rhetoric. The marvel to us today is that these Elizabethan parts could be done for Shakespeare by boys or men:[12] only the best of actresses would satisfy us today that they were getting out of them for us what Shakespeare put into them.

In the light of these general impressions of Shakespeare's use of emotional rhetoric, a more detailed consideration of sophistic rhetoric in the plays will be undertaken, beginning

---

Burbage elegy in MSS from Warwick Castle; E. K. Chambers, *The Elizabethan Stage*, II, 309; J. P. Collier, *Memoirs of the Principal Actors in the Plays of Shakespeare*, pp. 52-53; and J. P. Collier, *English Dramatic Poetry and Annals of the Stage*, I, 411-412. These references take up the matter of the *Funeral Elegy* on Burbage and the different versions.

12. This line in *Antony and Cleopatra* (V, ii) may indicate criticism on Shakespeare's part:

"Some squeaking Cleopatra boy my greatness."

with the traditional kind. Act II of *Titus Andronicus* opens with Aaron's soliloquy in the expository vein and closes with a splendid example of the traditional lament—the lament of Marcus over the maimed Lavinia. In the next act, Titus speaks lines upon lines of lamentation at the sight of his disfigured daughter. As the act progresses, his rhetoric becomes more and more unbridled as his grief drives him maddened to seek revenge. Aaron, the insatiate villain, speaks his villainy at length in Act IV and again in Act V. Titus's cutting of the throats of Chiron and Demetrius is framed in a speech of denunciation and anathema typical of the Senecan tragedy of revenge.

The *Henry VI* plays reveal the traditional use of declamatory rhetoric. Talbot's spirited rhetoric dominates *1 Henry VI*—his lament over Salisbury and Gargrave (I, iv); his denunciation of Sir John Fastolfe (IV, i); his defiance of the French at Bordeaux; his vain plea to his son to flee the field of battle; his lament over his son's death just before his own death (IV, ii-vii). Act I, scene i, of *2 Henry VI* closes with a good soliloquy by York in the expository vein. In this play there is much sophistic rhetoric in soliloquies and much rhetorical dialogue. Henry, York, the Cardinal, Gloucester, the Duchess of York, and Queen Margaret are the vehicles of rhetoric. The grand-opera type of rhetoric runs away with things in Act III, scene ii, in the fine example of Margaret's facility in the use of sophistic denunciation—here, her denunciation of the King. In *3 Henry VI*, York continues to be the vehicle for rhetoric, as also does the King. The King's soliloquy opening Act II, scene v is a good example of artificial rhetoric. *Richard III*, studiedly modeled on the Senecan tragedy of blood and revenge, contains an abundance of the traditional sophistic rhetoric. The women are made the vehicles for some of the best of Shakespeare's Senecan emotional rhetoric—Anne's lament at the coffin of Henry VI (I, ii); Margaret's denunciation of the fiendish Richard, certainly a rival of the stock medieval anathema that started at the top of a man's head and cursed him right on down to the heels (I, iii); her lengthy gloating over Queen Elizabeth's wretchedness (IV, iv). Gloucester, like Aaron, finds sophistic rhetoric the convenient weapon of the villain—smoothly insinuative, ridiculously audacious, but persistently persuasive.

The position of *King John* is pivotal in the history of Shakespeare's rhetoric. Here is a rewriting of an earlier play. In the reconstruction, Shakespeare used the utmost freedom in condensing the material within the compass of an average five-act play and in the treatment of characters. For this discussion of rhetoric, the elaboration of the characters of Constance and Philip is of significance. These characters are made to carry much sophistic rhetoric; but here for the first time in history plays do we find rhetoric revealing an individual touch that makes us want to call it by another name. Intensely emotional rhetoric it is in the speeches of Constance. At times it verges upon the purely sentimental and hysterical, but in the main it remains true to the best utterance of motherly love. A great actress is needed to portray Constance in order to keep her rhetoric, emotional as it is, from taking away from the depth of feeling intended in the character—from making an intendedly noble character melodramatic. Consider her speeches at the opening of Act III. Philip, spectacular, smart-talking, carefree, natural man as he is, naturally breaks out in declamatory rhetoric. He has the last word in every act except the third, closing Act II with the memorable "Commodity" soliloquy. *King John* gives us an understanding of what Shakespeare accomplished in the history of sophistic rhetoric in the Elizabethan drama. He transformed sophistic rhetoric from the mere mechanical declamation designed for theatrical effect apart from character into the spontaneous expression of individual emotion growing out of the interplay of character and circumstance. In this way, he indicated the proper place of sophistic rhetoric

Sophistic Rhetoric in Shakespeare 53

in drama; from *King John* on, Shakespearean drama ceases to be rhetorical drama.

Shakespeare's use of sophistic rhetoric can be followed through history play, comedy, and tragedy. *Richard II* is full of sophistic rhetoric. Richard himself is made the vehicle for much speaking. Emotional as he is, he is given to indulging the expression of his emotion; and, because he is poetical by nature, his speeches often take a poetical turn. To recall a few of what seem the best: his speech after meeting Bolingbroke, who has returned from exile (III, iii); his rhetorical outbursts when confronted with the proposal of resignation (IV, i); his long soliloquy in Pomfret Castle just before his death (V, v). The play contains also Gaunt's famous speech (II, i).

In the *Henry IV* plays, Shakespeare advances in his delineation of character by emphasizing character contrast. Hotspur is introduced as a foil to the Prince and reveals his character in his rhetorical speeches in the very first act. Lady Percy is made the vehicle for emotional rhetoric in both plays; her speech in Part I (II, iii) is comparable with the plea of Portia in Act II, scene i, of *Julius Caesar*. The ordered rhetorical conversation between the King and Prince in Act III, scene ii, in which the King seeks to persuade the Prince to assume the responsibilities of his position, is made pivotal in plot development and interpretation of character; and the ordered rhetorical conversation of Hotspur with Blunt (IV, iii), in answer to Blunt's delivery of the King's proffered adjustment of grievances, is also interwoven with the unraveling of the plot action and is, as well, indicative of character. In the Second Part, there is a good deal of good declamatory rhetoric. In the opening scene of the play, we have declamatory narrative; in the closing scene of Act IV, the rhetoric becomes emotionalized in the conversation between father and son. Just before this conversation the Prince soliloquizes on the crown in some striking emotional rhetoric, reminding us of the father's famous "Sleep Soliloquy" at the opening of Act III. *Henry V* registers some of Shakespeare's best achievements in rhetoric of the history plays. The King's long reflective soliloquy on *Ceremony* and his prayer following, IV, i, are excellent examples of Shakespeare's sophistic rhetoric at its best.

When comedy comes up for consideration, as a rule greater economy is found in the use of rhetoric than in the history plays. This is naturally to be expected in view of the greater prominence of rapid conversation, the lighter movement characteristic of comic incident, and reliance on repartee and word-play as a means of securing humor.[13] Moreover, in comedy the speaking parts are generally more concentrated. In *Love's Labour's Lost*, Biron is the character in whom Shakespeare concentrates most of the speaking; and the tempered rhetoric of the speeches of this play stands out in contrast to the traditional sophistic rhetoric of the early history plays and *Titus Andronicus*. In *Comedy of Errors*, Adriana and Luciana are made the vehicles for emotional rhetoric. Adriana's denunciation speech in Act II, scene ii, and the conversation between Luciana and Antipholus S. in Act III, scene ii are quite artificial. In the *Two Gentlemen*, the emotional speeches of the lovers show that here, as in *King John*, Shakespeare's interest in character development is going hand in hand with a sense for integrating sophistic rhetoric with character interpretation. Throughout this play, there is felt, it would seem for the first time in comedy, that problem of differentiating between sophistic rhetoric and rhetorical poetry which becomes all the more insistent in some of the later plays. In *Midsummer Night's Dream* and *Twelfth Night*, there is much of the best of Shakespeare's emotional rhetoric tinged with poetry that grows out of the love motive dominating the plays. In *Midsummer Night's*

---

13. Emotional rhetoric of the conventionally artificial type is a tragic, not a comic convention. In Shakespeare, the emotional rhetoric of comedy often becomes poetic in a way unknown elsewhere in Elizabethan drama.

Sophistic Rhetoric in Shakespeare

Dream, Helena's part calls for much extended speaking of "passionate words." The fairies come in for declamatory speaking of the more conventional artificial kind. In *Twelfth Night* Shakespeare practices much economy and distribution in the use of emotional rhetoric on the part of the lovers, and the speaking of the play gains in life-likeness as a result. In this play, as in *As You Like It*, much extended speaking is in prose; and, being thus like speech in ordinary life, is not rhetorical. The opening speech of the Duke, the soliloquy of Viola at the end of Act II, scene ii, and Sebastian's soliloquy at the opening of Act IV, scene iii are examples of extended rhetorical speaking. In *As You Like It*, the Duke waxes rhetorical at the beginning of Act II; so does Adam in his conversation with Orlando and Orlando in his conversation with the Duke in the same act; Jaques, of course, comes in for a goodly share of declamatory rhetoric. In Act III, scene v, Phebe and Rosalind are vehicles for extended emotional rhetoric. In Act IV, scene iii, Oliver indulges in some extended declamatory rhetoric. In *The Taming of the Shrew* excellent use is made of sophistic rhetoric in the interpretation of the characters of Petruchio and Katherine. In *Much Ado*, Claudio and Leonato break out in some sophistic rhetoric against Hero in Act IV. In *All's Well*, Helena's emotional rhetoric dominates the speaking in the play. Compare her disclosure to the Countess of the state of her affections in Act I, scene iii, and her soliloquy in Act III, scene ii.

Troilus and Cressida and *Pericles* revive the "grand opera" kind of rhetoric to be found in *Titus Andronicus*, *Richard III*, and the *Henry VI* plays. In both cases, as has been noted, these are problem plays in the matter of authorship and collaboration. *Troilus and Cressida* abounds in extended declamatory rhetoric. Ulysses, Agamemnon, Nestor, Aeneas, Troilus, Paris, Hector are all large speaking parts. The play begins formally with a lengthy prologue and ends in a highly melodramatic vein. *Pericles* has all the spectacular trappings of the rhetorical drama—the prologue-like Gower speeches and the dumb-shows. The role of Pericles offers great possibilities for the display of the skill of a declamatory actor.

Cymbeline and *A Winter's Tale* reveal that, as has been pointed out, what Shakespeare did for Elizabethan drama is comparable to what Gluck did for opera. Both plays are conceived on a grand scale—*Cymbeline* presents a certain spaciousness of action; *A Winter's Tale* leaps over sixteen years between Act III and Act IV. Both plays contain much rhetorical speaking, and the solo parts are prominent. But both plays are so held together by development of plot action and development of character that the rhetoric is integrated in the dramatic action. The First Gentleman in *Cymbeline* delivers an expository speech near the beginning of the play. Iachimo and Cymbeline, presenting as they do a great character contrast, become the vehicles for a great deal of rhetorical speaking, both in soliloquy and in conversation. There is much emotional rhetoric in the speeches of Imogen. Belarius delivers a long expository speech in Act III, scene iii. At the end of Act II Posthumus delivers an emotional soliloquy and, later in the play, is made the vehicle for several emotional soliloquies. In *A Winter's Tale*, Hermione, Leontes, Paulina, and Perdita are speaking parts. The denunciatory outbursts of Leontes are highly theatrical, but are so written in terms of character that they do not become melodramatic.

In tragedy, Shakespeare developed dramatic plot technique at its best and also illustrated the best use of rhetoric in poetic. In all the tragedies he has made emotional rhetoric a vital part of character interpretation. At once the soliloquies of the great tragedies are recalled as examples of emotional rhetoric at its best. In *Romeo and Juliet*, much of the declamatory rhetoric is likely to impress one as lyric or descriptive rather than sophistic, especially the Queen Mab speech of Mercutio and some of the love speeches of Romeo and Juliet. Some of the more heightened emotional speeches, however, show a lingering influence of Senecan rhetoric; for example, Juliet's outbursts after the death of Tybalt and the Friar's long speech just after Romeo threatens to stab himself (III, iii).

In the great tragedies Shakespeare perfected his skill in psychological studies of eccentric, abnormal, or subnormal characters.[14] These psychological studies employ emotional rhetoric in the expression and interpretation of states of mind. The traditional, mechanical, sophistic rhetoric of a mere theatrical performer he transforms into the expression of emotional thinking generated in character from within. The rhetoric thus becomes not just a mere adornment displaying the dramatist's skill in putting on stunts with words, but something organic in the drama because it is a part of character. And the psychological aspect of sophistic rhetoric in the tragedies is one of the most interesting observations made in the study of Shakespeare's rhetoric.

Julius Caesar marks the beginning of this period of perfecting psychological analysis. In Act I, scene ii, the rhetorical conversation between the introspective Brutus and the insinuating Cassius reveals the minds of these two men. Later in the same act, the conversation between Cassius and Casca again discloses the mind of Cassius. In Act II, the mind of the idealist Brutus is laid bare in his conversation with the conspirators; and, after they leave, the emotional rhetoric of Portia, some of the finest in Shakespeare, reveals the thinking of the ideal wife. Throughout the play, the role of Brutus, as well as that of his foil, Cassius, calls for the high-

14. The *Psychomachia* of Prudentius, with its allegory of soul-struggle, passed on to the Middle Ages the allegory which presented personified abstractions by means of appropriate costume, gesture, and speech. Its influence during the Middle Ages is attested by frequent citation, and it was printed in the sixteenth, seventeenth, and eighteenth centuries. Its influence is to be noted particularly in the Morality plays when the English drama became allegorical in method and psychological in point of view. For a brief discussion of Prudentius and the *Psychomachia*, see Baldwin, *MRP*, pp. 103-105.

est type of emotional acting. And, of course, the part of Antony tests all the ability of the emotional orator. These great parts in Shakespeare are misinterpreted as soon as their rhetoric is made suggestive in any way of the melodramatic and not kept integral in character and plot development.

The danger of lapsing into melodrama is all the more threatening in the case of *Hamlet*. Here is a play which is Senecan in conception, and much of the rhetoric can easily be made the traditional mouthing rhetoric of the rhetorical drama. The play contains a great deal of rhetoric; the leading characters take their turn in rhetorical speaking. But plot, action, and character were regarded by Shakespeare as the dominant elements in the play, not the dialogue and the theatrical acting. Plainly, Shakespeare was not writing rhetorical drama here. The rhetoric of the soliloquies and the rhetorical conversation were intended as a part of the psychological analysis. Any other interpretation misses Shakespeare; what one gets is not Shakespeare but the actor; and when actor and actress are emphasized at the expense of character and situation, the play becomes melodrama. To Shakespeare the critic, as revealed in his plays,[15] *Hamlet* as melodrama would have been, one is tempted to say, *reductio ad absurdum*.

Again, *Othello*, as Shakespeare conceived the play, was a psychological study of character clashing with character and circumstance. The rhetoric of the villainous Iago, the jealous Othello, the enraged Brabantio, the suffering Desdemona, and, toward the end of the play, the exasperated Emilia, was not written just to let you hear villainy, jealousy, and rage ranting on the stage nor to let you hear innocence suffering aloud;[16] it was intended to let you see Iago thinking villainy, Othello thinking jealousy, Brabantio and Emilia thinking their rage, Desdemona thinking thoughts of suffer-

---

15. See discussion in Chapter IX of Shakespeare the critic as revealed in his plays, and in *Hamlet* in particular (pp. 240-242).

16. See note 14.

Sophistic Rhetoric in Shakespeare 59

ing innocence. Only actors and actresses capable of interpreting the psychological states of these characters can do justice to Shakespeare's emotional rhetoric in this play.[17]

The role of King Lear can likewise be misinterpreted if his ravings are made purely melodramatic. Here is another example of Shakespeare's intense interest in this period in various psychological problems. This is another study of minds unbalanced through emotions stirred by clashes with antagonistic minds and disturbing circumstances. The "Lear" part is by far the dominant speaking part in *King Lear*. His emotional rhetoric is a part of his madness—it is his unbalanced mind thinking out aloud. The leading part is well supported in its rhetoric. The perverted Edmund reveals in his speeches his poison-concocting mind. The fearful Edgar assumes the part of a mad beggar and is made the vehicle for a rhetoric of the declamatory sort, as he philosophizes at the end of Act III, scene vi, or recounts his experiences to Edmund in Act V, scene iii. Kent is made the vehicle for expository rhetoric, as he tells the Gentleman of the beginning of the French invasion (III, i).

And what has just been said of these great tragedies is applicable to the remaining tragedies. Macbeth and Lady Macbeth break out in emotional rhetoric as they betray the workings of their villainous minds and suffer the remorse of minds diseased by their own villainy. At times, the ravings of Macbeth are punctuated by ironical touches of sober-

---

[17]. Disraeli, in *Vivian Grey*, refers to *Othello* made ballet and opera: Vivian, in talking to the ladies at Ems, refers to Vigano as the one who "has raised the ballet of action to an equality with tragedy. I have heard my father mention the splendid effect of his *Vestale* and his *Othello*."

Violet: "And yet I do not like *Othello* to be profaned. It is not for operas and ballets. We require the thrilling words."

Vivian: "It is very true; yet Pasta's action in the opera was a grand performance; and I have myself seldom witnessed a more masterly effect produced by an actor in the world than I did a fortnight ago at the Opera at Darmstadt, by Wild in *Othello*."

Near the end of *Vivian Grey*, Vivian attends Rossini's *Othello* at Reisenberg.

ing poetry. Timon's misanthropy breaks through, in Act IV, scene iii, in a deluge of curses—one protracted damning right and left without any reservation.

There is an abundance of rhetoric in *Antony and Cleopatra*, and it is often richly colored with poetic imagery. The "barge" speech of Enobarbus (II, ii) comes at once to mind as an extended example of this colorful rhetoric; and later, in Act IV, Enobarbus is made the vehicle for convincing emotional rhetoric just before his death. The emotional rhetoric of the lovers reveals with remarkable sincerity the intensity of their passion. In fact, the heightening of the characters of the lovers which Shakespeare achieves in the play depends in large measure upon his skilful use of sophistic rhetoric as revelation of character. The various mental attitudes of the Shakespearean Antony are revealed in his speech of direction to Enobarbus at the end of Act I, scene ii, his conversation with Cleopatra in Act I, scene iii, about Fulvia, his mental fencing with the other triumvirs in Act II, scene ii, his speech of despair for himself as he dismisses his attendants in Act III, scene xii, his outbursts of anger against Cleopatra and Thyreus in Act III, scene xiii, his melancholy broodings with Cleopatra and their attendants in Act IV, scene ii, his shouted boastings before Cleopatra in Act IV, scene viii, as he fancies ultimate triumph, his outburst of anger and despair in Act IV, scene xii, as he glimpses ultimate defeat in the words of Scarus:

>   Antony
> Is valiant, and dejected; and by starts,
> His fretted fortunes give him hope and fear,
> Of what he has and has not.

The closing lines of Antony reveal the mind of the passionate lover and passionate warrior soberly and eloquently and philosophically speaking its thoughts as it looks back upon the past and out upon the future. We are recalling, of course, Antony's matchless rhetoric in Act IV, scenes xiv and xv—rhetoric which casts about the warrior-lover's death an atmos-

Sophistic Rhetoric in Shakespeare   61

phere of magnificent tragedy peculiarly Shakespeare's own. As Antony passes, the rhetoric of Cleopatra heightens and dominates the interest of the remainder of the play. Antony's body is borne off as Cleopatra utters the eloquence of

> No more but e'en a woman.

And in Act V her last speeches lift her character up to the eminence of the closing scene, which matches in magnificence the scene of the death of her lover. In this play, Shakespeare reaches the supreme heights of his own sophistic rhetoric.

In *Coriolanus*, the passionate shoutings of Coriolanus against the people and the people's wishes are the audible workings of a stubborn aristocratic mind that lacks imagination to see out of itself and recognize the others' point of view. In the emotional rhetoric of Coriolanus, as we have said, Shakespeare seems to have risen to some of his best utterance.

There remains only *Henry VIII*. This play, problematical as to authorship, presents a succession of spectacular scenes and speech after speech of showy rhetoric. The play marks a lapse to drama of the rhetorical sort. Katherine, Buckingham, King Henry, Wolsey, Griffith and Cranmer help to swell the volume of the rhetoric, but rhetoric as integral in characterization is in large measure absent; or, if present, inferior.

It might be well to sum up here the impressions of Shakespeare's use of declamatory and emotional rhetoric in his plays.

First, Shakespeare's declamatory and emotional rhetoric is very different from the conventional rhetoric of the earlier Elizabethans and that of his contemporaries. When narrative or descriptive, his rhetoric was saved by his poetic genius from being the tiresome and dull type that characterizes so much of Elizabethan dramatic literature.[18] When the rhetoric

---

18. The conventional ornate rhetoric of Elizabethan drama was a phase of the vogue of expression that manifested itself also in artificially ornate Elizabethan prose.

was emotional, his psychological insight into character and his skill in integrating character development and plot action saved it from being mere declamation and gave it a certain intellectual appeal that the traditional emotional rhetoric lacks.

Second, sophistic rhetoric in the hands of Shakespeare, as in the hands of any other dramatist, when used in extended speeches inevitably brings the "solo" parts into prominence. However, Shakespeare, when working independently, avoids the conventional "grand opera" treatment of solo parts for their own sake. This he does by subordinating the solo parts to dramatic situation and plot development. It seems that even where he is collaborating, or revising, or consciously imitating, he achieves a certain toning down of the conventional declamatory rhetoric popular in his day.

Third, a proper sensing of Shakespeare's personal distrust of this conventional declamatory rhetoric and his aversion to melodrama is essential in the interpretation of the speaking parts in his plays.[19] Faithful acting of Shakespeare keeps in mind that Shakespeare's plays hold a "mirror up to nature"; and any acting which gives the impression that Shakespeare's personal interest in his sophistic rhetoric concerned itself with mere exhibition of skill in writing or mere histrionic acting inevitably misinterprets Shakespeare. Moreover, faithful interpretation of Shakespeare's characters through sympathetic rendering of their emotional rhetoric calls not only for trained memory and skill in expression, but for judgment and feeling as well. We cannot help wondering how we of today would have been impressed by the acting of Shakespeare's plays before an Elizabethan audience—particularly the acting of the matchless women parts; successful interpretation of these parts by men and boys attests the remarkable training of Elizabethan actors.

19. On the delivery of the set speech as a test of acting, see *Hamlet*, II, ii.

CHAPTER IV

Classification and Sources

RHETORICIANS IN GENERAL agree as to the number of classes of orations. Aristotle, Cicero, Quintilian, and Wilson agree upon three classes; and, in our own day, orations are still thought of as falling into one of these three classes. In the matter of the content of each class, too, rhetoricians agree as to the kinds of orations to be placed in each class. Sometimes it is difficult to draw a hard and fast line separating the classes, but in the main the classifications agreed upon below are fairly easily maintained.

Aristotle's *Rhetoric* (Bk. I, Chap. iii) gives the three kinds of rhetoric: deliberative, judiciary, and demonstrative. The treatise thus describes each kind:

"The first of these comprises two parts, viz., persuasion and dissuasion; for, whether in private or public debate, one or other of them is generally achieved.

"The second kind has also two subordinate parts, namely, accusation and defense, for the general result of the advocate's pleading turns upon either of the two.

"The third kind also contains under it two parts, encomium and inculpation."[1]

Cicero has this to say about classification:

"But of such subjects as are distinct from general questions, part come under the head of judicial proceedings, part under that of deliberations; and there is a third kind which is employed in praising or censuring particular persons. There are also certain commonplaces on which we may insist in judicial

---

1. See D. M. Crimmin's translation, p. 41.

proceedings, in which equity is the object; others, which we may adopt in deliberations, all of which are to be directed to the advantage of those to whom we give counsel; others in panegyric, in which all must be referred to the dignity of the persons commended."[2]

Quintilian, while he suggests that a division into judicial and extra-judicial may be sufficient, thinks it better to adopt the classification used generally by rhetoricians before him.

"There is, then as I have said, one kind of oratory in which praise and blame, are included, but which is called, from the better part of its office, the panegyrical, others, however, term it the demonstrative or epideictic. The second kind is the deliberative and the third judicial."[3]

Wilson's *Arte of Rhetorique* has the following on classification:

"The oration demonstrative standeth either in praise, or dispraise of some one man, or some one thing, or of some one deed doen.

"An oration deliberative, is meane whereby we doe perswade, or disswade, or entreate, or rebuke, exhorte or dehort, commend, or comforte any man.

"Oration Iudiciall, is an earnest debating in open assemblie, of some weightie matter before a Iudge, where the complainaunt commenceth his action, and the defendant thereupon answereth at his perill, to all such things as are laied to his charge."[4]

As Wilson suggests in his treatise, it is difficult to maintain hard and fast lines separating the classes. However, Wilson's classification has furnished in the main the basis for our classification of orations in Shakespeare. This classification by Wilson has been modified, first, by a comparison with ancient and modern conceptions of classification, and second, by a

2. *De Oratore*, Bk. I, Chap. 31. See J. S. Watson's translation, p. 40.
3. *Institutes of Oratory*, Bk. III, Chap. 4. See J. S. Watson's translation, pp. 182-183. London, 1899.
4. Pp. 11, 29, 86, G. H. Mair's edition.

Classification and Sources 65

consideration of the content of orations found in Shakespeare's plays. It is easy to classify orations of the law-courts. The term "forensic" seems to be more generally used today than the term "judicial," so we have used both of these terms for classifying orations of the bar. The difficulty arises in separating orations that are not forensic into two classes. In attempting this separation, I have thought of the word "deliberative" as signifying what it meant for Aristotle, Cicero, Quintilian, and to a certain extent, Wilson. Wilson's "entreate or rebuke, exhorte or dehort, commend or comforte," suggesting emphasis on appeal to the emotions or expression of emotions, we have transferred to the class of orations that make greatest use of emotional rhetoric—the epideictic, demonstrative, or occasional orations.[5] Expository orations I have put in the "occasional" class, also,—they are essentially "demonstrative."

In presenting in tabular form the orations in Shakespeare, I have used the generally accepted four-period division of his plays as given in Neilson and Thorndike's *Facts About Shakespeare*.[6]

5. Frankly, I am not at all satisfied that "entreate, exhorte or dehort" should be, without reservation, shifted from deliberative to demonstrative; moreover, I am not at all sure that Wilson has his words paired correctly. For an example of a hortatory speech I feel to be deliberative, see the speech to Nikokles by Isocrates, analyzed in Chapter V. However, in the case of Shakespeare's orations, the shift to the occasional class has proven a workable one.

6. P. 76. This book does not investigate the oration in "The Shakespeare Apocrypha." However, Tucker Brooke's discussion of *Sir Thomas More* in his Introduction (pp. li, lii) to *The Shakespeare Apocrypha* should be recalled. He begins his discussion of the "insurrection scene" (II, iv) thus: "The first 172 lines of the 'insurrection scene' appear to me more thoroughly in the tone of Shakespeare than any other passage in the doubtful plays." He then goes on to discuss the scene and the oration of More—the dramatic utility of the scene and the Shakespearean-like manner and matter of the oration—concluding, by way of summary, "it is exactly the sort of scene we should expect Shakespeare to write, had he been called upon to revise the play, full of his well-known sentiments, and expressed in a style which is very remarkably like his own during the period 1590-5." The scene is in Hand D, regarded by some as very likely the handwriting of Shakespeare, which handwriting Professor Brooke regards as lending added reason for believing the scene probably Shakespeare's.

66   *The Oration in Shakespeare*

Comedies		History Plays		Tragedies
		Period 1		
Love's Labour's Lost	1591	1-Henry VI		
		2-Henry VI	1590/92	
		3-Henry VI		
Comedy of Errors	1591	Richard III	1593	
Two Gentlemen of Verona	1591/95	King John	1593/96	Titus Andronicus 1593/4
		Period 2		
Midsummer Night's Dream	1594/95	Richard II	1594	Romeo and Juliet
Merchant of Venice	1596	1-Henry IV	1597/98	1591 or 1594/5
Taming of the Shrew	1596/97	2-Henry IV		
Merry Wives of Windsor	1598/99	Henry V	1599	Julius Caesar
Much Ado About Nothing	1599			1599
As You Like It	1599/1600			
Twelfth Night	1601			
		Period 3		
Troilus and Cressida	1601/02			Hamlet 1602/3/4
All's Well That Ends Well	1602			Othello 1604
Measure For Measure	1603/04			King Lear 1604/5
				Macbeth 1605/6
				Timon of Athens 1607
Pericles	1607/8			Anthony and Cleopatra 1607/8
				Coriolanus 1609
		Period 4		
Cymbeline	1610/11			
Winter's Tale	1611			
Tempest	1611	Henry VIII	1612	

7. A speech of defense comes in answer to an accusation advanced. In Shakespeare, the accusation is sometimes advanced in a speech of an oratorical nature. The following speeches delivered in connection with a trial should be considered along with the speeches of defense:

PLAY	SPEAKER
C of E, I, i	Duke
C of E, V, i	Adriana
1 H VI, III, i	Queen
2 H VI, IV, vii	Cade (prose)
R II, I, i	Bolingbroke
1 H IV, V, i	King
2 H IV, V, ii	King Henry V (particularly his judgment of the defense at end of scene)
M of V, IV, i	Duke
M of V, IV, i	Portia
Oth, I, iii	Brabantio
W T, III, ii	Officer (Reading indictment)
H VIII, II, iv	Katherine (Accusation of Wolsey)
H VIII, V, iii	Chancellor and Gardiner (The king's speech—judge and advocate.)

Classification and Sources

TABLE I
FORENSIC ORATIONS

Play	Act	Scene	Setting	Speaker	Spoken to	Purpose
					Period 1	
C of E	I	i	Hall, Duke's palace	Aegeon	Duke (and others)	Defense[7] of himself
C of E	V	i	Street before Priory	Ant. Eph.	Duke (and others)	Defense of himself
1 H VI	III	i	Before Parliament	Winchester	King and Lords	Defense of himself (brief and incomplete)
2 H VI	III	i	Abbey at Bury Saint Edmund's	Gloucester	Royalty and Lords	Defense of himself
2 H VI	IV	vii	Smithfield	Say	Cade and Company	Defense of himself
T A	I	i	Senate House	Tamora	Titus, Senators, Tribunes, and others	Defense of son
					Period 2	
R and J	V	iii	Tomb of Capulets	Friar Lawrence	Capulets, Montagues, and others	Exposition of situation. In defense of himself
R II	I	i	Palace	Mowbray	King and Lords	Defense of himself
1 H IV	V	i	Camp near Shrewsbury	Worcester	King and Lords	Defense of himself
2 H IV	V	ii	Westminster Palace	Chief Justice	King (attended)	Defense of himself
M of V	IV	vii	Court of Justice	Shylock	Duke, Magnificoes, and others	Defense of himself
					Period 3	
M for M	II	ii	Angelo's House	Isabella	Angelo, Provost, Lucio	Defense of Claudio (not sufficiently public)
Oth	I	iii	Council Chamber	Othello	Duke and Council	Defense of himself
T of A	III	v	Senate House	Alcibiades	Senators	Defense of friend
					Period 4	
W T	III	ii	Place of Justice	Hermione	Leontes, Lords off	Defense of herself
H VIII	II	iv	Black Friars	Katherine	King, Lords, and others	Defense of herself
H VIII	II	iv	Black Friars	Wolsey	Queen, King, and others	Defense of himself
H VIII	V	iii	Council Chamber	Cranmer	Lord Chancellor, Duke, and Lords	Defense of himself (broken and incomplete)

[7]See p. 66 for note.

TABLE II
DEMONSTRATIVE ORATIONS
Period I

Play	Act	Scene	Setting	Speaker	Spoken to	Purpose
1 H VI	I	i	Westminster Abbey	Messenger	Lords and others	Exposition: narrative of battle in France
2 H VI	I	i	Palace	Gloucester	Lords	Rebuke of the king's marriage
2 H VI	III	i	Abbey at Bury St. Edmund's	Queen	King and Lords	Denunciation of Gloucester
2 H VI	III	ii	Bury St. Edmund's	Salisbury	King and others	Exposition: epideictic
3 H VI	I	iv	Battlefield	Q. Margaret	York and others	Denunciation of York
3 H VI	I	iv	Battlefield	York	Queen Margaret and others	Denunciation of Queen
3 H VI	II	i	Plain near Mortimer's Cross	Warwick	Edward, Richard, Armies	Exposition: Battle of Saint Albans and the political situation
3 H VI	V	iv	Plain near Tewksbury	Q. Margaret	Lords and Soldiers	Battle oration
R III	II	i	Palace	Gloucester	King, Queen, Peers	Exposition: allegiance speech
R III	II	i	Palace	King Edward	Derby, Queen, Peers	Rebuke at suggestion of pardon for servant
R III	III	vii	Baynard's Castle	Gloucester	Buckingham	Answer to offer of kingship
R III	V	iii	Bosworth Field	Richmond	Soldiers	Battle oration
R III	V	iii	Bosworth Field	Richard	Soldiers	Battle oration
K J	I	i	Palace	Robert	King, Queen, Pembroke, and others	Exposition: claim to father's land
K J	II	i	Before Angiers	Chatillon	King and forces	Battle oration
T A	I	i	Before Senate House	Marcus Andronicus	Tribunes, Son of Emperor, and others	Eulogy of Titus or exposition on occasion of the election of Titus
T A	I	i	Before Senate House	Titus Andronicus	Gothic captives and others	Funeral oration
T A	I	i	Before Senate House	Marcus Andronicus	Titus and others	Presentation speech
T A	I	i	Before Senate House	Titus Andronicus	Marcus and others	Answer to offer
T A	IV	iv	Rome, before palace	Saturninus	Lords and others	Exposition: comment on Titus's action
T A	V	iii	Balcony	Marcus and Lucius	Aemilius, Tribunes, Senators, and others	Occasional and expository after deaths of principal characters

Classification and Sources

TABLE II (Continued)

Play	Act	Scene	Setting	Speaker	Spoken to	Purpose
					Period 2	
R II	I	iii	Lists at Coventry	Richard	Mowbray and Bolingbroke in presence of others	Pronouncing sentence
H V	I	ii	Palace Presence Chamber	Henry	French Ambassadors	Announcement of intended invasion
H V	II	ii	Council Chamber	Henry	Traitors	Pronouncing sentence
H V	III	i	Before Harfleur	Henry	Soldiers	Battle oration
H V	III	vi	English Camp	Montjoy	Henry in presence of others	Message from France
H V	III	vi	English Camp	Henry	Montjoy in presence of others	Answer to message
H V	IV	iii	English Camp	Henry	Soldiers	Exhortation; Saint Crispin's Day
J C	I	i	Rome, Street	Marullus	Commoners	Rebuke for holiday
J C	III	ii	Forum	Brutus	Plebeians	Funeral oration
J C	III	ii	Forum	Antony	Plebeians	Funeral oration
					Period 3	
T and C[a]	I	iii	Greek Camp	Agamemnon	Nestor, Ulysses, and others	Exhortation
T and C	I	iii	Greek Camp	Nestor	Agamemnon, Ulysses, and others	Exhortation
T and C	I	iii	Greek Camp	Ulysses	Agamemnon, Nestor, and others	Exposition: trouble with the Greek Camp
T and C	I	iii	Greek Camp	Aeneas	Agamemnon, Nestor, and others	Delivering challenge
H	I	ii	Room of State	King	Lords and others	Exposition: policy and state affairs
Cor	II	ii	Rome, Capitol	Cominius	Senators, Tribunes, and others	Commending Coriolanus
					Period 4	
Cym	V	v	Cymbeline's tent	Iachimo	Cymbeline, Lords, Officers, attendants, and others	Exposition of his cunning
W T	III	ii	Place of Justice	Paulina	Leontes, Lords and Officers	Rebuke of Leontes
Temp	V	i	The magic circle	Prospero	Alonso and friends	The breaking of the magic
H VIII	II	i	Westminster	Buckingham	Lords and commoners	Farewell speech
H VIII	II	iv	Black Friars	King	Lords and others	Exposition: explanation of position on marriage
H VIII	III	ii	Ante-Chamber to King's apartments	Wolsey	King and nobles	Allegiance speech
H VIII	V	v	Palace	Cranmer	King and Lords and Ladies of State	Christening of Elizabeth

[a] See p. 71 for note.

70 The Oration in Shakespeare

TABLE III
DELIBERATIVE ORATIONS

Period 1

Play	Act	Scene	Setting	Speaker	Spoken to	Purpose
L L L	IV	iii	Park	Biron	King and Lords	Change of Policy
1 H VI	III	iii	Plains near Rouen	La Pucelle	Burgundy and others	Winning allegiance
1 H VI	IV	i	Paris; a hall of state	King Henry	Rival Lords	Peace between lords
3 H VI	II	ii	Before York	Clifford	King, Queen, Prince, Northumberland	Making King decide to act for his house
R III	III	vii	Baynard's Castle	Buckingham	Gloucester	Persuading Gloucester to accept kingship
K J	II	i	Before Angiers	King John	Citizens of Angiers	Winning admission to the town
K J	II	i	Before Angiers	Philip	Citizens of Angiers	Winning admission to the town
K J	II	i	Before Angiers	Citizen	King John and King Philip	Persuading marriage of Blanche and Dauphin
K J	III	i	French King's pavilion	Pandulph	Kings and attendants	Persuading French desertion of English
T A	I	i	Before Senate	Tamora	Saturninus, Titus, and others	Reconciliation

Period 2

Play	Act	Scene	Setting	Speaker	Spoken to	Purpose
R II	IV	i	Westminster Hall	Carlisle	Lords as Parliament	Keeping Bolingbroke from throne
H V	I	ii	Presence Chamber, palace	Canterbury	King and Lords	Persuading the invasion of France
H V	III	iii	Before Harfleur	King Henry	Citizens of Harfleur	Winning admission to the town
H V	V	ii	Palace	Burgundy	French and English	Persuading peaceful settlement
M A N	IV	i	Church	Friar Francis	Royalty and attendants Leonato, attendants	Persuading use of disguised death of daughter

Period 3

Play	Act	Scene	Setting	Speaker	Spoken to	Purpose
Cor	I	i	Rome, a street	Menenius	Citizens	Winning kindly attitude to Senators
Cor	III	i	Rome, a street	Coriolanus	Patricians	Maintenance of power by Patricians
Cor	III	i	Rome, a street	Menenius	Citizens	Deterring from violence to Coriolanus
Cor	V	iii	Tent of Cor.	Volumnia	Coriolanus, Aufidius, and others	Persuading son to spare Rome

Period 4

Play	Act	Scene	Setting	Speaker	Spoken to	Purpose
H VIII	I	ii	Council Chamber	Katherine	King and others	Persuading favorable consider-

Classification and Sources

TABLE IV
Types by Periods

Period	Type of Speech	Comedies	Histories	Tragedies	Total Each	All
1	Forensic	2	3	1	6	
	Deliberative	1	8	1	10	
	Demonstrative	0	15	7	22	38
2	Forensic	1	3	1	5	
	Deliberative	1	4	0	5	
	Demonstrative	0	7	3	10	20
3	Forensic	1	0	2	3	
	Deliberative	0	0	4	4	
	Demonstrative	4	0	2	6	13
4	Forensic	1	3	0	4	
	Deliberative	0	1	0	1	
	Demonstrative	3	4	0	7	12
	Total	14	48	21	83	83

TABLE V
Types by Plays

Types of Orations	Periods	Comedies	Histories	Tragedies	Total
Forensic	1	2	3	1	
	2	1	3	1	
	3	1	0	2	
	4	1	3	0	
Total		5	9	4	18
Deliberative	1	1	8	1	
	2	1	4	0	
	3	0	0	4	
	4	0	1	0	
Total		2	13	5	20
Demonstrative	1	0	15	7	
	2	0	7	3	
	3	4	0	2	
	4	3	4	0	
Total		7	26	12	45
Sum of Totals		14	48	21	83

8. Note on *Troilus and Cressida:* The temptation is very great to include the rhetoric of Ulysses urging Achilles to fight (III, iii) as a deliberative oration. The speech in Homer is included in *A Collection of Orations from Homer to McKinley*, ed. Mayo W. Hazeltine; also the speech of Achilles in answer. In Shakespeare, however, the setting is informal, and, according to my definition of the oration in the drama (Chap. II), the speech of Ulysses falls under the head of rhetorical conversation—but *highly* rhetorical indeed!

As naturally to be expected in view of the variety of speeches included, the demonstrative or occasional oration is by far the kind most frequently used in Shakespeare's plays; more than half of the orations recorded are demonstrative.

The use of the oration is more frequent in the earlier plays than in the later plays. Nearly half of the total number of orations are found in the plays of the first period. From the end of the first period on, there is a constant falling off in the number of orations introduced. As Shakespeare's art develops, orations diminish in number as they gain in perfection, in structure, and dramatic integration.

Orations occur most frequently in history plays. Of the eighty-three orations recorded, forty-eight are set in history plays. In the first period, approximately two thirds of the number of orations are found in history plays. In the second period, approximately three fifths are found in history plays. And in the fourth period, the one history play, of doubtful authorship, contains more than half the number of all the orations recorded.

In the third period, the period of the great tragedies, the figures present a number of significant comparisons and contrasts with the figures of the first and second periods. In the first place, there is to be noted, as already mentioned, a falling off in the number of orations introduced: in this period, only thirteen orations have been recorded as compared with thirty-eight set in the first period and twenty in the second period. Then, of the thirteen orations recorded in the third period, five are found in one play, *Coriolanus*, four in *Troilus and Cressida*; and one each in *Measure for Measure*, *Timon of Athens*, *Hamlet*, and *Othello*. In other words, nearly half the number are found in one play, a tragedy; exactly half the remaining number in one play, a comedy; and only one each in the three remaining tragedies. No oration is recorded from *Macbeth*, *King Lear*, or *Antony and Cleopatra*.[9]

---

9. With the absence of orations from these great tragedies is worth

Classification and Sources 73

This survey leads to several observations as to the use of orations in Shakespeare. First, Shakespeare introduces the oration most often in his early plays, showing signs of experimentation and imitation; furthermore, among these early plays, he introduces the oration most often in the type of play in which he is the most imitative and most generally given to experiment in language, the chronicle history play. Second, Shakespeare, like his predecessors, finds the oration a convenient vehicle for rhetorical display. In many of the orations of the early plays, especially those introduced in history plays of the first and second periods, there are from time to time distinct reminders of the Senecan rhetoric which we discover in such profusion in pre-Shakespearean drama. Shakespeare's early orations thus reveal traces of his indebtedness to his predecessors in the matter of rhetorical style. Third, the use of the oration is particularly noticeable in those plays of Shakespeare developed about classical stories. In these plays, the lofty tone of the oration fits in naturally and harmoniously with the development of the plot as a whole. Fourth, Shakespeare early gives evidence of primary interest and marked success in plot development; and with the interest and success in plot development comes a decrease in the number of orations introduced and an increase in sustained effort in the development of the individual oration. That is to say, along with the development in plot structure comes discrimination and concentration in the use of the oration. Fifth, there is noted a growing interest and a developing skill in Shakespeare's use of the trial scene and the forensic. The tenseness of situation characteristic of a trial scene furnishes occasion and opportunity for unusually effective use of a carefully worked out speech of defense.

A review of the purposes for which orations of each class

---

noting the absence of orations from the great comedies of the second period—*Midsummer Night's Dream, Taming of the Shrew, All's Well, As You Like It, Twelfth Night*.

are used in Shakespeare's plays reveals their faithfulness to the traditions of rhetorical theory. Forensic or judicial orations in Shakespeare come in each case in answer to charges brought forward against a defendant; and, in several cases, the accusation is presented in a speech of a formal oratorical nature. In fifteen out of eighteen cases, the defense is made in defense of one's self; in the remaining three cases, the forensic is an advocate's speech in defense of someone else. Deliberative orations in Shakespeare are used in seventeen out of twenty cases for the purpose of persuading to action; in the remaining three cases, for the purpose of dissuading from action. Thus judicial and deliberative orations in Shakespeare are true to the classical and Elizabethan traditions of rhetoric as to classification of orations.

Of the forty-five orations in Shakespeare classed as demonstrative, twenty-four are speeches of the occasional type, including eulogies, rebukes, denunciations, battle orations, funeral orations, exhortations, a presentation speech, and a farewell speech. The remaining twenty-one demonstrative orations are speeches of the expository type. The demonstrative orations in Shakespeare are true, therefore, to the classical traditions of rhetorical theory and, with the modification already pointed out, to Elizabethan theory as set down by Wilson.

There remains but to point out the formal public setting of orations recorded in Shakespeare. In the case of only one forensic—that of Isabella in *Measure for Measure*—does there seem to be any deficiency in the formal public setting; but the excellence of the speech makes us forget entirely that there are only three persons making up the audience. In every other case, the setting seems to be entirely satisfying for the occasion of the speech. Among the deliberative orations, the only one which gives us pause as to its failure to measure up in every way to a sufficiently public speech is the speech of Tamora in *Titus Andronicus,* advocating reconcilia-

Classification and Sources

tion between Saturninus and Titus. This speech begins in the formal public manner; then suddenly a stage direction *(Aside to Saturninus)* makes fourteen lines not public address. The remaining lines of her speech resume the public manner. The stage direction would indeed be hard to manage; but certainly Tamora's duplicity in counseling a show of reconciliation along with the proposition,

> And then let me alone:
> I'll find a day to massacre them all
> And raze their faction and their family,
> The cruel father and his traitorous sons,
> To whom I sued for my dear son's life,
> And make them know what 'tis to let a queen
> Kneel in the streets and beg for grace in vain.

is not for just anyone's ears, but only those of Saturninus. In spite of this deficiency in the speech, we have included it because of the generally formal public nature of its setting. All of the demonstrative or occasional orations seem to us to satisfy the requirements of public address. We shall return to the matter of setting of the oration when we take up dramatic integration.

We pass now to the consideration of orations in Shakespeare with reference to source material. This consideration we think one of the most interesting matters in connection with Shakespeare's orations. Tables VI and VII furnish a basis for our discussion of Shakespeare's use of source material in writing orations:

TABLE VI
Sources Other Than Chronicles

Play	Speaker	Reference to Source Material	Evidence
L L L	Biron	An epistle of Erasmus "to persuade a yong Gentleman to marriage." Quoted by Wilson in *Arte of Rhetorique*, p. 39, Mair's Edition	Idea in source
C of E	Aegeon	Story not in Plautus's *Menaechmi*	
T A	Ant. Eph.	Plautus's *Menaechmi*	Hints
	Titus and other speakers	Though play not as yet traced to source material, German play *Tito Andronico* in *Deutsche National Litteratur*, Vol. XXIII, worthy of consideration for orations	Similarities of situation and wording
M of V	Shylock	Declamation 95, Silvayn's *Orator*	Hints
R and J	Friar Lawerence	Brooke's *Romeus and Juliet*	Hints
M A N	Friar Francis	Twentieth Novel of Bandello, story of Timbreo di Cardona	Hint of scheme, change of originator, combination
M for M	Isabella	*Die Schoene Phoenicia*, by Jacob Ayres Whetstone's *Promos and Cassandra*; cf. Prose narrative in *Heptameron*	Hints
H	King	Compare *Tragoedia Der Bestrafte Brudermord oder Prinz Hamlet aus Daennemark*; also, "Historie of Hamblet, Prince of Denmark" (1608) Translation of Belleforest's story of Hamlet in *Histoires Tragiques*	Hints
Oth	Othello	Cinthio's *Hecatommithi*, Decade III, Novel 7	Hint
Cym	Iachimo	Boccaccio's *Decameron*, Day II, Novel 9	Outline of narrative
W T	Paulina	Greene's *Pandosto*	Change of speaker; no hint for speech
	Hermione	Greene's *Pandosto*	Hints for situation and outline
J C	Marullus	Plutarch's *Julius Caesar*	Slight hints for occasion, outline, and effect
	Antony	*Antonius*, *Caesar*, *Brutus*	
	Brutus	*Brutus*, *Caesar*	
T C	Agamemnon	Homer's *Iliad*	Hints
	Nestor, Ulysses, Aeneas	Wilson's *Arte of Rhetorique*	
T of A	Alcibiades	Plutarch's *Alcibiades*	Hints as to speaker, invention of occasion and speech
Cor	Menenius	Plutarch's *Coriolanus*	Hint for situation; close rendering of story
	Coriolanus	Plutarch's *Coriolanus*	Close in parts in phrasing
	Menenius	Plutarch's *Coriolanus*	Hint
	Comminius	Plutarch's *Coriolanus*	Combination
	Volumnia	Plutarch's *Coriolanus*	Very close rendering

Classification and Sources 77

The hint for the speech of Biron may be found in Wilson's *Arte of Rhetorique*. Biron's speech has the same central idea as the epistle of Erasmus "to perswade a yong Gentleman to marriage," which is quoted in the *Arte of Rhetorique*.[10] Compare this statement from Erasmus with reference to the naturalness of love and marriage: "What is more unmanly then that man should go against the lawes of mankind?" with Biron's proposition

> To fast, to study, and to see no woman;
> Flat treason 'gainst the kingly state of youth.

This similarity of idea furnishes one of the instances in *Love's Labour's Lost* of what seems to be possible evidence of Shakespeare's knowledge of Wilson's book. Moreover, the central idea of the epistle of Erasmus is the same as the central idea of Shakespeare's play.

The story told by Aegeon in the opening scene of *The Comedy of Errors* is not found in Plautus' *Menaechmi*. The plot of the parents of the twins is Shakespeare's, and the oration of Aegeon is, therefore, also entirely independent of source material. However, there are two parts of the speech of Antipholus of Ephesus before the Duke which remind us of the play of Plautus: the reference to the dinner episode reminds us of a similar episode in the *Menaechmi*; the reference to Pinch, of the role of Medicus.

In the case of *Titus Andronicus*, some have suggested that the tragedy represents a recasting of two English originals, which are likewise thought to have furnished the source material for the German play, *Tito Andronico*, and the Dutch play, *Aran en Titus*, respectively.[11] A comparison of the

---

10. P. 40, Mair's edition. Cf. E. C. Knowlton's discussion of the "serious theme" in *Love's Labour's Lost:* "it is contrary to nature, or human nature, not to love and marry"—the same view that Luther held. "Nature and Shakespeare," *PMLA*, LI (Sept., 1936), 733.

11. See the Editor's notes on *Titus Andronicus* in the *Cambridge Shakespeare*, edited by William Allan Neilson. J. Churton Collins, in Essay II, on "Shakespearean Paradoxes," in *Studies in Shakespeare*, discusses at length the authorship of *Titus Andronicus* with expression of the belief

Shakespeare play with the German play reveals that the German play does not have the funeral of Titus's sons killed in the war; but there are similarities of situation and wording of corresponding speeches in the German play by way of comparison with the oration of Tamora, pleading for her sons, the oration of Marcus offering the crown to Titus, the oration of Titus in answer to the offer, and the oration of Saturninus commenting upon Titus's revengeful actions.[12]

While Shylock's speech is in the main independent of the declamation of the Jew in Silvayn's *Orator*, both in outline and in phrasing, there are in a few places distinct reminders of the declamation in Silvayn's work. We quote from the *Orator*:

"A man may aske why I would not rather take silver of this man, then his flesh."

"I might also say—that I would have it to terrifie thereby the Christians for ever abusing the Jews anie more hereafter: but I will onelie say, that by his obligation he oweth it me."

"Surely, in that it is a thing not vsuall, it appeareth to be

---

that the metre argues against Shakespearean authorship, but that some passages bear the stamp of Shakespearean contributions to the play. See T. M. Raysor, *Coleridge's Shakespearean Criticism*, I, 3-4. Chambers does not attach much importance to the German or Dutch play in connection with the play in the Folio nor does he accept the inference that the Folio *Titus Andronicus* is a recasting of two English plays, *Titus and Vespasian*, and *Titus Andronicus* of Henslowe's records. Chambers does think, however, that it may be that the Folio *Titus Andronicus* is a revision in 1594 of a play, *Titus and Vespasian*, that may have been given by Lord Strange's company (*William Shakespeare*, I, 318-319). J. Q. Adams thinks it very likely that Shakespeare merely revised a play, *Titus Andronicus*, written mainly by Peele (*Life of William Shakespeare*, p. 134). My own feeling about the Folio *Titus Andronicus*, from a study of the dramatic integration of the orations (see discussion of *Titus Andronicus* in Chap. VI), is that it is worthy of being regarded as a Shakespearean play—if a revision, so thorough a revision as to warrant Henslowe's calling it "new" (Chambers, *William Shakespeare*, I, 316). Moreover, a study of Peele's plays leads me to accept the conclusion reached by Arthur M. Sampley, in his article "Plot Structure in Peele's Plays," *PMLA*, LI (Sept., 1936), 688-701, that it is "hard to understand how Peele could have been responsible" for this, "on the whole, well-constructed" play.

12. See Actus Primus, Actus Tertius, Actus Quintus, Actus Septimus of *Tito Andronico*, in *Deutsche National-Litteratur*, Vol. XXIII.

Classification and Sources

somewhat the more admirable, but there are divers other that are more cruell, which because they are in vse seeme nothing terrible at all: as to binde al the bodie vnto a most lothsome prison, or vnto an intollerable slauerie."[13]

The speech of Friar Lawerence follows, in outline and detail, the friar's account at the tomb given in Brooke's *Romeus and Juliet* (ll. 2915-2970). The oration contains a detail which points to the use of the poem rather than the prose version in Painter's *Palace of Pleasure:* the name of Friar John, from Brooke's version, is used, and not Anselm, from Painter's version.[14]

In *Much Ado,* Shakespeare makes the Friar suggest the scheme of giving out the rumor that Hero is dead, a scheme which he believes will bring about repentance on the part of Claudio. In Bandello's story of Timbreo di Cardona, Lionato, the father, is the one who suggests the scheme of giving out that Fenicia, his daughter, is dead, and suggests it without reference to the possibility of its bringing about repentance on the part of Timbreo.[15] In Ayrer's play, *Die Schoene Phoenicia,* the father is the one who suggests the scheme, expressing, at the same time, belief that the report will bring about the repentance of his daughter's former suitor.[16] The speech of Shakespeare's Friar is distinctly reminiscent of the corresponding part of Bandello's story.

Shakespeare has made the oration of Isabella independent of his source material in both outline and development. There are, however, evidences of hints as to idea in the de-

13. Silvayn's *Orator,* Declamation 95, of a Jew who would for his debt have a pound of the flesh of a Christian, quoted in Furness, p. 310, and W. C. Hazlitt, *Shakespeare's Library,* I, i, 355-358.

14. The poem and prose version are given in Hazlitt, I, i, 75-260. It has been generally noted, from Malone on, that Shakespeare's play follows the Brooke poem more closely in detail than the Painter version. For a listing of Malone's reasons for thinking Shakespeare was more indebted to Brooke than Painter, see Introduction to the consideration of *Romeo and Juliet* by Collier in *Shakespeare's Library,* I, i, 65.

15. Twentieth Novel, translation in Furness, pp. 318-319.

16. Translation of selected passages in Furness, pp. 329-337; see translation from Act III, p. 334.

velopment of the plea. In Whetstone's *Promos and Cassandra,* Cassandra argues that her brother is a young man who violated the law as a lover, not as a criminal, that the law is established for the criminal in the interest of preserving order, and that rulers can show mercy.[17] Isabella's impassioned plea for mercy to be shown in the case of her brother condemned by the law, reminds us from time to time of the points made in the plea of Cassandra. But Shakespeare's achievement is markedly independent of Whetstone's in both outline and development, and Isabella's speech is distinctly more substantial, more ornate, and more effective than the speech of Cassandra.

In the prose tale, the *Hystorie of Hamblet,* translation of Belleforest's story of "Amleth," Chapter VI tells "How Hamlet having slaine his uncle and burnt his palace, made an oration to the Danes, to show them what he had done: and how they made him king of Denmarke, and what followed." Hamlet's oration to the Danes begins thus:

"If there be any among you (good people of Denmark) that as yet have fresh within your memories the wrong done to the valiant king Horuendile, let him not be mooved, nor thinke it strange to behold the confused, hydeous, and fearfull spectacle of this present calamatie."[18]

Compare this opening with the opening of the oration of the King in *Hamlet.* After the introduction, the oration in Shakespeare's play goes on to a discussion of the move made by Fortinbras and the king's policy in dealing with the foreign trouble; of this episode there is nothing to be found in the prose tale. With the speech of the king in Shakespeare's *Hamlet* should be compared, also, the speech by the King in the play, *Der Bestrafte Brudermord oder Prinz Hamlet aus Daennemark,*[19] acted by English players in Germany in the

---

17. Part First, Actus II, scene iii. See also Whetstone's *Heptameron.* Both in Hazlitt, II, ii, 209-304; I, iii, 157-166.

18. In Hazlitt, I, ii, 223-279.

19. See Act I, scene 7 of play in *Deutsche National-Litteratur,* Vol. XXIII.

Classification and Sources

seventeenth century and taken by some to be the representative of the earlier *Ur-Hamlet* tragedy ascribed by some to Kyd.[20] The speech of the King in the German play begins thus:

"Obschon unsers Herrn Bruders Tod noch in frischem Gedächniss bey jedermann ist, und uns gebietet, alle Solemnitäten einzustellen, werden wir doch anjetzo genöthiget, unsere schwarze Trauerkleider in Carmosin, Purpur, und Scharlach zu verändern, weil nunmehro meines seeligen Herrn Bruders hinterbliebene Wittwe unsere liebste Gemahlin worden; darum erzeige sich ein jeder freudig, und mache sich unser Lust theilhaftig."[21]

The speech of the King in the German play then goes on to attempt to persuade Hamlet to cast off his grief and mourning, give up his schooling at Wittenberg, and remain at court.[22]

A consideration of Cinthio's story of the *Moor of Venice* shows that there is in it no hint as to the speech of Othello before Duke and Council. The content of Othello's oration is, therefore, from beginning to end, Shakespeare's invention. There is in Cinthio's story, however, a hint as to the situation which leads up to Othello's speech. We refer to this passage near the beginning of Cinthio's story: "Their passion was so successful that they were married, although her relations did all in their power to make her take another husband."[23]

---

20. See Introduction of Kyd's works, edited by F. S. Boas, p. xlviii.
21. Erster Act, Scene VII—*Deutsche National Litteratur*, XXIII, 158. Translation in Furness, II, 126:
> King: "Although our brother's death is still fresh in the memory of us all, and it befits us to suspend all state show, we must nevertheless change our black mourning suits to crimson, purple and scarlet, since my late departed brother's widow has now become our dearest consort. Therefore, let each one show himself cheerful and make himself a sharer in our pleasure."

22. Compare with the King's conversation with Hamlet later in I, ii of Shakespeare's play.
23. Cinthio's *Hecatommithi*, seventh novel of the third decade. Quoted with translation in Hazlitt, I, ii, 285-308. Reference for Othello's oration, pp. 285-286. See also Furness, pp. 376-389.

The speech of Iachimo follows in general the narrative found in the ninth novel of the second day of Boccaccio's *Decameron*, giving the story of Bernabo da Genovo.[24]

In the case of Paulina's rebuke of Leontes, Shakespeare has made a change in the speaker. In Greene's *Pandosto*, the lords attempt to persuade the king of Bellaria's innocence and to dissuade him from his cruelty toward her and her child. Moreover, in Greene's story, there is no set speech as in Shakespeare's play. In the case of Hermione's defense, however, Shakespeare found definite hints for situation and outline. These he followed; but his speech is, in development, independent of Bellaria's speech in Greene's story. The oracle is given in *Pandosto* before Bellaria makes her speech; in *Winter's Tale*, it is given after Hermione's oration; but the oracle as given by Shakespeare follows very closely in phrasing—in fact, almost word for word—the oracle as given by Greene.[25]

All of the orations recorded in *Julius Caesar* are developed from slight hints in the source material. In only a few lines in the speech of Marullus do we find echoes of the hints in *Plutarch's Life*.[26] Hints for the occasion, the outline, and the effect of Antony's speech are found in the *Lives* of Antonius, Caesar, and Brutus.[27] Hints for the occasion and purpose of the speech of Brutus are found in both the *Life of Brutus* and *Life of Caesar*.[28]

In Book II of Homer's *Iliad*, Jupiter sends a vision to Agamemnon to persuade him to lead the Greek army to battle. The general, thinking that the army is discouraged because of the absence of Achilles, the presence of the plague,

---

24. Translation in Furness, pp. 455-456. See also Hazlitt, I, ii, 179-193.
25. *Shakespeare Classics*, pp. 19, 26-29. See also Hazlitt, I, iv, 35, 40-42.
26. *Shakespeare Classics*, I, 85; Hazlitt, I, iii, 172.
27. *Classics*, II, 22; I, 104; I, 137-138. Hazlitt, I, iii, 331; I, iii, 186; I, iii, 212.
28. *Classics*, I, 135; I, 103. Hazlitt, I, iii, 210, 186.

Classification and Sources

and the length of time that has been already consumed in besieging Troy, tests the attitude of the army by proposing a return to Greece. The proposal is accepted, but the army is kept from carrying out the proposal through the intervention of Ulysses. An assembly of the Greeks is called, several speeches are made, and the advice of Nestor is followed, the advice of Nestor being to muster the troops, divide them into groups by nations, and proceed to battle. In Book VII of Homer's *Iliad*, Hector issues his challenge to the Greeks, offering to fight a Greek in single combat.[29] In these two books of Homer's epic, we have hints for the speeches in Shakespeare's *Troilus and Cressida*. Deighton points out, in his edition of *Troilus and Cressida*, that the speech of Ulysses might have been inspired by these lines in Chapman's Homer:

We must not all be kings. The rule is most irregular
Where many rule. One lord, one king, propose to thee: and he
To whom wise Saturn's son hath given both law and empery
To rule the public is that king.[30]

Mair points out in his introduction to the *Arte of Rhetorique* the similarity of idea in the speech of Ulysses and that part of Wilson's *Arte of Rhetorique* in which Wilson praises "order" or "disposition" of the ancient rhetoricians. We quote from Wilson:

"I knowe that al things stande by order, and without order nothing can be. For by an order we are borne, by an order we live, and by an order we make our ends. By an order one rules as head, and other obey as members. By an order Realmes stande and Lawes take force. Yea, by an order the whole worke of Nature, and the perfite state of all the Elements have their appointed course. By an order wee learne and frame our doings to good purposes,—An army never get-

---

29. See Chapman's translation.
30. Book II, lines 172-175. See Appendix I, pp. 203-205, of the Arden Edition of *Troilus and Cressida*, ed. K. Deighton, particularly the note by M. J. Foster Palmer, in *Notes and Queries*, VI (Oct., 1900), 316-317.

teth victorie that is not in araie, and set in good order of battaile.[31]

> 31. Pp. 156-157. See suggestion in Mair's Introduction, note on p. xxxiv. We submit here in addition for comparison the speech of Beatrice at the end of Canto 1 in Dante's *Paradise* (Hazelfoot's Translation):
>
>> And she began: All things an order share
>> Among themselves which is the form wherein
>> The universe is made God's mien to wear,
>> The highest creatures see the print therein
>> Of that eternal worth which is the end
>> The law now treated of is made to win.
>> In the order that I say, all natures tend,
>> As they are different in destiny,
>> More or less near to their first source to wend.
>> Wherefore they move o'er Being's wide-spread sea
>> To different ports; and there is given each
>> Instinct to bear it where it ought to be.
>> This makes the fire to lunar ambits reach;
>> This is in mortal hearts the motive force;
>> This keeps the earth compact and safe from breach.
>> Nor only creatures that have no resource
>> Of intellect, are shot forth by this bow,
>> But those who love and reason as of course.
>> The Providence that orders all things so,
>> Makes that heaven ever tranquil with its light,
>> Wherein revolves that which doth swiftest go
>> And thither now, as to a destined site,
>> Is bearing us the virtue of that string
>> Which at a joyous mark its shafts aim right.
>> 'Tis true that, as the form which Art doth bring
>> In being oft does not accord with Art's
>> Intent, which matter lags in answering;
>> So from this course the creature too departs
>> Sometimes, that, albeit thus impelled, has power
>> To swerve, and in a new direction darts
>> (As fire may from a cloud be seen to shower),
>> If the first impetus that stirs its flight
>> Is wrested earthwards in false pleasure's hour.
>> Thou shouldst not wonder more, if I am right,
>> At thy ascent, than that a stream should flow
>> Down to the bottom from a mountain height.
>> 'Twould be a marvel in thee if, with no
>> Obstruction, thou shouldst sit down low in place,
>> Like live fire taming down to earth its glow.
>
> J. Churton Collins, in *Studies in Shakespeare* (pp. 61-62), compares the soliloquy of Ajax, in *Ajax*, 646-92, and the speech of Jocasta, in *Phoenissae*, 528-85, with the orations of Agamemnon, Nestor, and Ulysses in *Troilus and Cressida*, I, iii. In his *Spenser's Theory of Friendship*, Charles G. Smith calls attention to other possible sources. He points out that Professor Gayley in *Shakespeare and the Founders of Liberty in America*

Classification and Sources

In Plutarch's *Life of Alcibiades*, references are made to the skill of Alcibiades as an orator and to his bravery as a soldier and shrewdness as a politician. The reason for his exile, however, as given by Plutarch, was his being brought to trial on the charge of breaking images of the deities and the profanation of their mysteries, and not the refusal of the Senate to listen to his plea for his friend, as given by Shakespeare.[32] Shakespeare's placing of Alcibiades in the position of an orator in *Timon of Athens* is reminiscent of the hint in Plutarch as to the skill of Alcibiades as an orator, and the following lines from the oration of Alcibiades are reminiscent of the hints in Plutarch as to the achievements of Alcibiades in war:

> Hard fate! he might have died in war.
> My lords, if not for any parts in him—
> Though his right arm might purchase his own time
> And be in debt to none—yet, more to move you,
> Take my deserts to his, and join 'em both;
> And for I know your reverend ages love
> Security, I'll pawn my victories, all
> My honour to you, upon his good returns.

But the occasion of the oration, the defense of one of his friends, seems to be Shakespeare's invention.

(New York, 1917), pp. 166-168, thinks Ulysses's speech on degree is indebted to a passage in Chaucer (*Troilus and Criseyde*, Book 3, stanzas 250-252) on the power of love, and finds similarity to Spenser's account of concord (*F.Q.*, 4, 10, 34-35); and in a footnote Dr. Smith records that Todd (in *Works of Edmund Spenser* (London, 1805) V, 411-412), thinks the Spenser passage is imitated from the passage in Boethius which Chaucer translated in *Troilus and Criseyde*. Dr. Smith emphasizes the closeness of both the Chaucer passage and the Spenser passage, as well as the "Concord" Chorus in Gascoigne's *Jocasta*, to the speech of Ulysses. He calls attention further, in a footnote, to the fact that Professor Gayley, following Verplanck, thinks the speech of Ulysses is indebted to Hooker's *Laws of Ecclesiastical Polity*, ed. R. W. Church (Oxford, 1905), Book I, pp. 13-14. In Bruno's *Heroic Enthusiasts*, trans. by L. Williams (London, 1887-1889), Part 2, pp. 53-54, Dr. Smith finds a passage he thinks even more suggestive of Ulysses's speech than the Spenser passage; and he thinks, further, that Shakespeare may have been indebted even to the French policists—Michel de L'Hôpital, François de la None, and Jean Bodin. *Spenser's Theory of Friendship*, pp. 21-24.

32. See Everyman Edition of *Plutarch's Lives*, I, 295, 297, 303, 305, 306.

In all of the orations in *Coriolanus*, we find ample reminiscence of Plutarch's *Life*. The oration that Menenius makes to the commons near the opening of the play is developed from a hint in Plutarch as to situation plus a close rendering of the "notable tale."[33] The oration of Coriolanus on the subject of "corn gratis" follows in idea the oration in Plutarch.[34] In phrasing, the Shakespeare oration is, in the main, independent of Plutarch; but in some places, as Shakespeare develops his speech, he keeps very close to the oration in Plutarch in phrasing as well as in idea. The speech of Menenius designed to quiet the mutinous rabble is developed from the hint in Plutarch that the consuls undertook to "pacify" the rabble and justify the action of the senate.[35] The speech of Comminius, spoken in praise of Coriolanus as a candidate for the consulship, is developed by combining information concerning the career of Coriolanus from Plutarch's *Life*;[36] but while Shakespeare follows Plutarch closely in the matter of outline, he makes his oration independent of Plutarch in the matter of phrasing. In the case of the oration of Volumnia, however, we have a very close rendering of Plutarch in phrasing as well as in outline; in this instance Shakespeare keeps very close to the source material throughout the speech.[37]

Of the eighty-three orations recorded in Shakespeare, forty-eight are found in history plays; and, with the exception of four, these orations in history plays can be referred to the chronicles. In the case of the *Henry VI* plays involving the problem of the 1594 and 1595 Quartos, we have noted the parallels to be found from comparison of the orations in *2* and *3 Henry VI* with corresponding speeches in the *First Part of the Contention* and *The True Tragedie*, respectively. The table furnishing references for history plays follows:

33. *Classics*, II, 145-146. Hazlitt, I, iii, 263-264.
34. *Classics*, II, 164-165. Hazlitt, I, iii, 277-278.
35. *Classics*, II, 167. Hazlitt, I, iii, 280.
36. *Classics*, II, 139, 140, 148, 149. Hazlitt, I, iii, 259, 261, 266.
37. *Classics*, II, 198-201. Hazlitt, I, iii, 304-307.

TABLE VII
THE CHRONICLES AS SOURCES
(See Boswell-Stone)

Play	Speaker	Reference to Source Material	Evidence
1 H VI	3 Messenger	Holinshed's, and Halle's *Chronicles*	Hints for details, variance as to date
1 H VI	Winchester	Holinshed's, and Halle's *Chronicles*	Situation in charge
1 H VI	La Pucelle	Holinshed's, and Halle's *Chronicles*	Hint for situation, variance in detail
1 H VI	King Henry	Holinshed's, and Halle's *Chronicles*	Hint for few lines
2 H VI	Gloucester	Holinshed's, and Halle's *Chronicles; The First Part of the Contention*	Parallels in quarto
2 H VI	Queen	Hardying's *Chronicles*	Hint in chronicles for few lines
2 H VI	Gloucester (defense)	Holinshed and Halle	Hint for setting
2 H VI	Salisbury	Holinshed and Halle	Hint for situation
2 H VI	Say	Holinshed and Halle	Hint for situation
3 H VI	Margaret	(The True Tragedie of *Richard Duke of Yorke*)	Close parallels in quarto, hint in chronicles
3 H VI	York	Holinshed's *Chronicles* based on Halle and Whethamstede	Close parallels in quarto, hint in chronicles
3 H VI	Warwick	("Tragedie") Holinshed and Halle	Variance with chronicles
3 H VI	Clifford	Holinshed and Halle	Hint for situation
3 H VI	Margaret (to followers)	("Tragedie") Halle's *Chronicles*	Hint in quarto, variance with chronicles
R III	Gloucester	(Not in source)	Hints
R III	Edward	Holinshed's, Halle's, and More's *Chronicles*	Hints
R III	Buckingham	(See also *The True Tragedie of Richard III* for the orations of Buckingham and Richmond)	Hints
R III	Gloucester		Hints
R III	Richmond		Hints
R III	Richard		Hints
K J	Chatillon	*The Troublesome Raigne of Iohn, King of England*	Hints in old play, variance with chronicles
K J	King John	"Troublesome Raigne," Holinshed's *Chronicles*	
K J	King Philip	"Troublesome Raigne," Holinshed's *Chronicles*	
K J	Citizen	"Troublesome Raigne," Holinshed's *Chronicles*	
K J	Robert	"Troublesome Raigne," Holinshed's *Chronicles*	Hint in chronicles, free re-writing of speech in play
K J	Pandulph	"Troublesome Raigne," Holinshed's *Chronicles*	Hint in chronicle and old play

TABLE VII (Continued)

Play	Speaker	Reference to Source Material	Evidence
R II	Mowbray	Holinshed's Chronicles	Hints, variance
R II	Richard	Holinshed's Chronicles	Hints
R II	Carlisle	Holinshed's Chronicles	Hints, part paraphrasing
1 H IV	Worcester	Holinshed's Chronicles	Hint, variance
2 H IV	Chief Justice	Holinshed's, and Stow's Chronicles; Elyot's Governour	Hint
H V	Canterbury	Holinshed's Chronicles; Lyly's Euphues and His England (See also The Famous Victories of Henry Fifth)	Close rendering, hints
H V	Henry to ambassadors	Holinshed's Chronicles	Hints
H V	Henry to traitors	Holinshed's, and Halle's Chronicles (Close rendering in phrasing at end)	Hint for situation
H V	Henry to soldiers	Holinshed's Chronicles	Bare hint
H V	Henry to citizens	Holinshed's Chronicles	Hint for situation
H V	Henry to Montjoy	Holinshed's Chronicles; see also The Famous Victories of Henry Fifth	Hints
H V	Henry "Crispian"	Holinshed's, and Halle's Chronicles	
H V	Henry to Montjoy	Holinshed's Chronicles	Situation
H VIII	Burgundy	Holinshed's, and Halle's Chronicles	Variance in situation, hint
H VIII	Katherine (for subjects)	Holinshed's, and Halle's Chronicles	Hints
H VIII	Buckingham	Holinshed's, and Halle's Chronicles	Hints, change in person spoken to
H VIII	Katherine (in defense)	Holinshed's, and Stow's Chronicles	Close rendering in parts
H VIII	Wolsey (in defense)	Holinshed's Chronicles	Hints for situation
H VIII	Henry (allegiance)	Holinshed's, and Stow's Chronicles	Close rendering in parts
H VIII	Wolsey	Not in source material	
H VIII	Cranmer (in defense)	Foxe's Actes and Monuments (The Book of Martyrs)	Hint for situation
H VIII	Cranmer (christening)	Holinshed's, and Halle's Chronicles	Hint for situation

Note: The speech of Buckingham and the speeches of Cranmer are usually assigned to Fletcher. See Note 90, p. 100.

Classification and Sources

The orations in *1 Henry VI* are characterized by perfect freedom in the use of the source material. The speech of the Third Messenger describes the battle of Patay, which took place seven years after the death of Henry V: in the same scene in which the Messenger delivers his speech, the death of Henry V is recorded also. Furthermore, historically, the battle is recorded as having taken place on June 18, 1429, six weeks after the siege of Orleans; in *1 Henry VI* the Messenger describes the battle before the dramatizing of the siege of Orleans in the play and gives as the date "the tenth of August last." The details of the battle, however, are in accord with the details of the battle of Patay as given in Holinshed's *Chronicles*.[38] In the case of the brief and incomplete plea of Winchester, the situation is hinted in the charge made by Gloucester, the last lines of Gloucester's speech giving two counts recorded in Holinshed and Halle.[39] Winchester's incomplete plea is developed independently. So is the appeal that La Pucelle makes to win the allegiance of Burgundy. And in this appeal we find an instance in which *1 Henry VI* is at variance with Holinshed and Halle; namely, saying that Orleans was set free without a ransom.[40] Holinshed and Halle contain hints for the following lines in Henry's speech which is prompted by the quarrel over the roses between Vernon and Basset:[41]

> Cousin of York, we institute your Grace
> To be our regent in these parts of France;
> And, good my Lord of Somerset, unite
> Your troops of horsemen with his bands of foot;
> And, like true subjects, sons of your progenitors,
> Go cheerfully together and digest
> Your angry choler of your enemies.

The remainder of Henry's speech is developed independently.

38. III, 601/2/17; Halle, *Chronicles*, p. 601.
39. III, 591/2/5; 591/2/2; Halle, p. 131.
40. III, 618/2/11; Halle, p. 192.   41. III, 619/1/2; Halle, p. 194.

In the case of the orations in *2 Henry VI* and *3 Henry VI*, parallels are found—old and altered lines—with corresponding speeches in the *First Part of the Contention* and *The True Tragedie*.[42] This difference is noted, however. In *2 Henry VI*, the orations represent, without exception, fuller treatment than the corresponding speeches in *The First Part of the Contention*; in *3 Henry VI*, the orations are close parallels to the corresponding speeches in *The True Tragedie*, with the single exception of the address of Margaret to her soldiers—this address being undeveloped in *The True Tragedie*.

Shakespeare's use of material in the chronicles is to be observed in the following instances in *2 Henry VI*:

In Gloucester's speech in rebuke of the King's marriage, the lines beginning "Suffolk, the new made duke" and those beginning "A proper jest" should be compared with passages in Holinshed and Halle.[43] In Holinshed and Halle are to be found hints for the setting of Gloucester's defense.[44] In connection with Salisbury's speech presenting the case of the commons against Suffolk, reference to Holinshed and Halle shows that the people "Began to make exclamation against the duke of Suffolke, etc."[45] The defense of Lord Say is markedly independent of both the chronicles and the *First Part of the Contention*. In the chronicles there are to be

---

42. For dicsussion of the problem of the relationship between *The First Part of the Contention* and *The True Tragedie* and the *Henry VI* plays, see Miss Lucille King's two investigations, "The Use of Halle's Chronicles in the Folio and Quarto Texts of *Henry VI*," *PQ*, XIII (1934), 321-332, and "Text Sources of the Folio and Quarto *Henry VI*," *PMLA*, LI (Sept., 1936), 702-718; Peter Alexander, *Shakespeare's Henry VI and Richard III*, pp. 3-4, 71; Tucker Brooke's discussion of source, authorship, and history of *2 and 3 Henry VI i*n the Yale Shakespeare Series; J. Q. Adams, *Life of William Shakespeare*, pp. 136-137; E. K. Chambers, *William Shakespeare*, I, 281-289; R. B. McKerrow, "A Note on the 'Bad Quartos' of *2* and *3 Henry VI* and the Folio Text," *RES*, XIII (Jan., 1937), 64-72.

43. Holinshed (hereinafter cited Hol.), III, 625/1/9, 625/1/64; Halle, p. 205.

44. Hol., III, 627/1/15, 627/1/68, 627/1/11; Halle, pp. 210, 209.

45. Hol., III, 631/1/16; Halle, p. 217.

Classification and Sources

found slight hints as to the situation. Holinshed records that Lord Say was charged with complicity in the cession of Anjou and Maine, and his arraignment is recorded in both Holinshed and Halle.[46] Only a very few lines of the *First Part of the Contention* appear in the oration in *2 Henry VI*. We quote from the Contention:

Say. Kent, in the Commentaries Caesar wrote,
 Termde it the cruel'st place of all this land,
 Then noble Country-men, heare me but speake,
 I sold not France, I lost not Normandie.
Cade. But wherefore doest thou shake thy head so?
Say. It is the palsie and not feare that makes me.[47]

The orations in *3 Henry VI* show use of material in the chronicles as follows:

Two versions of the "crown" episode are to be found in Holinshed: the first, an abridgment of Halle; the second, a translation from Whethamstede.[48] In having the indignities heaped upon York before and not after his death, Shakespeare is following the second of the two versions. He departs from the second, however, in having Margaret and not "they" set the crown upon York's head; he also departs from the second and uses the first in having Margaret put a paper crown upon York's head and not one of bulrushes. It is to be noted also that, in having Margaret and not Clifford put the crown upon York's head, Shakespeare departs from the first version. A study of the orations of Margaret and York in connection with the chronicles emphasizes, therefore, the freedom which Shakespeare used in dealing with the historical material which he had at hand. Save for the hint as to the putting of the crown upon the head of York, Margaret's speech is entirely independent of the chronicles; and save for the reference to the crown, York's speech is also entirely independent of them.

46. Hol., III, 632/1/31, 634/2/31; Halle, p. 221.
47. *First Part of the Contention*, scene xviii.
48. Hol., III, 659/2/37; Halle, p. 251; Whethamstede, p. 489.

92   *The Oration in Shakespeare*

Warwick's account of the battle of St. Alban's and his defeat recalls the following hints in the chronicles. After Warwick's defeat at St. Alban's, the Lancastrians purposed marching to London, but they retired to the north of England when

> true report came not onelie to the queene, but also to the citie; that the earle of March, having vanquished the earles of Pembroke and Wiltshire, had met with the earle of Warwike (after this last batell at Saint Albons) at Chipping Norton by Cotswold; and that they with both their powers were coming toward London.[49]

Halle gives an account of the battle of St. Alban's, and Holinshed, an account of the situation for the King left alone in the face of defeat.[50] In one instance, Warwick's speech in Shakespeare's play is at variance with the account given in the chronicles. Shakespeare has Warwick say to Edward that George, afterwards Duke of Clarence,

> was lately sent
> From your kind aunt, Duchess of Burgundy,
> With aid of soldiers to this needful war.

Isabella of Portugal, a granddaughter of John of Gaunt, and consequently a distant cousin of Edward, was Duchess of Burgundy in 1461. A passage in Holinshed derived from Halle shows that George was not in England during the historic time of *3 Henry VI*, II, i.[51]

There is no direct reference in the chronicles for Clifford's speech to King Henry in front of the town of York; but a hint for the speech may be found in Holinshed, following Halle in the remark that Queen Margaret was "fortunate in hir two battels (Wakefield and Second St. Alban's), but vnfortunate was the King in all his enterprises; for where his

---

49. Hol., III, 661/1/33; Halle, p. 252.
50. Hol., III, 660/2/14.
51. Hol., III, 661/1/45; Halle, p. 253.

Classification and Sources

person was present, the victorie still fled from him to the contrarie part."[52]

Margaret's spirited speech in the plains of Tewkesbury near the end of the play is much fuller than the corresponding speech in the *True Tragedie*. Shakespeare's portrayal of "a woman of this valiant spirit," as the Prince says, is at variance, however, with the passage in Halle which says that, when news of Barnet Field came to the Queen, "She, like a woman al dismaied for feare, fell to the ground, her harte was perced with sorrowe, her speache was in manner passed, all her spirites were tormented with malencoly."[53]

The orations in *Richard III* are, in the main, developed from mere hints in the sources. For the speech of King Edward voicing his feelings after Derby has asked for the life of a servant who has been condemned for murder, the chronicles suggest the occasion for the speech and the speech itself.[54] For the speeches of Buckingham and Gloucester on the occasion of the offer of the crown, the chronicles furnish suggestions for the situation and the development of the speeches.[55] But in the development of both these speeches Shakespeare has given us orations markedly independent of the source material in both arrangement and phrasing. The orations to the soldiers delivered by Richmond and Richard near the end of the play are suggested by the orations given in the chronicles.[56] But again, as in the case of the speeches of Edward, Buckingham, and Gloucester, Shakespeare has made these orations to the soldiers distinctly independent of the source material. In connection with the reference of the orations in *Richard III* to the source material in the chron-

52. Hol., III, 660/2/60; Halle, p. 252.
53. Halle, p. 297.
54. Hol., III, 703/1/66; Halle, p. 326.
55. Hol., III, 726/2/21, 727/1/16, 731/1/39; More, 75/20, 61/31, 65/12. See note on p. 385 of Boswell-Stone's *Shakespeare's Holinshed*.
56. Hol., III, 757/2/14, 757/2/49, 758/1/7, 758/1/59, 758/2/23, 758/2/50, 756/1/60, 756/2/17, 756/2/43; Halle, pp. 415, 416, 417, 418.

icles, there should be taken into consideration two references to the *True Tragedie of Richard III*. The first reference has to do with the oration of Buckingham in offering the crown to Gloucester. The earlier play merely refers to the oration as being delivered, but at the same time points out definitely the place where the oration is being delivered and the occasion for it.[57] In both place and occasion, the oration in Shakespeare agrees with the reference in the earlier play. The second reference has to do with the oration of Richmond to his soldiers. In the earlier play, the oration is called "Richmond's speech to Earle Oxford, P. Landys, & Captain Blunt."[58] Shakespeare's oration, while developed from suggestions in the chronicles both as to caption and as to content, is also reminiscent of the speech of Richmond in the earlier play; and the lines

> The prayers of holy saints and wronged souls,
> Like high-rear'd bulwarks, stand before our faces.

distinctly recall these lines in the earlier play:

> Whose guiltlesse blood craves daily at God's hands,
> Revenge for outrage done to their harmless lives.

In *King John* four of the orations recorded are to be found in Act II, scene 1: the speech of Chatillon bringing news of the English and their movements; the speech of King John delivered in the interest of winning admission to the town of Angiers; the speech of King Philip delivered with the same end in view; and the speech of the Citizen of Angiers delivered in the interest of bringing about a peaceful settlement through the marriage of Lady Blanch and the Dauphin. These orations are all based on corresponding speeches in *The Troublesome Raigne of John*:[59] but reference to the chronicles shows that these speeches represent free handling of the record in the chronicles. Chatillon's speech is not in the

---

57. Hazlitt, II, i, 84-85.   58. Hazlitt, II, i, 109-110.
59. Hazlitt, II, i, 238, 239, 243, 244, 247-248.

Classification and Sources

chronicles and is based entirely on the earlier play. There is no hint for the speeches of the Kings or the speech of the Citizen.[60] According to the account in the chronicles an assault is made on Angiers and the city is entered by means of force;[61] the two kings arrange the agreement about the marriage.[62] The appeal that Robert makes in behalf of his inheritance represents a free rewriting of the corresponding speech in the old play, the Shakespeare speech laying its emphasis on the details of the basis of the plea. In the chronicles there is a hint that King John was required to hear Robert's plea.[63] In the case of Pandulph's argument for King Philip's break with England, Shakespeare has used a hint in the old play furnished by a short speech by Pandulph as the basis of an oration of independent development. The speech in the old play follows:

"I charge thee Philip King of France and all the Kings and Princes of Christendome, to make war upon this miscreant: and whereas thou hast made a league with him and confirmed it by oath, I doo in the name of our foresaid father the Pope, acquit thee of that oath, as unlawful, beeing made with an heretike; how saist thou Philip, doost thou obey?"

In the chronicles, there is a hint for the speech when they record that Pandulph was appointed by the Pope "to exhort the French King to make warre vpon him, as a person for his wickednesse excommunicated."[64]

In the opening scene of *Richard II*, we find the stage soon set for a forensic. The scene takes place in the King's palace. In the presence of King Richard, John of Gaunt, and other nobles and attendants, Bolingbroke brings forward his charges against Mowbray, and Mowbray is permitted to make his speech of defense. Bolingbroke's charges follow closely, in order and detail, the charges given in Holinshed's *Chronicles* as those presented by the knight speaking for Hereford. But

60. Hol., III, 160/1/4/.
61. Hol., III, 170/1/27.
62. Hol., III, 158/2/25.
63. Hol., III, 162/1/44.
64. Hol., III, 175/2/17.

Mowbray's speech of defense is, except for the hints as to the answers to the charges brought forward by Bolingbroke, markedly independent of the *Chronicles*.[65] The speech made by Richard when he pronounces sentence upon Bolingbroke and Mowbray is developed by Shakespeare from bare hints as to situation and detail to be found in the chronicles; in outline and diction the speech is markedly independent of the source material.[66] In the case of Carlisle's plea for keeping Bolingbroke from the throne, we have a combination of free paraphrasing of the source material and independent phrasing and invention of idea. In the general outline of the statement of the facts of the case, Shakespeare follows the hints given in the chronicles; in the closing prophecy as to the dire consequences that will follow the elevation of Bolingbroke to the throne, Shakespeare acts independently of the chronicles.[67]

The speech of Worcester in *1 Henry IV* is, in both setting and development, distinctly independent of the chronicles. The chronicles furnish suggestions for the details of the charges brought against Henry IV which Shakespeare incorporates in the speech of Hotspur to Sir Walter Blunt[68] and the speech of Worcester to Henry IV. The speech of Hotspur makes use of the oath made by Henry upon his return from exile, that he was returning only to claim his title as Duke of Lancaster; of the deposing and murder of Richard; of the imprisonment and neglect of the earl of March; and of "diverse other matters." The speech of Worcester is developed mainly about Henry's perjury in the matter of the oath made at Doncaster as evidenced by his insinuating himself into the kingship during the absence of Richard in Ireland. In the matter of setting, however, Holinshed records

65. Hol., III, 493/2/16.
66. Hol., III, 494/2/41.   67. Hol., III, 512/2/29.
68. *2 Henry IV*, IV, iii. This speech by Hotspur is in many ways suggestive of the demonstrative oration. The exclusion of it from the table of demonstrative orations has been due to the impression that the setting is more that of conversation than that of the "set" speech.

Classification and Sources

the sending by messengers of the articles containing the details which Shakespeare puts into the speeches of Hotspur and Worcester.[69]

The speech of the Chief Justice in 2 *Henry IV* is based upon the mention in Holinshed of the Prince's calling to mind his striking the Chief Justice in the latter's performance of duty.[70] A fuller account of the incident is given by Sir Thomas Elyot in his *Governour*.[71] But Elyot gives the incident merely as illustrative of the virtue of placability, the Judge's conciliatory manner preventing the Prince from doing the Judge any bodily harm. In Act II, scene 1, of the *Famous Victories of Henry V*, the Prince strikes the Judge, and the Judge sends him to prison. The oration of Shakespeare makes use of the incident as recorded in the *Famous Victories*; but, in phrasing and development of the argument based on the proposition that the young king put himself in his father's place and judged of the Justice's action accordingly, the speech is entirely independent of any suggestion in either the story in Elyot or the *Famous Victories*.[72]

With the exception of the speech of Canterbury before King Henry and the lords, the speeches of *Henry V* are markedly independent of source material in both idea and phrasing. The section of Canterbury's speech dealing with the defense of England against Scotland is, in structure and phrasing, independent of Holinshed.[73] What has been called

---

69. Hol., III, 523/1/8.   70. Hol., III, 543/2/10.
71. Edited by Arthur Eliot, 1834, Book III, pp. 123-125. Passage quoted in Boswell-Stone's *Holinshed*, pp. 162-163. The copying of the passage by Stow (557-558) is also noted by Boswell-Stone.
72. A. F. Hopkinson, in his edition of the *Famous Victories*, points out in a note (p. 16) that the "striking" episode is without historical foundation.
73. Boswell-Stone records that "Chicele answers Henry's fear that the Scot might pour down upon defenceless England, by recalling the day (October 17, 1346) when David II was vanquished and taken prisoner, during Edward III's absence in France." (Avesbury, 145-146.) He also suggests that the "unhistorical assertion that David was sent to France" Shakespeare may have drawn from a hint given in Act IV of the play of *King Edward III*.

the "genealogical argument" of the Archbishop, however, represents a very close rendering of the argument given in Holinshed.⁷⁴ The section devoted to the work of the honey-bees is based on a passage in Lyly's *Euphues and His England*, which in turn is based on chapters in Pliny's book on natural history.⁷⁵

The speech of Henry to the French ambassadors is based upon the "Paris balles" incident in Holinshed.⁷⁶ Henry's speech to the traitors is entirely independent of the *Chronicles* until the part referring to Lord Scroop is reached.⁷⁷ The closing lines of the address to the traitors represent in part close rendering in phrasing of the corresponding speech in Holinshed.⁷⁸ In the case of Henry's address to his soldiers at Harfleur, Shakespeare developed the oration from the barest hint in Holinshed: "And dailie was the town assaulted."⁷⁹ Henry's address to the citizens of Harfleur is developed from a mere hint as to situation, and Shakespeare uses great freedom in making use of this hint.⁸⁰

We come now to Henry's speeches just before the battle of Agincourt: his two speeches to Montjoy and his "Saint Crispian" oration to his soldiers. For all of these speeches we find hints for situation; but, in the case of each one, we find it independent of sources in structure and phrasing.⁸¹ A comparison of Shakespeare's orations with corresponding passages in the *Famous Victories* shows the advance Shakespeare made over his predecessor.⁸² The speech in the older play corresponding to the Saint Crispian speech is devoted

---

74. Hol., III, 545/2/29, 545/2/46. The very close rendering found in Canterbury's speech should be compared with the very close rendering found in Volumnia's speech.

75. See R. W. Bond's edition of the *Works of Lyly*, II, 44, 45, 46. See also C. Plinii Secundi *Naturalis Historiae Opus*, Liber XI, Capita v-xx.

76. Hol., III, 545/1/1, 545/1/9. Cf. also the incident in *Famous Victories*; Hazlitt, II, i, 352-353.

77. Hol., III, 548/1/3.   78. Hol., III, 548/2/15.
79. Hol., III, 549/2/69.   80. Hol., III, 550/1/38.
81. Hol., III, 552/1/56, 553/2/44, 554/1/13.
82. Hazlitt, II, i, 363, 364.

Classification and Sources

principally to the plan for organization of the army and the plan of attack. Shakespeare's speech, therefore, devoted principally to making a patriotic appeal to the soldiers, is entirely independent of the speech in the older play. The speech of Burgundy is to a great extent Shakespeare's invention. There is no speech in the old play corresponding to the speech of Burgundy, and the hint for situation in Holinshed records the ambassadors—not Burgundy—as the ones who approach Henry in the interest of peace. The theme of Shakespeare's speech, however, is found in Holinshed.[83] Boswell-Stone points out that the lines

> And my speech entreats
> That I may know the let, why gentle Peace
> Should not expel these inconveniences
> And bless us with her former qualities.[84]

may have grown out of the recollection of the unsuccessful close of the conference at Meulan, recorded by Holinshed.[85]

Of the orations recorded in *Henry VIII*, the speech of Buckingham and the two speeches of Cranmer are staged in parts of the play which are generally ascribed to Fletcher. We shall consider first those orations which are generally ascribed to Shakespeare. In the two orations of Katherine, we find close rendering in parts of the phrasing found in Holinshed. The deliberative oration of Katherine urging immediate action with reference to the grievances of the subjects is based on several passages in Holinshed and Halle recording the grievances and rebelliousness of the subjects.[86] The judicial oration of Katherine before King Henry is based upon Katherine's speech as recorded in Holinshed; and in the opening and closing sections the speech in Shakespeare follows closely in phrasing the speech in the *Chronicles*.[87]

83. Hol., III, 572/1/18.
84. Boswell-Stone, *Holinshed*, p. 200.
85. Hol., III, 569/2/43.
86. Hol., III, 891/1/31, 891/1/70, 891/2/8. Halle, pp. 694, 697, 699.
87. Hol., III, 907/1/63; Stow, p. 912 from Cavendish (I, 149-152). Katherine's speech should be compared with Hermione's.

Wolsey's defense in the face of Katherine's charge that the Cardinal is the principal enemy who has brought about the estrangement between her and her husband is independent of the source material in structure and phrasing, and the speech is developed from a mere hint as to situation given in Holinshed.[88] The demonstrative oration of the King delivered just after the Queen has departed is the last of Shakespeare's great orations. In parts there are close renderings of the oration as recorded in Holinshed. In the main, however, Shakespeare's speech is independent in phrasing and structure.[89] Wolsey's allegiance speech is, apparently, entirely independent of source material in both setting and development, and seems to mark a decided falling away, in both structure and phrasing, from the standard set in the orations of Katherine and the King. It is worth noting in this connection that Wolsey's allegiance speech is practically the last of what is usually regarded to be Shakespeare's contribution to the play.[90]

Of the three orations usually assigned to Fletcher, Buckingham's farewell speech and the setting of Cranmer's eulogy can be traced to Holinshed's *Chronicles*, and Cranmer's speech before his accusers can be traced to Foxe's *Actes and*

   88. Hol., III, 908/1/35.
   89. Hol., III, 907/2/46; Stow, p. 914.
   90. The following parts are usually assigned to Shakespeare: I, i, ii; II, iii, iv; III, ii, 1-203. See *Larger Temple Shakespeare*, Vol. VIII, Preface to *Henry VIII*. Also Chambers, *William Shakespeare*, I, 496, and Adams, *A Life of William Shakespeare*, p. 435. For a concise statement of the Shakespeare-Fletcher authorship matter, see Cumberland Clark, *A Study of Shakespeare's Henry VIII*, Chapter IV, "The Question of Authorship," pp. 40-57. Professor Brooke, in his edition of *Henry VIII* in the "Yale Shakespeare Series," gives the scheme of scenes and authors which Spedding determined upon in his *Who Wrote Shakespeare's Henry VIII*, in the *Gentleman's Magazine* for August, 1850. Spedding ascribed the scenes given above to Shakespeare with V, i (altered) added; the remaining scenes he ascribed to Fletcher. H. Douglas Sykes, *Sidelights on Shakespeare*, gave the Shakespeare scenes to Massinger, with Fletcher as the companion author. I feel that Shakespeare, not Massinger, wrote the scenes in question; the character of the orations lends weighty support to this opinion.

Classification and Sources

Monuments. Buckingham's references to the details concerning his father's unfortunate end and his own unfortunate end, as well as the depiction of Buckingham's attitude toward his own fate, are based upon corresponding parts of the speech as recorded in Holinshed and Halle.[91] The eulogy by Cranmer is, of course, without source material in the chronicles; but the chronicles contain a hint for the setting (the christening date and ceremonies).[92] Cranmer's speech before his accusers can be traced to hints as to the situation to be found in Foxe's *Actes and Monuments*.[93]

Shakespeare exercises, then, extreme freedom in the use of his sources in the chronicles and develops his orations with striking independence and, at times, inventions. Leaving out of consideration the orations in the *2* and *3 Henry VI* plays, in which we find problematical parallels with corresponding speeches in the Quartos of *The First Part of the Contention* and *The True Tragedie*, there are but four instances of close renderings, and these are made only in parts of orations. Shakespeare usually develops his orations from hints—sometimes very bare hints—as to situation and detail, and in a few instances we find in Shakespeare's orations variations from the source material in the matter of time, speaker, person spoken to, and historical details. In comedies and tragedies, too, Shakespeare usually develops his orations from mere hints. In the case of only a few orations do we find long sustained close renderings from sources. Moreover, all the best orations are developed from hints. In three instances we note variance with source material; two instances of a change of speaker; one instance of a change of detail. Shakespeare's orations, then, represent, in the vast majority of cases, Shakespeare's independent work; in structure, imagery, and diction, they are in the main the creations of his own

91. Hol., III, 856/1/68, 856/2/4, 743/2/49, 744/1/50, 763/1/25. Halle, pp. 624, 394, 395, 424.
92. Hol., III, 934/2/5. Halle, pp. 805, 806.
93. II, 173/1.

rhetorical genius. And even in those instances in which we find close renderings in structure and phrasing of the source material upon which the orations are based, the orations are distinctly charged and enriched with the power and beauty of Shakespeare's matchless rhetorical style.

CHAPTER V

Structure of Orations

ONE OF THE DISTINCTIVE characteristics of an oration is that it is a speech exhibiting systematic, unified structure. Such a speech lends itself, therefore, to analysis into its component parts. The arrangement of these parts, the way in which these parts are made to fit into one another, reveals care and purpose on the part of the orator. The parts are carefully united to form an organic whole which functions for the purpose of developing one main idea, to which are related all other ideas, subordinate but contributing to the ultimate development of the main idea. The oration thus comes to be a composite unit, designed for the purpose of convincing in the interest of some one proposition. This kind of speech suggests the oration in its ideal form.

In studying the oration in Shakespeare there is need to analyze the speeches to observe his development of outline. In this connection, however, the distinction must be made at the outset between a slavish, mechanical working out of an outline and its spontaneous, artistic development. The former method of procedure results in a purely artificial, wearisome, ineffective composition, in which thought is likely to be sacrificed to language and the development of the main idea rendered unconvincing in the attempt to adhere to an outline. In other words, the spirit of the speech becomes lost in the mechanism; the life of the speech becomes organized out of it. On the other hand, the spirit of a speech is preserved and its appeal and convincingness are secured through a natural working-out of a simple but well-defined outline.

This type of outline may be so simple that it may be evident at a glance. Increase in the amount of detail and elaboration will render analysis correspondingly more difficult. But simple or complex, once the good oration is reduced to its parts, their interrelation becomes evident. Ideal structure is structure in which outline is made to serve the ultimate conformation of the composition. And in the consideration of the structure of orations in Shakespeare, it is our purpose to observe his achievement with reference to this ideal standard which has been suggested.

Whenever any one phase of Shakespeare's work comes up for consideration, the first observation to claim attention is that as his work progressed his art revealed a steady, orderly development. This observation is true in connection with the use of the oration in his plays; it seems there can be made out a gradual advance in degree of perfection as the oration appears in successive periods. This advance can be observed in both structure and dramatic integration.

Right away, in his very earliest plays, Shakespeare reveals a grasp of organic rhetorical structure. As a matter of fact, we somehow feel that, even in the plays of doubtful authorship, the orations reveal the touch of Shakespeare's hand in the vast majority of cases. *1 Henry VI* offers a problem in authorship. The speech of the Messenger is purely expository and thus does not betray Shakespeare's individual rhetorical style. The incomplete forensic of Winchester is broken off by Gloucester's abrupt interference that fires the exchange of snappy personalities between the two, but the part existing in the play might well be Shakespeare's. The deliberative oration of La Pucelle that makes Burgundy exclaim:

> I am vanquished. These haughty words of hers
> Have batt'red me like roaring cannon shot,
> And made me almost yield upon my knees.

has throughout, however, all the ring of Shakespeare's rhetor-

Structure of Orations

ical method: directness, economy, orderly procedure through a rounded period of convincing argument. And the same is true of the deliberative oration of King Henry designed to bring about peace between the rival lords. When we consider the orations in the problematical *2* and *3 Henry VI*, we find that some of the demonstrative speeches echo the prevailing Senecan rhetoric of the times; but the echoes generally have a distinctly Shakespearean sound—very clear and reverberating at times, perhaps, but not metallic nor hard on the ears.

Biron's speech is extremely mechanical and in a sense academic. Shakespeare is playing with words here and exercising with the colors of rhetoric. Consequently, the outline sticks out and betrays the work of the conscious experimenter in rhetorical form. But in *Comedy of Errors*, the two defense speeches, as simple in structure as they are and as artificially "set" as they are made, reveal Shakespeare's early grasp of the possibilities of the use of the forensic in the drama. And when we turn to those plays that are unmistakably Senecan imitations, *Richard III* and *Titus Andronicus*, the rhetoric of the orations is in most cases strikingly Shakespearean in contrast with a great deal of the Senecan sophistic rhetoric in the plays. We have already pointed out the orderly procedure of the orations in *King John* contrasting with the sophistic rhetoric of Constance. By the end of the first period, Shakespeare's use of outline has already emerged from the experimental stage; and, from this point on, outline is subdued, never obtrusive.

Shakespeare's orations in *Richard II* reveal a maturing sense for the use of argumentative rhetoric in the drama. Mowbray's defense against Bolingbroke's charges takes up the charges one by one and answers them; and, in this speech of only some twenty-five lines, we have anticipated the elaborate defense of Hermione some fifteen or more years later. Carlisle's speech before the lords arguing against the elevation of Bolingbroke to the throne looks forward to the impassioned argumentative speeches in *Coriolanus;* his speech wrings from Northumberland the admission,

> Well have you argued, sir;

before he pronounces

> and, for your pains, of capital treason
> we arrest you here.

In the two *Henry IV* plays, Shakespeare introduced a forensic, one in each, very simple in structure but successfully argumentative in tone. And in *Merchant of Venice,* and later in *Measure for Measure,* he elaborates and intensifies the forensic in the defendant's speech of Shylock and the advocate's speech of Isabella. In *Much Ado,* there is the cool, calm deliberation of the Friar arguing the disguised death of Hero as a means of ameliorating a very distressing situation. In *Henry V,* there is that splendid array of ten orations in which Shakespeare seems to center his attention consciously on the revelation of the various possibilities of a judicious use of rhetoric in poetic. Henry assumes the role of orator as statesman, judge, and soldier; and, while some of his oratory soars fairly high at times on the wings of emotion, it is always kept from flying away with the speech through Shakespeare's sense for the restraining effect of unified rhetorical structure. Six of his orations are of the occasional or expository kind; the seventh is a direct businesslike argument to win admission to Harfleur. Canterbury's speech, arguing the justice of invading France, is an ambitious exercise in deliberative oratory; and Burgundy's argument for a settlement between the French and English Kings, while much shorter and simpler in conception, is none the less direct and convincing. In *Julius Caesar,* there is the concentration of the oratory in a single scene at the crisis of the play, a concentration of rhetoric in poetic managed with an

Structure of Orations

effectiveness which Shakespeare revealed likewise in *Merchant of Venice*, in which he showed he had mastered the technique of the forensic in the drama. In *Julius Caesar*, he showed he had mastered, possibly to an even greater extent, the technique of the occasional oration in the drama. In fact, in Antony's oration he undertook the setting of an appeal to the emotions into the framework of a methodically worked-out oration on a scale found nowhere else in his plays. This speech represents Shakespeare's first serious and ambitious attempt to introduce the oration in tragedy.

His third period is the period of great orations. In *Troilus and Cressida*, Shakespeare again concentrates the rhetoric of oratory in a single scene. Agamemnon, Nestor, Ulysses, and Aeneas, all deliver their orations in Act I, scene iii. The speeches of Agamemnon and Nestor represent Shakespeare's hortatory rhetoric at its best when highly colored by the imagery of poetry. The speech of Ulysses is the most ambitious expository oration in Shakespeare. The speech progresses in an orderly fashion step by step to explain the trouble in the Grecian camp and to offer a solution; and the diction is so well managed that the heightening effects of poetry do not take away in any respect from the prevailing rhetorical purpose underlying the exposition. In elaborateness of outline, we associate with this speech of Ulysses that of King Henry VIII explaining his position with reference to his marriage; but the diction of this later speech does not maintain the level of the earlier one. In *Hamlet*, crowded as it is with speaking, the only speech which we record as an oration is the expository address of the King announcing his policy and the condition of state affairs. This speech possesses all the characteristics of the rhetoric of oratory; directness, logical procedure, formal diction, periodic structure. Whenever Shakespeare's hand touches the oration in the third period, the maturity of his genius creates a work of finished rhetorical art.

To this period belong his forensic achievements in *Measure for Measure*, *Othello*, and *Timon of Athens*. The speech of Isabella in defense of her brother and the speech of Alcibiades in defense of his friend reveal the effective dramatic possibilities of an elaborately worked out advocate's speech; the speech of Othello in his own defense reveals even more successfully the possibilities of a defendant's plea. In *Coriolanus*, commendatory rhetoric reaches a high-water mark in the oration of Comminius. The facts of Coriolanus's valor are marshaled in order and presented in a style which lifts the speech at once into the realm of emotional oratory but which uses word and phrase and figure with such spontaneity and discretion as to make it a model of the art of praise. Deliberative oratory in the drama finds its happiest expression in the four deliberative orations in *Coriolanus*. In the first speech of Menenius to the citizens, the apt story is used to enforce the argument; in the later one, the orator resorts to mere plain, pointed argument to appeal for the exercise of patience and reason in dealing with the imperious patrician. The oration of Coriolanus pleading against "corn gratis" is a model of deliberative rhetoric. Impassioned as the speech becomes because of the earnestness and decision of the orator, the speaker never loses sight of the fact that his purpose is to make an intellectual, not an emotional, appeal. Under analysis, therefore, the speech reveals articulate organic structure; but so spontaneous and sincere and convincing is the rhetoric of the orator that the inner mechanics of the structure and the functioning of the parts of the speech never obtrude to detract from the artistic effect of the oration as a whole. The speech fails to achieve its purpose, but its failure is a glorious failure from the standpoint of rhetorical art. More successful in its purpose is the plea of Volumnia for the salvation of Rome. And the marvel of Shakespeare's oration becomes all the greater when we reflect that, in this speech, Shakespeare has followed Plutarch very closely all the way

Structure of Orations

through. The alchemy of Shakespeare's rhetorical genius indeed transmutes here a not to be despised baser metal into very fine gold.

In the fourth period, Shakespeare worked out a variety of oratorical speeches. We have already referred to the oration of Henry VIII in explanation of his position as to his marriage to Katherine. As in Volumnia's speech, Shakespeare is writing with his eye frequently on his source material; and his oration is again a remarkable example of the power of his genius to transform the old into the new. Henry's oration is an excellent speech to analyze. Analysis is very easy here because the parts are, as it were, visibly held together in solution. All the way through, Henry lets us know when we are passing from one part of the argument to another. But so consistently is the speech devoid of mechanical tricks of rhetorical style and so thoroughly infused with the principle of articulation characteristic of logical presentation of the case in hand, that the obviousness of the structure detracts in no way from the success of the speech as a piece of oratory in the best sense. Buckingham's farewell speech and Cranmer's eulogy, if not Shakespeare's, are in the Shakespeare tradition; and there are parts in both speeches that sound so very much like Shakespearean rhetoric itself that we wonder if the speeches may not after all be his. The speeches are both good examples of the occasional oration. We have already commented on the apparent weakening to be observed in the broken "allegiance" speech of Wolsey. The speech lacks fire, perhaps, because the speaker does, and thus may represent not a weakening of Shakespeare's rhetoric but speech eminently in character. The King's ironical "'Tis nobly spoken" would seem to bear out the latter impression. Katherine's petition for a favorable consideration of their subjects' grievances shows no weakening anywhere of Shakespeare's deliberative rhetoric. Its earnestness of purpose, its studied restraint, its directness in expression, and its periodicity of effect all place it among the best of Shakespeare's orations.

In the fourth period, Shakespeare succeeds in giving us the forensic in the drama in its most finished form. The oration of Hermione applies all the principles of oratorical structure to rhetoric in poetic. Her defense represents the crowning achievement which was promised earlier in the speech of Shylock and that of Othello. Katherine's defense contains several reminders of Hermione's defense, but the later speech does not maintain the level of the rhetorical excellence to be found in the earlier.

Of the two expository orations of the fourth period, Iachimo's exposition of his cunning is interesting from the standpoint of emotional oratory. Here, the speaker announces at the very outset

> Thou'll torture me to leave unspoken that which
> to be spoke, would torture thee.

And, as he proceeds, he works upon the feelings of his audience, teasing the father by putting off, line after line, coming to the "matter" of the speech, and finally drives the lover to cry out frantically

> Ay so thou dost,
> Italian fiend! Ay me, most credulous
> fool

and so on, until, maddened, he strikes Imogen to the ground. Here Shakespeare gives the oration a distinctly "grand opera" setting and develops it in a style which contains many echoes of the rhetorical drama. Moreover, it is interesting to note that, in working up all of these theatrical effects, Shakespeare follows the story of Boccaccio rather than the circumstances represented in Act I, scene iv. The other expository speech, that of Prospero on the occasion of breaking the magic spell, is lighter in movement and encompassed by the atmosphere of poetry. The benignity of the orator tempers

Structure of Orations

the style of the oration; the magic circle might be taken as symbolic of the periodic movement of the orator's art; the simplicity and spontaneity that characterize the expression are typical of rhetoric in poetic at its best. It is not a great speech, but it is an entirely successful use of the oration in the drama.

This chronological review of Shakespeare's orations from the standpoint of their structure shows a gradual development from the artificial and, in a way, declamatory rhetoric of Biron to the spontaneous persuasive rhetoric of the later plays. Shakespeare's earliest orations show evidences of the influence of the early Elizabethan orations. Early Elizabethan rhetoric in the drama, imitative and experimental as it is, results generally in a set display, the profuse exhibition of showy rhetorical expression. Structure is often artificial at the expense of sincerity and convincingness. But even the rhetoric of Shakespeare's early orations is characterized by a restraint which marks at once an advance upon the earlier Elizabethan rhetoric.

And as Shakespeare's art develops, there come an enriching in expression, an increasing ease with which an outline is worked out, and a subduing of outline in the attainment of the total ultimate effect. There is a softening of outline accompanied by a sympathetic working out of detail. Outline becomes more and more subdued as more and more effort and skill are devoted to feeling and expression. The meticulously artificial, mechanical exhibition of Biron becomes transformed into the forceful, heart-to-heart, clearly thought-out reasoning of Coriolanus; the bare relation of Aegeon's story of his misfortune becomes transformed into the confident appeal and picturesque narrative of Othello and the passionate reasoning and appeal of Hermione. In the hands of Shakespeare, the oration is transformed from a mere artificial exhibition in rhetorical display into a spontaneous yet painstaking vehicle of purposeful rhetorical thought. In comedy, the oration seems to reach its triumph in the trial scene in the *Merchant of Venice* and again in that in the *Winter's Tale;* in tragedy, on the funeral occasion in *Julius Caesar,* in the forensic of Othello, and in the plea of Coriolanus before the patricians. The speeches in *Henry V* come as a crowning achievement in rhetoric in the history play.

Moreover, a consideration of the purpose for which orations in Shakespeare are delivered reveals their fidelity to the best classical tradition of the function of rhetoric. Mechanical and artificial as Biron's rhetoric is, his speech is made at the King's command to make a speech of persuasion:

> Then leave this chat; and, good Biron, now prove
> Our loving lawful, and our faith not torn.

Orations of the deliberative type, by their very nature, emphasize persuasion as their purpose, and so do orations of the judicial type. All of Shakespeare's orations of the deliberative type are spoken for the purpose of persuasion or dissuasion. The most successful deliberative orations seem to be those in *Coriolanus*. His orations of the judicial type are delivered to influence a judge and jury in favor of one's own case or the case of another. His forensic oratory is truest to the classical tradition in the oration of Hermione. The demonstrative oration, which offers great opportunities for indulgence in showy and emotional rhetoric, is the type which would present the temptation to abandon the classical tradition. But Shakespeare's orations of the demonstrative or occasional type, even those that are expository and narrative, are speeches of persuasion. Antony's oration over Caesar marshals the forces of emotional rhetoric to rouse to action. Ulysses's analysis of the trouble with the Greek camp is designed to bring about a remedy. The speech of the Third Messenger telling of the "dismal fight" between Lord Talbot and the French issues in the beginning of an offensive move on the part of the English.

Structure of Orations   113

As a basis for a more detailed study of Shakespeare's use of outline in individual speeches, some examples of each type arranged in order of time of writing, using the threefold division generally adopted today, are now presented:

FORENSIC ORATIONS

FIRST PERIOD

Comedy of Errors, I, i (A hall in the Duke's Palace) Aegeon to the Duke, officers, and other attendants
    I. Introduction
    II. Discussion: the story of his life
    III. Conclusion

SECOND PERIOD

Merchant of Venice, IV, i (Venice: A court of justice) Shylock to the Duke, Magnificoes, and others
    I. Introduction
    II. Discussion
        A. Reason for insistent demand
            1. Instances of humor
            2. Application to case in hand
        B. Intention to claim bond
            1. Instance of right of possession
            2. Application to case in hand
    III. Conclusion

THIRD PERIOD

Othello, I, iii (A Council-Chamber) Othello to Duke and councillors
    I. Introduction
    II. Discussion
        A. Confidence in the righteousness of his case
            1. Plainness of speech
            2. Willingness to tell the story
            3. Willingness to have the lady testify
        B. The statement of his case
    III. Conclusion

FOURTH PERIOD

The Winter's Tale, III, ii (Sicilia: A place of justice) Hermione to Leontes, Lords, and officers
    I. Introduction

II. Discussion
      A. The one accused
         1. Acknowledged righteousness of past life
         2. Call to plead for life and honor
         3. Appeal
            a. Acknowledged merit of past life
            b. Confidence in rectitude in case in hand
      B. The accusation
         1. Not guilty of infidelity: loved Polixenes honorably and as husband commanded
         2. Not guilty of conspiracy
            a. Unacquainted with conspiracy
            b. Camillo, an honest man
            c. His departure, not understood
      C. Readiness to receive sentence
         1. With blessings of life denied
         2. Not afraid to die
   III. Conclusion

DEMONSTRATIVE ORATIONS

FIRST PERIOD

Richard Third, V, iii (Bosworth Field) Richmond to his soldiers
   I. Introduction
   II. Discussion
      A. The fight, a fight against
         1. The enemy of the human race
         2. The enemy of God
      B. The reward
         1. As soldiers of God
         2. As soldiers of humanity
   III. Conclusion

SECOND PERIOD

Henry V, III, i (Before Harfleur) Henry to his soldiers
   I. Introduction
   II. Discussion
      A. Call to assume warlike mien
      B. Call to do honor to forbears
   III. Conclusion

Structure of Orations 115

THIRD PERIOD

Troilus and Cressida, I, iii (The Greek Camp; before Agamemnon's tent) Aeneas to Greeks
  I. Introduction
  II. Discussion
     A. The one challenging
     B. The one challenged
     C. The challenge
  III. Conclusion

FOURTH PERIOD

Henry VIII, V, v (The palace) Cranmer to King and Court
  I. Introduction
  II. Discussion
     A. Her good and blessed reign
     B. The good and blessed reign of her successor
  III. Conclusion

DELIBERATIVE ORATIONS

FIRST PERIOD

King John, II, i (France before Angiers) King John to citizens of Angiers
  I. Introduction
  II. Discussion
     A. French preparation for siege
     B. The parle due to the arrival of the English
  III. Conclusion

SECOND PERIOD

Henry V, III, iii (Before the gates of Harfleur) King Henry to citizens of Harfleur
  I. Introduction
  II. Discussion
     A. The consequence of refusal to yield
     B. His indifference to consequent violence
     C. The wisdom of surrender
  III. Conclusion

THIRD PERIOD

Coriolanus, I, i (Rome: A street) Menenius to a company of mutinous citizens
  I. Introduction

II. Discussion
　　　　A. The erroneous position taken by plebeians through malice, or through folly
　　　　B. The story
　　　　　　1. The accusation
　　　　　　2. The answer
　　　　C. The application to the case in hand
　　III. Conclusion

FOURTH PERIOD

Henry VIII, I, ii (The council-Chamber in the palace) Queen Katherine to the King for subjects
　　I. Introduction
　　II. Discussion
　　　　A. Grievances of the subjects
　　　　　　1. Cause of grievances
　　　　　　2. Voicing of grievances
　　　　B. The burdensome exactions
　　　　　　1. In general
　　　　　　2. In particular
　　　　C. The prevalent spirit of rebellion among subjects
　　III. Conclusion

These analyses, however, do not reveal the distinctive oratorical structure of the best of Shakespeare's orations. As the best of Shakespeare's oratorical structure reflects the best classical traditions, we shall review these classical traditions before presenting additional analyses of Shakespearean orations.

Aristotle has this to say about the parts of an oration:

"This (the exordium) is the commencement of a discourse resembling what, in poetry, is called *prologue*, and in instrumental music *prelude*, or *overture*. It is, as it were, the opening of an avenue, in order to proceed forward upon our destination."

"The matters which regard the hearer, that is to say, the judge, consist, on one side, in gaining his good will, and on the other, in whetting his resentment against our adversary;

Structure of Orations 117

sometimes in calling his attention to, and sometimes diverting it from, the subject."[1]

"This (narration) never occurs through one continuation, in demonstrative rhetoric, being only to be found by starts and portions . . . showing either 'that such a particular action has been done, provided it is difficult of belief'; or 'that it is such as is represented,' or 'considerably beyond the extent asserted'; or, finally, 'that it comprises all those qualities together.' "

"A defendant, in his narration of a fact, should take care not to say any thing which excites compassion, or may irritate the judge."

"Deliberative rhetoric has scarcely anything to do with the narration; for, as its subject is future, there can be little to relate, except of past occurrences, which might inspire a better resolution with respect to things proposed to be done at a distant period."[2]

"This (proof) should be demonstrative, and founded upon the force of argument."[3]

"Refutation never takes place without bringing an objection or opposing argument to argument."[4]

"For the composition of this (peroration), there are four requisites:
1. That we ourselves should stand well in the mind of the judge, while we produce a contrary disposition towards our adversary.
2. To strengthen or weaken the reasoning alleged on either side.
3. To excite the feeling of some passion in the judge. And,
4. To awaken his recollection of what has been said."[5]

Cicero says this with reference to arrangement:

". . . four, five, six, or even seven partitions (since they are differently divided by different teachers) into which

1. *Rhetoric*, III, xiv. Crimmin's translation, pp. 436-440.
2. III, xvi. Crimmin, p. 451.   3. III, xvii. Crimmin, p. 459.
4. III, xvii. Crimmin, p. 465. 5. III, xix. Crimmin, p. 473.

every oration is by them distributed; for they bid us adopt such exordium as to make the hearer favorable to us, and willing to be informed and attentive; then to state our case in such a manner that the detail may be probable, clear and concise; next, to divide or propound the question; to confirm what makes for us by arguments and reasoning, and refute what makes for the adversary; after this some place the conclusion of the speech, and peroration as it were; others direct you, before you come to the peroration, to make a digression by way of embellishment or amplification, then to sum up and conclude."[6]

"But we shall derive the greatest abundance and variety of matter of the exordia, either to conciliate or to arouse the judge, from those points in the cause which are adapted to create emotion in the mind; yet the whole of these ought not to be brought forward in the exordium; the judge should only receive a slight impulse at the outset, so that the rest of our speech may come with full force upon him when he is already impressed in our favor."[7]

"But every exordium ought either to convey an intimation of the whole matter in hand, or some introduction and support to the cause, or something of ornament or dignity.

"Your narrative will be clear if it be given in ordinary language, with adherence to the order of time and without interruption.

"It (narration) concerns the fortune of the whole cause, whether the case is stated with caution or otherwise, because the statement of the case is the foundation of all the rest of the speech.

"What follows is, that the matter in question be laid down, when we must settle what is the point that comes under dispute; then the chief grounds of the cause are to be laid down conjunctively, so as to weaken your adversary's supports, and

---

6. *De Oratore*, II, xix. Watson's translation, p. 104.
7. II, lxxix. Watson, pp. 177-178.

to strengthen your own; for there is in causes but one method for that part of your speech, which is of efficacy to prove your argument; and that needs both confirmation and refutation; but because what is alleged on the other side cannot be refuted unless you confirm your own statements, and your own statements cannot be confirmed unless you refute the allegations on the opposite side, these matters are in consequence united both by their nature, by their object, and by their mode of treatment. The whole speech is then generally brought to a conclusion by some amplification on the different points or by exciting or mollifying the judge; and every particular, not only in the former parts of the speech, but more especially toward the conclusion, is to be adapted to excite as much as possible the feelings of the judges, and to incline them in your favor."[8]

Quintilian makes these statements with regard to the structure of an oration:

"In giving an exordium (Greek Proem) at all there is no other object but to prepare the hearer to listen to us more readily in the subsequent parts of our pleading. This object, as is agreed among most authors, is principally effected by three means, by securing his good will and attention, and by rendering him desirous of further information; not that these ends are not to be kept in view throughout the whole pleading, but because they are pre-eminently necessary at the commencement, when we gain admission as it were into the mind of the judge in order to penetrate still farther into it."[9]

"It is most natural, and ought to be most usual, that when the judge has been prepared by the methods which have been noticed above, the matter, on which he is to give judgement, should be stated to him. This is the narrative or statement of the case."[10]

---

8. II, lxxx. Watson, p. 180.
9. *Institutes of Oratory*, IV, i. Watson's translation, p. 254.
10. IV, ii. Watson, p. 272.

"There are some writers who place the proposition after the statement of facts, as a division of a speech on any matter for judgement. To this notion I have already replied. In my opinion the commencement of any proof is a proposition which may be advanced not only in stating the principal question, but sometimes even to introduce particular arguments, especially those which are called epicheirema."[11]

"Partition is the enumeration, according to their order, of our own propositions; or those of our adversary, or both."[12]

"In fine, of the five parts into which we have distinguished judicial pleading, whatever other may occasionally be unnecessary in a cause, there certainly never occurs a suit in which proof is not required."[13]

"Refutation may be understood in two senses; for the part of the defender consists wholly in refutation; and whatever is said by either party in opposition to the other, requires to be refuted. It is properly in the latter sense that the fourth place is assigned it in judicial pleadings."[14]

"What *was* to follow, was the peroration, which some have termed the *completion,* and others the *conclusion.* There are two species of it, the one comprising the substance of the speech, and the other adapted to excite the feelings."[15]

Wilson adopts the sevenfold division in discussing arrangement:

There are feuen partes in euery Oration
   I. The Enterance or beginning.
   II. The Narration.
   III. The Propofition.
   IIII. The Deuifion or feuerall parting of things.
   V. The Confirmation.
   VI. The Confutation.
   VII. The Conclufion.

Orations in general confift vpon feuen partes

---

11. IV, iv. Watson, p. 304.
12. IV, v. Watson, p. 307.   13. V, Introduction. Watson, p. 313.
14. V, xiii. Watson, p. 379. The five parts of the judicial pleading are: exordium, statement of facts, confirmation, refutation, peroration.
15. VI, i. Watson, p. 407.

Structure of Orations

The Entraunce or beginning is the former parte of the Oration, whereby the will of the ſtanders by, or of the Iudge is ſought for, and required to heare the matter.

The Narration is a plaine and manifeſt pointing of the matter, and an euident ſetting forth of all things that belong vnto the ſame, with a breefe reherſall grounded vpon ſome reaſon.

The propoſition is a pithie ſentence comprehended in ſmall roome, the ſomme of the whole matter.

The Deuiſion is an opening of things, wherein we agree and reſt vpon, and wherein we ſticke and ſtande in trauers, ſhewing what we have to ſay in our owne behalfe.

The Confirmation is a declaration of our owne reaſons, with aſſured and conſtant proofes.

The Confutation is a diſſoluing, or wyping away of all ſuch reaſons as make againſt vs.

The Concluſion is a clarkly gathering of the matter ſpoken before, and a lapping vp of it altogether.[16]

A comparison of these quotations reveals the general agreement among rhetoricians as to the proper structure of an oration, the various parts into which an oration may be properly divided, and the purpose of each part. A comparison reveals further the indebtedness of Roman rhetoricians to Greek rhetoricians, and the indebtedness of Elizabethan rhetoricians to both. This indebtedness of Elizabethan rhetoricians to the classics finds ample illustration in Shakespeare's orations. As we break up Shakespearean orations into their parts and note the use of the various parts in the development of the orations as units of composition, we shall discover constantly reminders of the principles with regard to structure which we have found laid down in these treatises on rhetoric—ancient and Elizabethan.

Before submitting further analyses of Shakespeare's orations, the practice of ancient oratory should be reviewed and illustrated by analyses.

The place occupied by Isocrates in the history of Greek oratory is unique. A weak voice and a lack of nerve rendered

---

16. *Arte of Rhetorique*, p. 7.

him admittedly deficient so far as public speaking was concerned. The success as a public orator attained by Demosthenes, Isocrates could never hope to attain; and he himself frankly admitted that such success was utterly beyond the range of his natural gifts. But even Demosthenes drew from Isocrates in the matter of style. While to Demosthenes it was given to deliver his orations in public with eloquence and force, to Isocrates belongs the credit of giving to the written oration its fullest and most finished development in the matter of structure and prose style. It was as a prose analyst and stylist that Isocrates stood supreme in the realms of Attic oratory. The ability of Isocrates to amass an enormous array of material into a well-formed and, at the same time, ornamental composition is that which distinguishes him in the history of the Greek oration.

The arrangement of the speech into four parts—proemium, narration, proof, epilogue—was first employed, in practice, earlier, with slavish uniformity by Lysias; and, for this reason he is regarded as the inventor by some authorities. But Isocrates is generally said to have invented the fourfold division of the speech. The genius of Isocrates enabled him to break through the rigid uniformity characteristic of the speeches of Lysias and, with consummate skill and invention, to transpose and subdivide these main divisions. No matter which of the two stylists we regard as the inventor, certain beyond a doubt it is that Isocrates exerted immeasurably the greater influence upon the subsequent history of oratory, both in the literature of Greece and in the literature of Rome. The instruction in literary rhetoric which was necessary for all orators in the preparation of their orations and was the kind of work in which Isocrates excelled, influenced, more than the work of any other single man, the literary efforts of his contemporaries and the whole of subsequent history of oratory in his native land.

Of the six forensic speeches extant under the name of Isocrates, the *Aegenetikos* is the latest, and perhaps the best. These forensic speeches were written by Isocrates early in his literary career; in his later writings, he speaks of them with contempt, and commends himself for having given up this kind of oratorical writing for the writing of speeches upon loftier themes.

Analysis of *Aegenetikos*

I. Proemium: Speaker's delight at being able to speak in defense of himself
II. Narration and Proof
    A. Legal claim
        1. How he became heir
            a. Long intimacy with Thrasylochos
            b. Adoption as his son
        2. Legality of his claim to the inheritance
            a. According to the law of Aegima
            b. According to the law of Keos
            c. According to the law of claimant in own city
    B. Personal claim
        1. His interest manifested in Thrasylochos
        2. Claimant's lack of interest
III. Refutation
    A. Reasonableness of the will
    B. Justness of the will
IV. Epilogue: Summary of his claims for a verdict

As examples of his orations of the epideictic type, we have selected his eulogy of Evagoras, the father of the Cyprian King, Nikokles, and the hortatory speech addressed to Nikokles.

Analysis of *Evagoras*

I. Proemium
    A. Desire to extol
    B. Decision to attempt to do it in prose
II. Evagoras
    A. His lineage
    B. His acquisition of the throne
    C. His character
    D. His domestic reforms
    E. His wars with Persia

III. Hortatory Epilogue
  A. The noble character of Evagoras
  B. Its worth for imitation

Analysis of *To Nikokles*

I. Proemium
  A. King's need of preparation
  B. Isocrates' offering of advice
II. Advice
  A. Be intelligent
  B. Be a friend of mankind and of the realm
III. Epilogue: Exhortation to Nikokles to make good use of his and others' advice

An illustration of his orations deliberative, the field in which Isocrates achieved his greatest success, is the most famous of all Isocrates' works, the *Panegyrikos*, written to urge the formation of a union of the Greeks to carry on war against Persia.

Analysis of *Panegyrikos*

I. Proemium
  A. Need of unity among Greeks
  B. Attitude of speaker to his subject
II. Greece
  A. Narration: Greece now divided against itself
  B. Proposition
    1. Sparta, the obstacle to Greek unity
    2. Athens' claims over Sparta to sovereignty
  C. Proof
    1. Athens' claim to Empire
      a. Civil services
      b. Military services
      c. Moderation in rule
    2. Spartan ascendency
      a. Imperial Sparta
      b. Present condition of Greece
      c. Appeal to Sparta to mend her ways
III. Persia
  A. Narration: Divisions in Greece have given Persia time to gain a foothold in Grecian territory.

Structure of Orations

   B. Proposition: United Greece would be able to overcome Persia.
   C. Proof
      1. Confirmation
         a. Weakness of Persia
            (1) Persian repulses
            (2) Causes of
         b. Reasons for a war on Persia
            (1) Greek hatred of Barbarians (Persians)
            (2) Propitiousness of the moment
            (3) Sufferings in Greece
      2. Refutation: Treaty of Antalkidas no real obstacle to the war
IV. Epilogue
   A. Righteousness of the war
   B. Possible benefits of the war

From a consideration of these analyses,[17] it is observed that the presence of an introduction and conclusion is constant. The introduction gives the oration a start by commenting upon the position and attitude of the writer, or by suggesting pointedly what will be the central idea in what is to follow. The conclusion serves as a means of rounding off the speech by giving a final exhortation, by summarizing briefly and giving a closing plea to do what he has been urging, or by stating, in a summary and pointed manner, the grounds upon which the speaker claims a verdict. Between the introduction and conclusion, we find the body of the speech. In the simplest form of the oration—the eulogy of Evagoras and the hortatory speech to Nikokles—we find this to be contained within a single division. In the forensic speech, we find the body of the speech breaking up into a bringing forward of the arguments in favor of the speaker's claim and a refutation of the arguments brought forward by the advocates of his opponent. In the deliberative speech, we see the fullest development of the Isocratean sense for structure. The body

[17]. For summaries and analyses of the orations of Isocrates see Sir R. C. Jebb, *The Attic Orators*, II, 87-89, 108-113, 150-166, 217-219.

of the Panegyrikos divides into two main parts, each part containing its own narration of a situation, its own proposition in view of the situation, and its own process of proof.

The greatest disciple of Isocrates was Cicero. In Cicero were combined the ability to write and ability to speak in public. Moreover, Cicero was pre-eminently strong where Isocrates was weak. It is as the advocate that Cicero reigns supreme; in the art of public oratory his forensics are recognized models. Two well-known forensics have been chosen for analysis. The first is the speech in defense of Milo:[18]

Analysis of *Pro Milone Oratio*

I. Exordium
    A. Comment upon the audience and the case
    B. Method of defense he intends to pursue
II. Refutation
    A. Answer of first objection
        1. Argument of Milo's opponent
            (Milo has confessed to the slaying of Clodius)
        2. Counter-arguments of Cicero
            a. Precedents, slaying rightly and lawfully done
            b. Milo's right to self-preservation
    B. Answer of second objection
        1. Argument of Milo's opponents: The slaying of Clodius was contrary to the interests of the Republic
        2. Counter-argument of Cicero: Sentiment seems to prove opposite
    C. Answer of third objection
        1. Argument of Pompeius that a special inquiry is proper in this case: Motive is important in view of peculiar circumstances
        2. Counter-argument of Cicero: Real reason is a selfish one, as shown by appointment of judges and presiding officer
III. Narration: the incident as it occurred

---

18. See *Oratio Pro Milone*, with translation of Asconius' Introduction, Marginal Analysis and English Notes by the Rev. John Smyth Purton, Cambridge, 1891.

Structure of Orations

IV. Proposition: Generalizations in light of the narration—Question, Was he slain legally or illegally? To be answered by settling the question, Who laid the plot against whom?
V. Division
VI. Confirmation
    A. The question of who laid the plot
        1. Reason for Clodius, against Milo
        2. No reason for Milo, against Clodius
    B. Contrast in character (against Clodius) of Clodius and Milo
    C. History of relations between the two men (against Clodius)
    D. Evidence of the circumstances (against Clodius)
    E. Additional evidence
        1. More refutation
            a. The emancipation of the slaves
            b. Milo's return to Rome (a favorable reception)
        2. More confirmation
            a. Milo's attitude to subsequent charges against him
            b. Milo's claim upon the Roman people—he made possible their safety and happiness by slaying Clodius
VII. Conclusion: Plea for mercy for Milo
    A. Recalling Milo's attitude
    B. Manifesting intense personal interest in Milo and fear lest the speaker's effort has been in vain

In its orderly arrangement, its careful analysis, its rhetorical manner of expression, and its quantity of well-chosen illustration, Cicero's defense of the appointment of Pompey to the command of the Roman forces in western Asia is a finished model of a public oration.

Analysis of *De Imperio Cnaei Pompeii Oratio*

I. Proemium: Opening comment upon his own position and the case in hand
II. Narration: The situation in the East
III. Proposition: Consideration of what is to be done in the face of the situation

IV. Division
V. Confirmation
   A. The nature of the war
   B. The extent of the war
   C. The choice of a commander
VI. Refutation of
   A. The objections of Hortensius
   B. The objections of Catullus
VII. Conclusion, or Epilogue
   A. Pompey, the ideal commander
   B. The urgent need for the passage of the Manilian bill
   C. Purity of the speaker's own motives

Like Isocrates, Cicero was a literary artist. His ingenuity as an advocate enabled him to vary his order of arrangement to suit the particular case in hand. (Compare the arrangement in *Pro Milone Oratio* with that in *De Imperio Cnaei Pompeii Oratio*.) However, irrespective of the order or arrangement, the parts themselves are always constant, and the function of each part is always the same. The fourfold division of the forensic of Isocrates has become, in the hands of Cicero, a sevenfold division by the addition of the proposition, and the division of the author's argument in support of his case, and the separation, from this argument of the author, of the narration of the facts in the case. These two additions and the breaking of one Isocratean division into two parts are devices on the part of Cicero for the purpose of making absolutely clear to the audience the trend and structure of his speech.

We come now to Thomas Wilson. In his *Arte of Rhetorique*, as we have already pointed out, Wilson recalls Cicero's "Partitions" in the use of the sevenfold division of the oration.[19] Wilson constantly refers to Cicero, too, in regard to matters of diction and sentence structure. In the second

---

19. Wilson's *Arte of Rhetorique* is the subject of a doctoral dissertation by Russell Halderman Wagner, Cornell University, 1928. An abstract has been printed. For Wilson's writing of orations, see the *Discourse Upon Usury* in the form of dialogue and orations.

Structure of Orations

book of his text, Wilson takes up each division in detail, and, in the third book, discusses in detail the matter of elocution, "the apt chusing and framing of words and sentences together." In both these books, Wilson frequently refers to "that most excellent oratour *Tullie*." For instance in the second book, there is, in Wilson's detailed discussion of *The Division*: "Now, *Tullie* would not have a division to be made, of, or above three parts at the moste, nor yet lesse than three neither, if need so require." And, again, in the third book, in the discussion of the choice of words, is this sentence: "Therefore, to avoide such folly, we may learne of that most excellent Orator *Tullie*, who in his third booke, where he speaketh of a perfect Orator, declareth under the name of *Crassus*, that for the choice of words fower things should chiefly be observed." Then follows an enumeration of the four things to be observed, with a detailed discussion of aptness and the use of figures. In his discussion of the use of figures, Wilson makes the statement: "Therefore, to the end that they (figures) may be knowne, such as most commende and beautifie an Oration, I will set them forth here in such wise, as I shall best be able, following the order which *Tullie* has used in his Booke, made of a perfect Oratour."

Shakespeare's orations may now be considered in the light of what has been recalled of ancient oratory. First, the introductions and conclusions will be examined. Some introductions are quoted here:

Aegeon

A heavier task could not have been impos'd
Than I to speak my griefs unspeakable:
Yet that the world may witness that my end
Was wrought by nature, not by vile offense,
I'll utter what my sorrow gives me leave.

Othello

Most potent, grave, and reverend signiors,
My very noble and approv'd good masters,

That I have ta'en away this old man's daughter,
It is most true; true, I have married her:
The very head and front of my offending
Hath this extent, no more. Rude am I in my speech,
And little blessed with the soft phrase of peace;
For since these arms of mine had seven years' pith
Till now, some nine moons wasted, they have us'd
Their dearest action in the tented field,
And little of this great world can I speak
More than pertains to feats of broils and battle,
And therefore little shall I grace my cause
In speaking of myself. Yet by your gracious patience,
I will a round unvarnish'd tale deliver
Of my whole course of love, what drugs, what charms,
What conjuration and what mighty magic,
(For such proceeding I am charg'd withal),
I won his daughter.

Ulysses

                Agamemnon,
Thou great commander, nerve, and bone of Greece,
Heart of our numbers, soul and only spirit
In whom the tempers and minds of all
Should be shut up, hear what Ulysses speaks.
Besides the applause and approbation
The which, (To Agamemnon) most mighty for thy place
   and sway,
(To Nestor) And thou most reverend for thy stretch'd-
   out life,
I give to both your speeches, which were such
As Agamemnon and the hand of Greece
Should hold up high in brass, and such again
As venerable Nestor, hatch'd in silver,
Should with a bond of air, strong as the axle-tree
On which the heavens ride, knit all Greek ears
To his experienc'd tongue, yet let it please both,
Thou great, and wise, to hear Ulysses speak.

Henry VIII

                      My Lord Cardinal,
I do excuse you; yea, upon mine honour,
I free you from't. You are not to be taught

Structure of Orations

That you have many enemies, that know not
Why they are so, but, like to village curs,
Bark when their fellows do: by some of these
The Queen is put in anger. You're excus'd:
But will you be more justifi'd? You ever
Have wish'd the sleeping of this business: never desired
It to be stirr'd; but oft have hind'red, oft,
The passages made toward it. On my honour,
I speak my good Lord Cardinal to this point,
And thus far clear him. Now, what mov'd me to it,
I will be bold with time and your attention:

Alcibiades

Honour, health, and compassion to the Senate!

. . . .

I am an humble suitor to your virtues,
For pity is the virtue of the law,
And none but tyrants use it cruelly.

Coriolanus

Now as I live, I will. My nobler friends,
I crave their pardons,
For the mutable, rank-scented many, let them
Regard me as I do not flatter, and
Therein behold themselves. I say again,
In soothing them we nourish 'gainst our Senate
The cockle of rebellion, insolence, sedition,
Which we ourselves have plough'd for, sow'd and scatter'd,
By mingling them with us, the honour'd number,
Who lack not virtue, no, nor power, but that
Which they have given to beggars.

How! no more!

As for my country I have shed my blood
Not fearing outward force, so shall my lungs
Coin words till their decay against those measles,
Which we disdain should tetter us, yet sought
The very way to catch them.

Hermione

Since what I am to say must be but that
Which contradicts my accusation, and
The testimony on my part no other

But what comes from myself, it shall scarce boot me
To say "Not guilty." Mine integrity
Being counted falsehood, shall, as I express it,
Be so receiv'd.

Antony

Friends, Romans, countrymen, lend me your ears!
I come to bury Caesar, not to praise him.
The evil that men do lives after them,
The good is oft interred with their bones;
So let it be with Caesar. The noble Brutus
Hath told you Caesar was ambitious;
If it were so, it was a grievous fault,
And grievously hath Caesar answer'd it.
Here under leave of Brutus and the rest,—
For Brutus is an honourable man;
So are they all, all honourable men—
Come I to speak in Caesar's funeral.

The corresponding conclusions follow:

Aegeon

But here must end the story of my life;
And happy were I in my timely death,
Could all my travels warrant me they live.

Othello

This only is the witchcraft I have us'd.
Here comes the lady; let her witness it.

Ulysses

To end a tale of length,
Troy in our weakness stands, not in her strength.

Henry VIII

Therefore, go on;
For no dislike i' the world against the person
Of the good queen, but the sharp thorny points
Of my alleged reasons, drives this forward,
Prove but our marriage lawful, by my life
And kingly dignity, we are contented
To wear our mortal state to come with her,
Katherine our queen, before the primest creature
That's paragon'd o' the world.

Structure of Orations

Alcibiades

Must it be so? It must not be. My lords,
I do beseech you, know me.

. . . . . .

Call me to your remembrances.

. . . . . .

I cannot think but your age has forgot me;
It could not else be, I should prove so base,
To sue, and be deni'd such common grace.
My wounds ache at you.

Coriolanus

                  Therefore, beseech you,
You that will be less fearful than discreet,
That love the fundamental part of state
More than you doubt the change on't, that prefer
A noble life before a long, and wish
To jump a body with a dangerous physic,
That's sure of death without it, at once pluck out
The multitudinous tongue; let them not lick
The sweet which is their poison. Your dishonour
Mangles true judgement and bereaves the state
Of that integrity which should become't
Not having the power to do the good it would,
For the ill which doth control't.

Hermione

           Therefore proceed,
But yet hear this: mistake me not; no life,
I prize it not a straw, but for mine honour,
Which I would free,—if I shall be condemn'd
Upon surmises, all proofs sleeping else
But what your jealousies awake, I tell you
'Tis rigour and not law. Your honours all,
I do refer me to the oracle:
Apollo be my judge!

Antony

Here was a Caesar! when comes such another?

These quotations suggest the various types of introductions and conclusions found in Shakespeare's orations. The note of formality struck in the introduction serves to set the oration off at the very outset from the rest of the scene. The introduction usually contains a direct address to the audience for the purpose of gaining attention and consideration. Sometimes there is a statement of the speaker's willingness to speak; sometimes there is an indication of what is to follow or the reason for what is to follow. Whatever may be the special method the speaker adopts in his introduction, the general purpose of the introduction is to secure for the speech an attentive sympathetic hearing. The ideal introduction is suggestive of a spirit of humility combined with confidence. The introduction of the oration of Coriolanus is a notable exception: the speaker ignores the conventional form of opening in his emphasis on unrelenting opposition to "corn gratis" for the people. As a rule, however, Shakespeare's introductions are true to the best classical conventions. In addition to the speeches just quoted are the forensic of Isabella, the speech of the Citizen in *King John*, the plea of Worcester in *1 Henry IV*, Canterbury's speech in *Henry V*, La Pucelle's speech in *1 Henry VI*, Gloucester's in *Henry VIII*, which furnish examples of introductions in Shakespeare reminiscent of the exordia of classical oratory.

Like the introduction, the conclusion is characterized by its formality. In general, the conclusion may be said to round out the oration and complete its periodic effect. This is done by giving a terse summary gathering up of what has been said, a brief and pointed indication of the intended significance of the oration, the driving home of the point which has been uppermost in the speaker's mind, or an appeal to the feelings and sympathy of those to whom the speaker has been speaking. The conclusion serves to impress the idea of completeness, of something finished, a unit in itself. Moreover, the conclusion serves to intensify further the focusing upon the main idea. This intensifying may be concentrated in a single line; or a more or less full and extended sum-

Structure of Orations

ming up of what has been said may be made preparatory to a final telling thrust at the very end of the speech. In other words, the speaker may adopt the method of rounding out his effort with a brief pointed appeal to his audience, or he may make use of the method of presenting a gradual, accumulative reinforcement of what he wishes to press home upon his hearers. All of the following orations have more or less elaborate conclusions, reminiscent of the classic perorations: Biron's, Canterbury's, Volumnia's, Gloucester's rebuke of the King's marriage, Queen Margaret's denunciation of Gloucester, Queen Margaret's battle oration, Richmond's battle oration, Richard's battle oration, Henry's St. Crispin's Day Speech, and Paulina's rebuke of Leontes.

Shakespeare's earliest orations reveal structure along classical lines. Biron's speech contains introduction, narration with division, proposition, refutation, confirmation, and conclusion. La Pucelle's speech divides into introduction, narration, proposition, confirmation, and conclusion. Richmond's oration before his soldiers reveals the fourfold division into introduction, narration, confirmation, and conclusion. King Henry's speech to the rival lords contains introduction, narration, proposition, confirmation, and conclusion. The nature of the discussion varies, of course, with its use in the individual speech. Its content and division, therefore, depend upon the individual question in hand. Whatever the content and method of the treatment, however, the note of formality struck in the introduction and repeated in the conclusion is preserved throughout the body of the speech. From beginning to end, however impassioned and personal it may become, the oration is a formal utterance.

As Shakespeare's dramatic skill develops, his skill in the use of the rhetoric of oratory grows also. This development of rhetorical skill expresses itself especially in the breadth and depth of artistic perception displayed in the handling of the parts of the body of the oration. Shylock's speech is distinctly refutatory in nature. The Friar's plea in *Much Ado* is psychological in point of view. The oration of Ulysses is both psychological and philosophical in its approach to the matter in hand. The forensic of Isabella, after first attacking and undermining, in the refutatory vein, the antagonistic attitude of the Deputy, subtly but none the less directly makes her positive argument so personal and plain that his antagonism weakens by the end of the speech.

In history plays we note the same maturing of rhetorical art. The speeches of the Kings and the Citizen in *King John* betray a certain academic consciousness of working out an exercise in rhetorical composition; but the unmistakable periodicity of the three speeches, the pervading sense for logical procedure in making an appeal to reason, and the wave-swell motion of the rhetorical style capped from time to time with the imagery of poetry combine to qualify them as examples of rhetoric in the best classical tradition. In *Henry V*, Shakespeare's grasp of rhetorical structure enabled him to work out the deliberative rhetoric of Canterbury and the occasional rhetoric of Henry on the ambitious scale that he did without the consciousness of his art which the speeches in *King John* betray. The qualities of the Katherine speeches and that of Henry VIII have already been commented upon; there is only need to emphasize here how well they illustrate the use of the parts of the classical oration.

Now tragedy should be considered. The academic consciousness of the rhetorical structure of the Friar's speech at the end of *Romeo and Juliet* has been overcome by the time the impassioned plea of Antony develops in *Julius Caesar*. And all the orations in *Coriolanus* exhibit complete mastery of all the principles of the rhetoric of oratory. Analyses of these orations reveal the presence of the parts of the classical oration used with a freedom and artistic assurance which, as has already been noted, set Isocrates apart from his contemporaries as a literary artist.

Structure of Orations

In the course of his use of the oration in his plays, Shakespeare shows the greatest amount of development in the use and structure of the forensic. Aegeon's defense consists merely of an introduction, the story of his life, and a conclusion. Gloucester's defense introduces accusation and answer. Shylock's speech is made up largely of refutation in answer to questions raised by his opponents. Isabella assumes the role of advocate and matches wits with Angelo in defense of her brother. Othello's oration is a well-rounded forensic. A formal address to his audience is followed by his proposal, poor speaker as he is, to state his case. To the direct question as to his guilt, he asks that Desdemona be brought forward as a witness; and, while waiting for her, he presents his argument in his own defense in the form of a picturesque story of his courtship. The oration is rounded out by a brief pointed conclusion. The speech of Alcibiades, which recalls the speech of Isabella not only in its structure but also in its phrasing at times, marks a certain advance in concentration over the speech of Isabella. Hermione's oration is pure rhetoric; the speech is exposition and argument throughout. An introduction stating her difficult position is followed by a narration recalling her life as queen. The narration is followed by her proposition: innocence. Her proof is divided into two parts answering the two counts in the indictment. She refutes the idea that death will be a frightful punishment by giving four reasons why life is no longer worth while. Her speech closes with a conclusion which reiterates her prizing of honor, not life; denounces condemnation on a basis of the indictment as unjust; and appeals to the oracle of Apollo. The defense of Katherine begins in a way that reminds us of the oration of Hermione, and throughout the speech there are hints of the earlier speech; but Shakespeare does not achieve anything like the perfection in execution that he did in the earlier speech.

Before leaving the matter of outline, there should be submitted a few additional analyses of Shakespearean orations that reveal striking fidelity to the classical tradition.

Coriolanus: To Representatives of Patricians and Plebians

I. Proemium
    A. Unrelenting opposition to "corn gratis"
    B. Determination to continue to contend for one supreme power in the state—the patricians
II. Narration
    A. Evidence of danger in giving the "people" power equal with that of patricians
    B. The resulting confusion of authority
III. Proposition: Free gifts of corn to "the people" aid destruction of the state—unwise proposal.
IV. Proof
    A. "The people" undeserving
    B. Consequences of "corn gratis"
        1. Courting disunion in the State
            a. Weakening of the supreme power of the Senate
            b. Strengthening of the possibility of the people's getting power
        2. Fostering instability in the State
V. Epilogue
    A. Appeal to patricians to silence the plebeians
    B. Reason for his appeal—the preservation of the unity of the State

Antony: Before the Romans

I. Proemium
    A. Address to the Roman people
    B. Introductory comment
    C. Occasion
        1. What Brutus has already said
        2. Brutus' permission to Antony to speak
II. Narration
    A. Caesar's lack of ambition
        Thought of doing Brutus no direct wrong
    B. Caesar's worth
        Thought of doing Brutus no direct wrong

Structure of Orations

    C. Caesar's claim upon the Roman people
    D. Caesar's Will, referred to
        Thought of doing Brutus no direct wrong
III. Proof: Main appeal to the Roman people—the meaning of Caesar's death for the Roman people
    A. Revealed by the mantle
    B. Revealed by the will
IV. Epilogue: Concluding comment (the people now in motion)

Ulysses: To Agamemnon

I. Proemium
    A. Address to Agamemnon and Nestor
    B. Request for hearing
II. Narration: The situation in the Greek camp—army disorganized
III. Proposition: Disregard of rank spells chaos
IV. Proof
    A. Effects of order and disorder
        1. In the physical world
        2. In states
    B. The bane of disorder
        1. In general
        2. In particular application to the Grecian situation
V. Epilogue: "To end a tale of length,
        Troy in our weakness stands, not in her strength."
VI. Extended detailed illustration of disorder in Grecian camp

Henry VIII: To his Court

I. Proemium
    A. Excusing the Cardinal
    B. Promising explanation of his own position
II. Narration: The occasion which disturbed his conscience
III. Proof: Process of his subsequent thinking
    A. Conscience-sickness
        1. Question of disfavor of Heaven
        2. Question of judgment upon him
        3. Question of danger to his realms
    B. Search for a remedy
        1. In private with Lord Lincoln
        2. In public on the present occasion
IV. Epilogue: Willingness to have the investigation continue and to abide by the findings

There remains to point out one other matter in connection with the development of outlines in Shakespeare. This is the mechanical means of articulation of the parts of the oration. Reference is had here to such expressions as: Thus, hence, therefore, now, I say, say, so, whereof, then, I do protest, I this infer, consider, I beseech you, and the like. These expressions help to emphasize the formal nature of the oration, and at the same time, to make clear the process of development in thought.

The eloquence of Shakespeare's orations can now be discussed. It has already been said that Shakespeare's earliest orations reveal from time to time the lingering influence of the grandiloquent rhetoric to be found in the work of his predecessors. Biron's oration makes use throughout of mechanical tricks of style: scholastic and meticulously careful arrangement, enumerating and balancing of parts; a striving for the decorative and the carefully balanced and antithetical in expression; a conscious effort toward the attainment of a richly rounded periodic effect. But, with the exception of the oration of Biron, the early orations are remarkably free from the excessively mechanical style characteristic of so much of Elizabethan rhetoric. With an early grasp of organic rhetorical structure we find an early restraint in the use of the mechanics of style.

With the maturing of Shakespeare's art, his rhetoric of oratory becomes true eloquence in the sense of lofty, impassioned, convincing utterance. Rhetorical device and the imagery of poetic are introduced to serve the interests of exposition and argument; they are employed, not for their own sake, but for the sake of the speech as a whole.[20] Shakespeare has already grasped this idea of true eloquence when writing

20. "The Colors of Rhetoric in Shakespeare" is a thesis that would compare Shakespeare's use of the mechanics of style with the traditional medieval use. Professor Benjamin S. Harrison has already discussed "The Colors of Rhetoric in Chaucer" (Yale dissertation). See also his article, "Medieval Rhetoric in the Book of the Duchesse," *PMLA*, XLIX (June, 1934), 428-442.

Structure of Orations

the speech of Shylock. A few years later he reaches the heights of true eloquence in the funeral oration of Antony. These heights are kept in the speech of Ulysses, the forensics of Othello, Isabella, Alcibiades, and Hermione, the speeches in *Coriolanus*, the speech of rebuke by Paulina, and, in a measure, the expository speech of Henry VIII. The oration in Shakespeare witnesses the revival of the Aristotelian ideal.

This is no attempt to analyze the eloquence of Shakespeare's orations, and it is with hesitation that the following passages are quoted from them; they should all be taken entire if they are to be rightly appreciated. However, it is always of value to recall some of the greater passages of sustained eloquence that have become universally memorable:

Shylock

>   Now for your answer:
> As there is no firm reason to be rend'red
> Why he cannot abide a gaping pig;
> Why he, a harmless necessary cat;
> Why he, a woollen bagpipe; but of force
> Must yield to such inevitable shame
> As to offend, himself being offended,
> So can I give no reason, nor I will not,
> More than a lodg'd hate, and a certain loathing
> I bear Antonio, that I follow thus
> A losing suit against him—Are you answer'd?

Ulysses

> The heavens themselves, the planets, and this centre
> Observe degree, priority and place,
> Insisture, course, proportion, season, form,
> Office, and custom, in all line of order;
> And therefore is the glorious planet Sol
> In noble eminence enthron'd and spher'd
> Amidst the other; whose medicinable eye
> Corrects the ill aspects of planets evil,
> And posts, like the commandment of a King,
> Sans check to good and bad. But when the planets
> In evil mixture to disorder wander,

What plagues and what portents! what mutiny!
What raging of the sea! shaking of earth!
Commotion in the winds! Frights, changes, horrors,
Divert and crack, rend and deracinate
The unity and married calm of states
Quite from their fixture! Oh, when degree is shak'd
Which is the ladder to all high designs,
Then enterprise is sick! How could communities,
Degrees in schools, and brotherhoods in cities,
Peaceful commerce from dividable shores,
The primogenitive and due of birth,
Prerogative of age, crowns, sceptres, laurels,
But by degree, stand in authentic place?
Take but degree away, untune that string,
And, hark, what discord follows! Each thing meets
In mere oppugnancy. The bounded waters
Should lift their bosoms higher than the shores
And make a sop of all this solid globe.
Strength should be lord of imbecility,
And the rude son should strike his father dead.
Force should be right; or rather, right and wrong,
Between whose endless jar justice resides,
Should lose their names, and so should justice too.
Then everything includes itself in power,
Power into will, will into appetite;
And appetite an universal wolf,
So doubly seconded with will and power,
Must make perforce an universal prey,
And last eat up himself.

Isabella

Too late? Why, no, I, that do speak a word,
May call it back again. Well, believe this,
No ceremony that to great ones longs,
Not the king's crown, nor the deputed sword,
The marshal's truncheon, nor the judge's robe,
Become them with one half so good a grace
As mercy does.
If he had been as you and you as he,
You would have slipt like him; but he, like you,
Would not have been so stern.

I would to heaven I had your potency,
And you were Isabel. Should it then be thus?
No; I would tell what 't were to be a judge,
And what a prisoner.

. . . .

                            Alas, alas!
Why, all the souls that were were forfeit once;
And He that might the vantage best have took
Found out the remedy. How would you be,
If He, which is the top of judgement, should
But judge you as you are? O, think on that;
And mercy then will breathe within your lips,
Like man new made.

. . . .

Could great men thunder
As Jove himself does, Jove would ne'er be quiet;
For every pelting, petty officer
Would use his heaven for thunder,
Nothing but thunder! Merciful Heaven,
Thou rather with thy sharp and sulphurous bolt
Splits the unwedgeable and gnarled oak
Than the soft myrtle; but man, proud man,
Dress'd in a little brief authority,
Most ignorant of what he's most assur'd,
His glassy essence, like an angry ape,
Plays such fantastic tricks before high heaven
As makes the angels weep; who, with our spleens,
Would all themselves laugh mortal.

                    Hermione

                        Sir, spare your threats—
The bug which you would fright me with I seek;
To me can life be no commodity.
The crown and comfort of my life, your favour,
I do give lost; for I do feel it gone,
But know not how it went. My second joy
And first-fruits of my body, from his presence
I am barr'd, like one infectious. My third comfort,
Starr'd most unluckily, is from my breast,
The innocent milk in it most innocent mouth,
Hal'd out to murder, myself on every post

Proclaimed a strumpet; with immodest hatred
The child-bed privilege deni'd which longs
To women of all fashion; lastly, hurried
Here to this place, i' the open air, before
I have got strength of limit. Now my liege,
Tell me what blessings I have here alive,
That I should fear to die?

Carlisle

I speak to subjects, and a subject speaks,
Stirr'd up by God, thus boldly for his king.
My Lord of Hereford here, whom you call king,
Is a foul traitor to proud Hereford's king;
And if you crown him, let me prophesy,
The blood of English shall manure the ground,
And future ages groan for this foul act.
Peace shall go sleep with Turks and infidels,
And in this seat of peace tumultuous wars
Shall kin with kin and kind with kind confound.
Disorder, horror, fear, and mutiny
Shall here inhabit, and this land be called
The field of Golgotha and dead men's skulls.

Chief Justice

If the deed were ill,
Be you contented, wearing now the garland,
To have a son set your decrees at nought?
To pluck down justice from your awful bench?
To trip the course of law and blunt the sword
That guards the peace and safety of your person?
Nay, more, to spurn at your most royal image
And mock your workings in a second body?
Question your royal thoughts, make the case yours:
Be now the father and propose a son,
Hear your own dignity so much profan'd
See your most dreadful laws so loosely slighted,
Behold yourself so by a son disdained;
And then imagine me taking your part
And in your power soft silencing your son.

Henry V

God's will! I pray thee, wish not one man more.
By Jove, I am not covetous for gold,

Nor care I who doth feed upon my cost;
It yearns me not if men my garments wear;
Such outward things dwell not in my desires;
But if it be a sin to covet honour,
I am the most offending soul alive.
No, faith, my coz, wish not a man from England.
God's peace! I would not lose so great an honour
As one man more, methinks, would share from me
For the best hope I have. O, do not wish one more!
Rather proclaim it, Westmoreland, through my host,
That he which hath no stomach to this fight,
Let him depart. His passport shall be made,
And crowns for convoy put into his purse.
We would not die in that man's company
That fears his fellowship to die with us.

La Pucelle

Look on thy country, look on fertile France,
And see the cities and the towns defac'd
By wasting ruin of the cruel foe.
As looks the mother on her lowly babe
When death doth close his tender dying eyes,
See, see the pining malady of France!
Behold the wounds, the most unnatural wounds,
Which thou thyself has given her woeful breast.
O, turn thy edged sword another way;
Strike those that hurt, and hurt not those that help.
One drop of blood drawn from thy country's bosom
Should grieve thee more than streams of foreign gore.
Return thee therefore with a flood of tears,
And wash away thy country's stained spots.

Margaret

What though the mast be now blown overboard,
The cable broke, the holding-anchor lost,
And half our sailors swallow'd in the flood?
Yet lives our pilot still. Is't meet that he
Should leave the helm and like a fearful lad
With tearful eyes add water to the sea
And give more strength to that which hath too much,
Whiles, in his moan, the ship splits on the rock,
Which industry and courage might have sav'd?

Ah, what a shame! ah, what a fault were this!
Say Warwick was our anchor; what of that?
And Montague our topmast; what of him?
Our slaught'red friends the tackles; what of these?
Why, is not Oxford here another anchor?
. . . .
And, though unskilful, why not Ned and I
For once allow'd the skilful pilot's charge?
We will not from the helm to sit and weep,
But keep our course, though the rough wind say no,
From shelves and rocks that threaten us with wreck.
As good to chide the waves as speak them fair.

Coriolanus

O good but most unwise patricians! why,
You grave but reckless senators, have you thus
Given Hydra here to choose an officer,
That with his peremptory "shall," being but
The horn and noise o' the monster's, wants not spirit
To say he'll turn your current in a ditch,
And make your channel his? If he have power,
Then vail your ignorance; if none, awake
Your dangerous lenity. If you are learn'd,
Be not as common fools; if you are not,
Let them have cushions by you. You are plebeians,
If they be senators; and they are no less,
When, both your voices blended, the great'st taste
Most palates theirs. They choose their magistrate,
And such a one as he, who puts his "shall,"
His popular "shall" against a graver bench
Than ever frown'd in Greece. By Jove himself!
It makes the consuls base; and my soul aches
To know, when two authorities are up
Neither supreme, how soon confusion
May enter 'twixt the gap of both and take
The one by the other.
. . . .
                              No, take more!
What may be sworn by, both divine and human,
Seal what I end withal! This double worship,
Where one part does disdain with cause, the other
Insult without all reason, where gentry, title, wisdom,

> Cannot conclude but by the yea and no
> Of general ignorance,—it must omit
> Real necessities, and give way the while
> To unstable slightness; purpose so barr'd, it follows
> Nothing is done to purpose.

To know such passages as these is to know the best of the rhetoric of oratory. To see the beauty of poetic imagery as it spontaneously emerges to give grace and color to expression of thought; to feel the rhythm of rhetorical movement imparted by the ebb and flow of the progress of thought; to experience the sense of exaltation as both poetry and rhetoric rise to lofty heights of beautiful or impassioned oratory; to become aware of the sense of completeness as the peroration rounds out the composition; to perceive the purpose of the orator that has steered the oration through to its conclusion—this is to appreciate the oration in Shakespeare. The true eloquence of Shakespeare's orations depends on no schematized, mechanical, high-sounding, or showy rhetoric that dazzles the eye, strikes the ear, amuses one's fancy, or flatters one's wits. It rather grows out of rhetoric that delights because it is rightly but unaffectedly beautiful, teaches because it seeks to impart the truth, and persuades because it appeals to reason. And when these things are said about Shakespeare's rhetoric of oratory, qualities are claimed for it which were judged ideal for rhetoric by Aristotle, Cicero, Quintilian, and Wilson.[21] The structure of Shakespeare's orations reveals their fidelity to the best classical tradition.

21. For an eighteenth-century presentation of the Aristotelian classical theories of rhetoric, see Hugh Blair, *Lectures on Rhetoric and Belles Lettres*. In the nineteenth century, the *Lectures on Rhetoric and Oratory* by John Quincy Adams seem to me the clearest presentation of the Aristotelian theories of the rhetoric of oratory I have read. They present these theories, moreover, from the practical viewpoint of the legal profession. It is of interest in this connection to note that Elyot, in his *Governour*, discusses rhetoric in the chapter devoted to the study and practice of law (pp. 36-37 in the Eliot edition).

CHAPTER VI

Dramatic Integration

A DISCUSSION OF THE dramatic integration in Shakespeare's orations should be begun by noting Aristotle's discussion of rhetoric in poetic:

"Under Thought is included every effect which has to be produced by speech; in particular,—proof and refutation; the excitation of the feelings, such as pity, fear, and anger, and the like; the heightening or extenuating of facts. Furthermore, it is evident that the dramatic incidents must be treated from the same points of view as the dramatic speeches, when the object is to evoke the sense of pity, fear, grandeur, or probability. The only difference is that the incidents should speak for themselves without verbal exposition; while the effects aimed at in a speech should be produced by the speaker, and as a result of the speech."

We have pointed out in Chapter III how Shakespeare integrated his sophistic rhetoric. We emphasized that this integration of his emotional rhetoric was achieved by making it integral in character development. We are concerned here with his integration of the oration—principally "proof and refutation"; in some cases, "the heightening or extenuating of facts." Dramatic integration of the oration is a matter of making rhetoric integral in plot development. This discussion of the dramatic integration of Shakespeare's rhetoric of oratory must be built up, then, upon a consideration of Shakespeare's poetic.

We have already pointed out that from the first Shakespeare seems to grasp the significance of rhetorical structure

Dramatic Integration

of the Aristotelian oratory. The more Shakespeare's early plays are studied, the more evident it becomes that he seems to grasp too the significance of Aristotelian poetic. On the surface, *Titus Andronicus* and the *Henry VI* plays are excessively overlaid with declamatory rhetoric; but clear all this rhetoric away and expose the sequence of the incidents, and there is found much more consistency in plot development than should be expected.[1]

Begin with *Titus Andronicus*. This play is, of course, saturated with the Senecan conception of poetic—a rhetoricated poetic. But take the rhetoric away and reduce the movement of the action to its simplest terms, and the play stands true to the Aristotelian poetic: movement from a beginning at the end of Act I, in Tamora's duplicity to cover up her vengeance; through a middle, Act III, scene i, when her vengeance, committed through her sons, drives Titus to seek aid of the Goths to wreak counter-vengeance; to an end presenting the wholesale slaughter as the lines of vengeance meet. Note, now, the setting of the orations in this plot movement. As poor technically as Tamora's deliberative oration on reconciliation is, it comes at a point of focusing in plot action, the initial action: from her oration the subsequent lines of action issue. Her unsuccessful forensic pleading for the life of her sons precipitates the initial action. The funeral oration of Titus precipitates the forensic of Tamora; and the occasional speeches of Marcus eulogizing Titus are directly in line with the friction between Titus and Saturninus, which in turn

---

1. J. Churton Collins' essay, "Shakespearean Paradoxes," in *Studies in Shakespeare*, discusses at length *Titus Andronicus* from the standpoint of Shakespearean authorship. Of special interest in connection with my discussion here is Collins' point as to the unity of plot in *Titus Andronicus*, pp. 123-125. William John Tucker, however, in his discussion of *Titus Andronicus* in *College Shakespeare*, thinks "Nor is it easy to see, with Boas, that the play bears the unmistakable stamp of unity. On the contrary, there is a decided lack of consistency and definiteness in the portrayal of the characters. Further, the defects of its versification, the absence of dramatic spirit and poetic imagery, and the savage atrocities of the story all weigh against its authenticity."—p. 26.

occasions the oration of Tamora at the point of the initial action. Later in the play, the oration of Saturninus on Titus' turn against Rome comes directly in line from the crisis when Titus turns to the Goths; and the occasional orations of Marcus and Lucius at the end of Act V clear the air—in fact, voice the catharsis after the wholesale slaughter of the principal actors in the tragedy. Thus the orations in *Titus Andronicus* are every one of them made vital in plot development. In this play, crowded as it is with Senecan rhetoric, the dramatist holds true to Aristotelian rhetoric in poetic.

By their very nature, the *Henry VI* plays are not as consistent in plot structure as *Titus Andronicus*. History is essentially episodic in its progress; the plot structure of history plays, therefore, will be likewise episodic. As Aristotle points out, episodic plots may be the result of lack of dramatic skill on the part of the dramatist or the result of the deliberate providing of "parts" for actors. In providing parts for actors, the drama inevitably becomes rhetorical. The *Henry VI* plays reveal constantly the influence of the earlier Elizabethan rhetorical drama, and their plot structure is, from the very nature of their content, episodic. In episodic plots, orations cannot be as successfully integrated in dramatic action as they can be in a climactic plot. Consequently, we do not find the orations in the *Henry VI* plays worked into the texture of the play as we do in *Titus Andronicus*. The orations in the *Henry VI* plays, however, are, as a rule, infinitely better orations, and they mark points of focusing. The Third Messenger's speech issues in preparations to invade France. Winchester's forensic marks a moment of tension. La Pucelle's address to Burgundy is made pivotal, even though not critical, so to speak, as in a tragic plot. Henry's speech to the quarreling lords marks a moment of tension. The clash between England and France, impersonated in the play by La Pucelle and Talbot, contributes a sort of unity to the plot;

Dramatic Integration

and in the person of La Pucelle, as she passes from her shout of victory:

> Rescu'd is Orleans from the English! (I, vi)

through success in winning over Burgundy (III, iii), to the pathetic reversal in defeat and capture and insult at the end (V, iv), one feels a distinctly tragic progress in dramatic action. But we are not made to feel the consistency and cogency of plot that combine to knit the parts together and drive the action on to an inevitable issue as in great tragedy. Indeed, they do not combine in history as they do in tragedy. And the achievement in *1 Henry VI* of making material essentially episodic reveal upon analysis the elements of tragic progress in terms of a single character shows on the part of Shakespeare a grasp of the essentials of Aristotelian poetic in this play too, one of the earliest of the plays in point of date included in the First Folio.[2]

The *Second* and *Third Parts* of *Henry VI* do not reveal this underlying tragic progress in terms of a single character. Their plots are again essentially episodic, and what tragedy comes is incidental in the sense of occurring in the course of events, not inevitable as a result of character. The plots record the conflict between the houses of York and Lancaster; the end of *2 Henry VI* registers merely a pause in that conflict, and *3 Henry VI*, at best, only an apparent finish. In these episodic plots, the orations are incidental: they come in the course of events. They mark, however, as they always do, points of focusing. In *2 Henry VI*, Gloucester's oration opposing the King's marriage registers his opposition to the Cardinal and Suffolk and York; and his death, the turning point of events in the play. Salisbury's oration voices the turn of the commons against Suffolk. Lord Say's forensic is

---

[2]. It is to be noted, as has already been pointed out in connection with the orations, how much freedom the dramatist exercised in handling the source material for the plot. For a concise statement, see Neilson's introduction in the *Cambridge Shakespeare*.

occasioned by those commons taking action against the nobility. In *3 Henry VI*, the denunciatory orations at the end of Act I come at a moment of extreme tension in the history of the conflict between the houses. Warwick's expository oration reports events subsequent to Wakefield and fires Richard and Edward to action. Clifford's oration appeals to Henry to fight for the maintenance of the Lancaster line in power. Margaret's oration to her followers is a ringing appeal in the face of the battle on the plains near Tewksbury.

In *Richard III* and *King John*, Shakespeare is making great strides in working out Aristotelian rhetoric in poetic. In *Richard III*, the character of Richard not only unifies the plot but makes possible the working out of the catastrophe of tragedy; one feels that the disaster that Richard meets is more than just an episode in history, that it is the inevitable outcome of weakness in his character. The oratory is concentrated as in *Titus Andronicus*:[3] Gloucester's allegiance speech and Edward's rebuke of Derby for the request for the servant's life (II, i), Buckingham's speech urging Gloucester to accept the kingship and Gloucester's speech in reply (III, vii), the battle orations of Richmond and Richard (V, iii). The same concentration is noted in *King John:* Chatillon's battle oration, the speeches of the Kings before Angiers, the speech of the Citizen of Angiers—all in Act II, scene i; the speech of Pandulph is placed at the point of crisis in the play. In both plays the oratory is staged at critical moments in plot development; and in the case of the deliberative orations and the battle orations we have effective use of speech, rather than action, to influence plot development.

In his earliest comedies, Shakespeare achieved promising success in dramatic integration. The single oration in *Love's Labour's Lost*, as mechanically worked out as it is, marks a point of focusing to which preceding lines of action have been

---

3. This concentration of oratory at vital points in plot development I feel is a very dependable bit of evidence in support of dating *Richard III*, *Titus Andronicus*, and *King John* about the same time.

Dramatic Integration 153

converging and from which the remaining action of the play develops. In *A Comedy of Errors*, Aegeon's forensic furnishes a background for the subsequent action of the plot; the forensic of Antipholus of Ephesus begins the disentangling at the end. By the time Shakespeare puts his hand to the writing of *Merchant of Venice*, he has grasped and made his own the principles of Aristotelian poetic and has already achieved success in the working out of Aristotelian rhetoric in poetic.

Here should be stated, with reference to Shakespeare's dramatic integration of the oration, what has already been suggested in Chapter I, the Aristotelian conception of rhetoric of the oration in the drama. The ideal oration marks a point of focusing in the progress of dramatic action. For the moment, dramatic action comes to a standstill, and interest becomes centered in what the speaker has to say in the oration. The onward movement of the dramatic action becomes for the moment transmuted into movement about the central idea discussed in the oration. To this point of focusing, precedent lines of action converge; from it, subsequent lines of action issue. The oration thus comes to be a vital, organic, integral part of the dramatic action. Skill in dramatic integration and success in it are directly proportional to the effectiveness with which this vital relation is brought about. Furthermore, it is easy to see that the oration in the drama has the greater chance for possessing perfected dramatic integration in proportion to the greater amount of success achieved in plot structure.

With the opening of the second period, Shakespeare marks a distinct advance in the matter of plot structure and dramatic action; and with his advance, there comes a concern for discrimination in the use of the oration and for effectiveness in dramatic integration. In the trial scene in the *Merchant of Venice*, the oration of Shylock is made to grow materially out of the situation and to function as a vital part of the plot.

The main lines of action meet in this scene. Their meeting raises the question as to Shylock's next move. His oration is the answer to that question, and thus marks a point of focusing to which precedent lines of action converge. It also marks at the same time a point of focusing from which subsequent lines of action issue. The stand taken by Shylock leads to the solution of the Shylock-Antonio line of interest by bringing about victory for Antonio and defeat for Shylock. Moreover, the oration leads to a happy ending of the Portia-Bassanio line of interest, the other main theme in the play. In this way, the oration becomes an integral part of dramatic action.

From the *Merchant of Venice* on, there is observed a sudden decrease in the number of orations introduced, with a corresponding increase in successful and effective dramatic integration. In tragedy, dramatic integration seems to have been most effectively done in *Julius Caesar*, *Othello* and *Coriolanus*. Antony's oration grows out of the rise and success of the conspiracy and issues in swaying the mob in favor of Caesar and against the conspirators; the oration determines the destiny of the conspirators by setting in motion influences which lead ultimately to the defeat of the conspirators. Othello's speech grows out of the intriguing of Iago; the success of the oration, contributing to the defeat of Iago's conspiracy, prompts Iago to begin another line of intrigue. The oration of Coriolanus grows out of the change in popular sentiment toward him in consequence of his attitude toward the people; his opposition to "free corn" and the appeal that he makes to the patricians to oppose the plebeians in their demands lead ultimately to his banishment and the events that follow. In comedy, dramatic integration is well done in *Much Ado* and the *Winter's Tale*. The speech of the Friar in the church grows out of the accusation made by Claudio in consequence of the intriguing of John; it proposes a plan which leads ultimately to a happy ending to the play. Hermione's oration grows out of the accusation based upon the

Dramatic Integration

preceding dramatic action; the outcome of the trial—the verdict of the oracle and the setting aside of the verdict by the King—is followed immediately by developments which lead to the subsequent development of the plot. In history play, dramatic integration is effectively done in *Henry V* when the oration of Canterbury comes in answer to Henry's question as to the right to invade France; the success of the oration in persuading Henry that he has the right leads to the invasion of France, which constitutes the principal part of the plot structure of the play.

All these orations stand out prominently in the matter of dramatic integration because they are made to function as organic parts of the development of plot; they are made to sustain a vital relationship to dramatic action. The speech of Othello and that of Canterbury prepare for initial action; those of Shylock, Antony, Coriolanus, the Friar, and Hermione determine crisis. *Henry V* and *Coriolanus* contain orations at the three major points of dramatic plot structure. Canterbury's speech prepares for initial action; Henry's St. Crispin's Day speech and his answer to Constable determine the point of turning in the direction of the end; Burgundy's speech prepares for the denouement. The speech of Menenius at the opening of *Coriolanus*, in addition to furnishing exposition, sounds the note of conflict in the play and looks forward to the crisis; the speech of Coriolanus to the patricians and representatives of the people precipitates the crisis; the speech of Volumnia prepares for—in fact, determines—the denouement.

As he perfected plot structure, then, Shakespeare perfected also the weaving of the oration into the plot as an integral part of plot development. His achievement at once invites comparison with the classics. It will be interesting to work back.

Shakespeare took up the poetic of the Elizabethan drama where Marlowe left it off. Marlowe had done much in advance of his contemporaries in the direction of consistent and cogent plot structure. But Marlowe's drama, when he ceased to write, was dominated by the manner of rhetoric in the tradition of Seneca. This Senecan tradition was post-classical tradition of the drama—drama that appropriated the rhetorical style. In consequence, it became episodic and stringy in plot structure and heavy and gaudy in expression.

The Sophoclean tradition of drama was just the reverse. Sophoclean tragedy is compact and direct and crucial in plot structure; economical, restrained, but swift and sure in expression. Where Senecan tragedy is loose in dramatic structure, Sophoclean tragedy is tight; where Senecan tragedy emphasizes the utterance of one's feelings at the expense of interplay of character and circumstance, Sophoclean tragedy emphasizes above everything else interaction, contributing to a totality of impression at the end; where Senecan tragedy moves along in a leisurely fashion to a final episode at the end, Sophoclean tragedy moves swiftly to an inevitable catastrophe. These two poetic techniques, therefore, are as far apart as the poles; the one is extensive *ad libitum* in its movement; the other intensive within certain prescribed bounds.

Shakespeare inherited through Marlowe the extensive poetic of the post-classical period, and, as has been noted already, the lingering influences of the Marlowesque rhetorical drama. But, as has already been shown, too, *1 Henry VI*, *Titus Andronicus*, and *Richard III* contain beneath the rhetorical surface the unmistakable essentials of Sophoclean tragedy. And it has been seen that, in his earliest comedies, Shakespeare makes the Sophoclean poetic ideal—dramatic action above everything else—increasingly his poetic ideal; and that, in *King John*, he imperfectly works out a consistent, if not cogent, plot about King John as a centralizing figure.

From *King John* on, Shakespeare never loses sight of the Aristotelian ideal. In the history plays, of course, this ideal is inevitably overshadowed by rhetoric that goes along with

Dramatic Integration

the episodic movement inherent in this type of play. But even here, Shakespeare succeeds as no one else in harmonizing the two ideals of poetic. In comedy and tragedy, the Aristotelian ideal is always obvious or easily discovered.

This demonstrates what makes Shakespeare the supreme dramatist of the world. Shakespeare succeeded in making what we usually call the romantic drama of his immediate predecessors conform to the best classical dramatic tradition; he harmonizes the two poetic ideals. In doing this, he developed the best possibilities of the romantic drama by restriction and the best of the classical drama by extension. His drama is, therefore, neither romantic nor classical—it is pure drama: he made drama all it can possibly be.

All this has special significance for this study in that it helps formulate an appreciation of what Shakespeare made of rhetoric in poetic. The restriction which he placed upon the romantic drama subordinates speaking to action in the development of plot, the main element in classical drama. Shakespeare thus realized in practice Aristotle's theory of the poetic of the drama and his theory of the use of rhetoric in that poetic. The extension which he gave to the classical drama in range of character, situation, space, and time opened up possibilities for the introduction of rhetoric in poetic of which the classical dramatists and Aristotle never dreamed. In this liberation of the classical drama, Shakespeare made possible the use of all the types of classical orations in a great variety of situations but introduced them with such discrimination and such a fine feeling for drama as a work of finished art that he wove them into the fabric of the drama as a whole. Orations in Shakespeare do not obtrude; they fit into the play. They are worked out, not as ends in themselves, but as means to an end.

As Shakespeare's art in the weaving of the oration into the fabric of the drama progresses, we find him making distinct advances over his predecessors in the care and elaboration devoted to setting. Considerable elaboration in setting is to be noted in history plays. The *Henry VI* plays furnish several instances of the placing of the oration in scenes presenting spectacular stage setting appropriate to the occasion of the oration. The speech of the Third Messenger is staged in Westminster Abbey after the Dead March has been sounded and the funeral of Henry V has entered, "attended on by the Duke of Bedford, Regent of France; the Duke of Gloucester, Protector; the Duke of Exeter, the Earl of Warwick, the Bishop of Winchester, Heralds, etc." Winchester's brief and incomplete defense is spoken in the Parliament-House, in the presence of the King, Exeter, Gloucester, Warwick, Somerset, Suffolk, Richard Plantagenet, and others. King Henry's speech to the rival lords, Vernon and Basset, is delivered in a hall of state in Paris, in the presence of Gloucester, Bishop of Winchester, York, Suffolk, Somerset, Warwick, and Exeter. The speech of Gloucester in rebuke of the marriage of Henry to Margaret is spoken in the palace in the presence of Salisbury, Warwick, Cardinal Beaufort, York, Somerset, and Buckingham. The Queen's denunciation of Gloucester and Gloucester's defense are spoken in the Abbey at Bury St. Edmund's, after the King and Queen, the Cardinal, Suffolk, York, Buckingham, Salisbury, and Warwick have entered the Parliament. Salisbury's expository speech, presenting the position of the Commons in demanding the death or exile of Suffolk, is also delivered in Bury St. Edmund's, in the presence of the King, Lords, and Commons.

Richard II furnishes two good examples of elaborate and imposing state settings. Mowbray makes his defense of himself in the palace at London, in the presence of the King, John of Gaunt, and other nobles and attendants. The scene in which the Bishop of Carlisle makes his oration urging the keeping of Bolingbroke from the throne has this stage direction:

Dramatic Integration 159

London, Westminster Hall

Enter as to the Parliament Bolingbroke, Aumerle, Northumberland, Percy, Fitzwater, Surrey, the Bishop of Carlisle, the abbot of Westminster (and other Lords), Herald, and Officers.

Canterbury's speech to persuade Henry to invade France and the speech of Henry to the French ambassadors announcing his intention to invade France are delivered in the Presence Chamber of the King's Palace, in the presence of Lords and attendants. Burgundy's speech persuading a peaceful settlement is spoken in the palace of the French King, in the presence of King Henry and his lords, the French King, Queen Isabel, Princess Katherine, Alice, the other ladies, and other French. Henry's speech to the traitors is spoken in a council chamber at Southampton, in the presence of the traitors and three lords.

In *2 Henry IV*, the defense of the Chief Justice is made in the Palace at Westminster, in the presence of Warwick, Lancaster, Clarence, Gloucester, Westmoreland, and others, and Henry V and his attendants.

Henry VIII furnishes a number of instances of the use of spectacular setting. The scene in which Katherine makes her plea for favorable consideration of the subjects' grievances has these stage directions:

London. The council-chamber in the palace.

Cornets. Enter the King, leaning on the Cardinal's shoulder, the Nobles, and Sir Thomas Lovell; the Cardinal places himself under the King's feet on his right side.

. . . .

A noise within, crying, "Room for the Queen!" Enter Queen Katherine, ushered by the Duke of Suffolk: she kneels. The King riseth from his state, takes her up, kisses and placeth her by him.

The scene in which Katherine makes her defense, Wolsey makes his defense, and the King states his position with regard to his marriage, has these stage directions:

160   *The Oration in Shakespeare*

A hall in Black-Friars

Trumpets, sennet, and cornets. Enter two Vergers with short silver wands; next them two Scribes, in the habit of doctors; after them, the (Arch) bishop of Canterbury alone; after him the Bishops of Lincoln, Ely, Rochester, and Saint Asaph; next them, with some small distance, follows a Gentleman bearing the purse, with the great seal, and a cardinal's hat; then two priests, bearing each a silver cross; then a Gentleman usher bareheaded, accompanied with a Sergeant-at-arms bearing a silver mace; then two Gentlemen bearing two great silver pillars; after them, side by side, the two Cardinals; two Noblemen with the sword and mace. The King takes place under the cloth of state; the two Cardinals sit under him as judges. The Queen takes place some distance from the King. The Bishops place themselves on each side the court, in manner of a consistory; below them the Scribes. The Lords sit next the Bishop. The rest of the Attendants stand in convenient order about the stage.

Wolsey's speech of allegiance is made in the Ante-chamber to the King's apartment, in the presence of the King and nobles. The scene in which Cranmer attempts to make his defense has these stage directions:

The Council-chamber

A council-table brought in with chairs and stools, and placed under the state. Enter Lord Chancellor; places himself at the upper end of the table on the left hand; a seat being left void above him, as for Canterbury's seat. Duke of Suffolk, Duke of Norfolk, Surrey, Lord Chamberlain, Gardiner, seat themselves in order on each side. Cromwell at lower end as secretary. (Keeper at the door).

The following directions furnish an elaborate and impressive setting for the speech of Cranmer on the occasion of the christening of Elizabeth:

The palace

Enter trumpets, sounding; then two Aldermen, Lord Mayor, Garter, Cranmer, Duke of Norfolk with his marshal's staff, Duke of Suffolk, two Noblemen bearing great standing-bowls for the christening-gifts; then four Noblemen bearing a canopy, under

Dramatic Integration

which the Duchess of Norfolk, godmother, bearing the child richly habited in a mantle, etc., train borne by a Lady; then follows the Marchioness Dorset, the other godmother and Ladies. The troop pass once about the stage, and Garter speaks.

The funeral orations in *Julius Caesar* are delivered in the Forum from the pulpit. The expository speech of the King in *Hamlet* is delivered in a room of state in the castle before the Queen, Hamlet, Polonius, Laertes, Ophelia, lords, and attendants.

The great forensics are placed in elaborate settings. The speech of Shylock is spoken in a court of justice in Venice, in the presence of the Duke, the Magnificoes, Antonio, Bassanio, Gratiano, Salerio, and others. The oration of Othello is delivered in a council chamber in Venice, in the presence of the Duke and senators set at a table with lights; officers are attending. Othello makes his speech after a sailor and a messenger have come in with news for the Duke, and after Brabantio, Cassio, Iago, Roderigo, and officers have brought him to court. The defense of Hermione is made in a place of justice in Sicilia, in the presence of Leontes, lords, and officers and with Paulina and ladies attending. The speech of Alcibiades is made in the senate-house before senators and attendants.

Shakespeare's use of the oration in the court scene deserves special consideration. In the discussion of the structure of orations a steady and marked progress in the development of the forensic as a unit of composition has already been noticed and there is an increasing skill on the part of the dramatist in the working up to a court situation and the setting of the oration in a trial scene. With the exception of the forensics of Antipholus of Ephesus, Say, and Worcester—which are spoken outside of buildings—Shakespearean forensics are delivered in appropriate places—a Hall in the palace of the Duke of Ephesus, Parliament House, Abbey at Bury St. Edmund's, Angelo's House, Council Chamber,

Place of Justice, Black Friars. In the case of all these trial scenes, there are appropriate personages present—a judge or judges and attendants. In all cases in which the forensic is spoken in defense of one's self, there is a formal indictment. Four of the forensics stand out above the others in effectiveness of setting: the Shylock speech in a court of justice; the Hermione speech in a place of justice; the Katherine speech in a hall in Black Friars; the Cranmer speech in a council chamber. These four stand out prominently in setting because in the scenes in which they are set the atmosphere of the courtroom and of the procedure of a trial is preserved most effectively throughout. The trial scene in which Hermione makes her defense seems the most effective of all because the oration is most fully and convincingly developed and the court procedure is most consistently and completely preserved.

Moreover, Hermione's oration represents the best of Shakespeare's work in dramatic integration. Her speech comes at the point of crisis near the middle of the play. It is made the natural and spontaneous outgrowth of a situation created by precedent dramatic action. The court scene—including the setting, the personages present, the methods of court procedure—is worked out more completely and more naturally than anywhere else in Shakespeare's plays. The outcome of her trial determines the direction taken by the remaining dramatic action of the play. Hermione's oration represents at once, therefore, the best of Shakespeare's work in the structure of the oration in itself and the best of his work in dramatic integration of the oration as a vital part of the plot development. Furthermore, her forensic achieves the introduction of rhetoric in poetic according to the best classical tradition in a play which represents Shakespeare's most ambitious effort in harmonizing the romantic and classical ideals of poetic of the drama.

In connection with dramatic integration, we note the in-

Dramatic Integration 163

stances in which an oration is made to be vitally related to the development of dramatic action through its connection with the part played by the mob.[4] Antony's oration gathers force and effectiveness through the appeal that is made to the emotions of the crowd. On two occasions in *Coriolanus*, Menenius makes an address to the crowd of citizens to prevent their resort to violence. Both King John and King Henry Fifth make appeals to citizens to sway the mind of the crowd. Lord Say undertakes a defense of himself against Cade and his crowd of followers. The speech of Marullus is directed to the commoners, rebuking them for making a holiday. The battle orations are appeals to the loyalty of soldiers through swaying the mind of the crowd. The study of the oration in Shakespeare, therefore, touches the study of the psychology of the Shakespearean mob: the oration is a natural means used in attempting to influence the thinking of the crowd, which is, in a number of instances in Shakepeare, made an important element in the development of dramatic action.

Consideration of the dramatic integration of orations in Shakespeare's plays reveals the secret of the dramatist's supreme contribution to the history of dramatic art. He made drama liberally classical in progress of plot and conservatively romantic in range of character, situation, space, and time. The poetic of his drama is essentially Aristotelian in conception; the rhetoric, likewise, both emotional rhetoric and the rhetoric of oratory, is unmistakably Aristotelian in its integration in poetic. Aristotle visualized the relationship between the two literary movements and the most artistic expression of each; Shakespeare realized fully Aristotle's restricted vision, in terms of art itself. As all criticism of the two inevitably builds up upon Aristotle, all expression of the two in art inevitably looks up to Shakespeare.

4. For a discussion of "The Shakespearean Mob" by Frederick Tupper, Jr., see *PMLA*, XX (1912), 486-526.

Moreover, our consideration of the integration of the oration has put us in touch with weighty evidence in support of the generally accepted chronology of his plays. The steady natural development observed both in the composition of orations and their interweaving in plot development rings true, with one little exception, to the chronological list of the plays given in Chapter IV. The one small exception is that, in the list, *Romeo and Juliet* is placed after *Titus Andronicus*, on a basis of the date of the First Quarto. This dating regards the play as approximately contemporary with *Merchant of Venice*—about 1595. The mechanical setting and structure of the Friar's speech at the end of *Romeo and Juliet* give it the appearance of being contemporary with Biron's oration in *Love's Labour's Lost* and the speeches of Aegeon and Antipholus in *Comedy of Errors;* and also the expository speech of the Third Messenger in *1 Henry VI.* As Professor Neilson points out,[5] frequence of rhyme, the lyrical quality of the poetry, and the abundance of verbal quibbling point to an early date; and my suggestion as to the Friar's oration fits in perfectly with this view. The obvious sense for tragic plot structure may be brought forward to favor a date later than that of the three plays mentioned above. But if one is willing to see the hand of Shakespeare revealing a sense for tragic plot development in *1 Henry VI* as I suggested, this contention for a later date can be easily relinquished. Furthermore, the assumption that the Nurse's reference to the earthquake of eleven years before is to the earthquake of 1580, weak as the assumption is regarded for determining date, would work along with my suggestion to date the play about 1591, contemporary with *Love's Labour's Lost, Comedy of Errors,* and *1 Henry VI.*[6] With this single

5. *Cambridge Shakespeare.*
6. William John Tucker, in *College Shakespeare,* has this to say about the date of *Romeo and Juliet:* "The date of *Romeo and Juliet* rests largely on a remark made by the old Nurse: 'I remember it well: 'tis since the earthquake now eleven years,' that Juliet was weaned. This is said to refer to the earthquake which occurred in England on April 6th, 1580.

Dramatic Integration 165

exception, my feeling for the stage of Shakespeare's development in the use of rhetoric in any play bears out the generally accepted dating of the play in the course of his development as a dramatic artist.

In addition, this study of Shakespeare's rhetoric and poetic discovers their kinship in conception as fine arts and their kinship in expression to all forms of great art. The ordered, careful, progressive, unified movement of the oration is akin to the ordered, careful, progressive, unified movement of the drama. And the qualities that Shakespeare's orations and Shakespeare's dramas possess are the qualities that characterize and distinguish all works of finished art—art expressed in the notes of a musical composition, art framed in colors when painted upon canvas, or art built in masonry when caught in stone. Moreover, the oration in Shakespeare takes its place as an expression of rhetoric as both a fine and practical art: a work of finished art in itself, it is made to function as a vital part of the art of the drama.

Eleven years later would bring us to 1591, the year in which the first sketch of the play is supposed to have been written. We are also told in the first quarto that the drama 'had been played many times with great applause before 1597."—p. 223. Coleridge, in *Marginalia and Notes on Individual Plays*, expresses the opinion that *Romeo and Juliet* is an early play, associates it in his mind with *Love's Labour's Lost* in the matter of time of composition. See T. M. Raysor, *Coleridge's Shakespearean Criticism*, I, 6.

CHAPTER VII

Elizabethan Oratory

IT HAS BEEN pointed out in connection with the discussion of Shakespeare's poetic that the early Elizabethan drama was episodic in movement rather than concentrated in plot structure, and that this episodic drama was characteristically rhetorical in manner and distinguished by its abundance of extended speaking. This type of narrative movement, inherited from the Middle Ages, is the characteristic type of narrative in the Elizabethan period. The prose romances of the time abound in set speeches. Their "set" quality is often made very prominent by the formal introduction and formal conclusions, and by the argumentative nature of their development. Speeches of defense, speeches of the deliberative kind, and occasional speeches, expository and narrative, are represented among them. Academic debates, too, are frequently found worked out to great lengths.[1]

The frequency with which these exercises in rhetoric are met in prose romances reveals not only the interest of the writers themselves in the set speech but also the interest of

1. I hesitate to point to specific examples because examples can be found anywhere in the romances of Lyly, Greene, Sidney, and, to a lesser extent, Lodge. To recall an example of each type of speech: in Lyly's *Euphues*, *The Anatomie of Wit*, Eubulus and Euphues engage in debate on opposite sides of a question of conduct. In Robert Greene's *Anatomie of Fortune*, Arbasto's speech in defense of his change of life from that of the kingly palace to that of a monk's cell is a good academic exercise in the forensic type of oratory. Lucille's soliloquy in Lyly's *Anatomie of Wit*, arguing to persuade herself either to change or not to change the direction of her love from Philautus to Euphues, reminds one of the Selimus speech in Greene's play. Arbasto's speech in Greene's *Anatomie of Fortune*, expository of his experiences in France, is in line with the narrative speeches we find in the Elizabethan drama.

[166]

the Elizabethan public in this form of entertainment. The custom of reading alone was only beginning to be a customary form of entertainment, and the gathering together in popular assemblies to listen to public speaking preserved for spoken literature the high place it had occupied throughout the Middle Ages and the Renaissance. As Morris W. Croll has indicated, "Both the customs and the spirit of the sixteenth century life demanded literary expression in oratorical forms."[2] People were drawn together from patriotic, political or religious interests, and these gatherings produced a constant demand for public speaking. Paul's Cross and Charing Cross were favorite places for orators to deliver speeches to enthusiastic open-air audiences. Moreover, the progresses of Queen Elizabeth were occasions upon which the Elizabethan public thronged to take advantage of the opportunity afforded for entertainment, and one of the distinctive features of these progresses was the delivery of orations.[3] And when, on her progress to a university, the Queen was greeted with an address in Latin or Greek, she was able to reply in the language used in the address. The Elizabethan public, therefore, was brought up on the oratorical style.

2. "Attic Prose in the Seventeenth Century," *SP*, XVIII (April, 1921), 79-128. For a discussion of the development of English prose, see this and Croll's other study, "The Cadence of English Oratorical Prose," *SP*, XVI (1919), 1-55, frequently referred to by Professor Baldwin in both his *Ancient* and *Medieval Rhetoric*. W. M. Patterson, in *The Rhythm of Prose*, approaches the study of prose expression from a modern scientific point of view. For an historical treatment, see George Saintsbury, *History of English Prose Rhythm*.

3. "In these progresses the queen's entertainers vied with one another in the novelty and elaboration of their preparations, which included besides addresses and orations of welcome in the learned tongues, allegorical pageantry, decorations, and fireworks, whole masques and dramas in Latin and English." F. E. Schelling, *Elizabethan Drama*, I, 103. In this connection, Professor Wallace's note on Queen Mary's coronation-procession is of interest: " 'In Paules church-yard against the schoole,' says Holinshed (*Chronicles*, 1577, 1586, p. 1091), 'one master Heiwood sat in a pageant under a vine, and made to hir an oration in Latin and English.' " *Evolution of the English Drama Up to Shakespeare*, p. 82.

In studies of English prose, Croll has pointed out the distinction between this oratorical or Asian style and the essay or Attic style. The oratorical style takes its character from those "colors of rhetoric" that have to do with words and their sounds. These colors are the "schemata verborum" that trace their lineage back to Gorgias and Isocrates through Cicero. The essay style takes character from the colors of thought, the "figurae sententiae."[4] The style of Euphuism, therefore, forms a chapter in the history of the "colors of rhetoric"; and, in its emphasis on word display and ingenuity in expression and on colorful word painting for its own sake, it reveals its kinship to the rhetoric of the First and Second Sophistic. This artificial style of affectation and display was general at the time in all countries; in England it reached its height in the prose of Lyly. As Lyly matured, his own style became less Euphuistic; and while Euphuism continued in Elizabethan prose after Lyly, we find English prose in general employing the Asian style less and less. As the sixteenth century passes on into the seventeenth, the English prose of Sidney, Lyly, Greene, and Lodge—prose diffuse, florid, and unrestrainedly rhetorical in the post-classical and medieval sense, designed primarily to entertain through exhibitions in language—gives way before the analytical, scholarly, elaborate but more restrained prose of Bacon and Browne—prose compact and learnedly rhetorical in the classical sense, designed primarily to teach through processes of thought. In preaching, the sensational, colloquial, artificially rhetorical speeches of Latimer and Knox and the other militant reformers give ground before the analytical, scholarly, and stately speeches of Bishop Andrews, Dr. Donne, and others of the more intellectual divines. Beginning with all the exuberance, experimentation, and zeal for display of

---

4. For a convenient grouping of the sixty-four "colors of rhetoric," see Synoptic Index at the end of Professor Baldwin's *MRP*.

Elizabethan Oratory

learning which the possession of classical learning added to the medieval delight in gaudy and high-sounding rhetorical expression, Elizabethan prose began to settle down, about the turn of the century, to a period of more ordered, restrained, and thoughtful expression that was to lead the way to the standardization of the Augustan Age.

The oratorical or Asian style colored the Elizabethan drama from its very beginnings. But before the set speech in the Elizabethan drama is considered, the story of its development should be briefly reviewed. Its beginning, though in some respects sudden, was none the less a natural outburst of dramatic effort resulting from the dramatic tendencies which had been quietly but constantly at work in England for at least four centuries. As early as the twelfth century, the Church utilized the possibilities of drama as a means of instructing communicants in the story of the Bible, the Christian faith, and the lives of saints and martyrs. Later, the guilds gave the mystery play permanent literary form. The cycles often reveal a certain dramatic sense in the handling of character and situation; and sometimes, especially in dramatizing the New Testament story, a sense for tragic plot-action. Later still came the moralities, in which the characters were the Vices and Virtues with the addition in still later times of allegorical personages to represent some human condition or quality. The abstract characters of the moralities finally gave place to historical characters celebrated for some specific human quality or condition. To amuse the audience while witnessing the presentation of a serious morality, short humorous pieces, called interludes, were later introduced. John Heywood isolated the interlude from the morality; and in his humorous plays he paved the way for the later distinctly and truly dramatic form of comedy. The introduction into England of classical and Italian models to work from gave these native tendencies in the direction of the true drama the stimulus needed for bringing into existence what developed into the drama that gave us Shakespeare.

The first stage was the stage of imitation and experimentation. Translations of classical and Italian models prompted representation of these plays on the stage and the writing of plays in English fashioned after the foreign models. In the early years of the Elizabethan drama the classical tradition was obediently followed and the result was a series of plays modeled upon Senecan tragedy and Plautine comedy;[5] and, in the case of some plays in which the medieval method of treatment was employed, the subjects were taken from the classics.[6]

After a score of years which had witnessed a reverent observing of classical tradition and obedient imitation of the classical drama, the native drama cut loose from the classical drama; from 1579-1580 on, there came the independent and individual achievements of Lyly, Peele, Greene, Lodge, Kyd, and Marlowe. The classical material and the classical form were appropriated by these dramatists in the writing of plays which were the products of their own native geniuses, plays stamped with the marks of individuality and of freedom in the choice of subjects and in method of development. The drama thus became romantic; and it was this romantic drama which greeted Shakespeare when he came to London about 1586 or 1587. In Shakespeare, the Elizabethan drama reached the culmination of this period of maturing art.

While Shakespeare was still alive, the third and last period in the history of the Elizabethan drama was already beginning. Great Ben Jonson and Beaumont and Fletcher stand at the beginning of this period of decadence. Magnificent though the decadence seemed, it was nevertheless real and

---

5. *Gorboduc* (1562), *Jocasta* (1566), *Gismond of Salerne* (1567-68), *Ralph Roister Doister* (1534-41).

6. *Horestes* (1567), *Cambyses* (1569-70), *Damon and Pithias* (1576-67-68), *Appius and Virginia* (1575-67-68).

constantly at work, undermining the constitution, so to speak, of the strong and healthy literature of Shakespeare's time. Catering to popular clamor, the dramatists representative of this age of decline substituted for the spontaneous expression of the earlier dramas, stereotyped, strained, and often unnatural expression, and allowed the scope of the drama to be narrowed in subject matter and treatment to appeal to the tastes of a particular class. Through the influence of the school of Massinger, Ford, and Shirley, the Elizabethan drama was sapped of its former strength and vigor, and was finally destroyed as a literary force.

Our main purpose in this chapter is to touch upon the set speech in general and the oration in particular as they appear in Elizabethan drama in these succeeding stages of its development. The set speech is always a distinctive feature of Elizabethan drama. Long narrative speeches are introduced to relate, often in minute detail, the course of events. What might be called character-choral speeches are devoted to the revelation of character. Speeches of debate, arguments pro and con, are drawn out at times to unwieldy lengths. Speeches of defense are spoken in answer to charges advanced against a defendant. Eulogies and denunciations and appeals to soldiers and to fellow-citizens are frequently and oftentimes elaborately worked out in Elizabethan plays. In fact, in the early Elizabethan period, many of the plays are little else than masses of long speeches following one another in rapid succession.

The frequency of speech-making in Elizabethan drama seems to have grown out of a number of contributing causes. In the first place, there was the primitive and bare nature of the Elizabethan stage. On the Elizabethan stage, speeches were used for stage business which has been managed since by an ever increasing amount of stage machinery. Hence, we find in Elizabethan plays numerous speeches of description and narration, as well as of explanation, to build up a word setting. Again, the nature of the classical drama exerted a decided influence upon speech-making in English drama. Plays modeled upon the drama of Seneca abound in prologues and epilogues and chorus speeches reminiscent at once of the abundance of such speeches in Seneca;[7] and long examples of rhetorical description and narration and speeches of the argumentative type, also, are to be found in the plays which represent adaptation of the classical tradition to the prevailing spirit of the native drama.[8] Then too, incentive to the crowding of speeches into plays was given the dramatist by the interest of the Elizabethan audience in public speaking. The abundance of the rhetoric in Elizabethan plays, modeled as it was on the post-classical tradition, came in response to a popular appeal.

What of the oration, as we have come to know it in Shakespeare's plays, during the development of the Elizabethan drama? This question opens up another subject: the oration in the Elizabethan drama. The aim here can be only to sketch what seems to be the history of the oration in Elizabethan drama as a whole and relate the oration in Shakespeare to it.

The oration does not seem to appear as a a speech of definite character and serious dramatic purpose before the beginning of the romantic drama. The poetic of early Elizabethan plays consists mainly in the linking together of incidents, strung along one after another without an attempt to weave them together into a closely knit plot. In such a stringing together of incidents, the oration can at best occupy only a detached position. In these early Elizabethan plays, however, we find promises of the future oration in the drama, promises which are oftentimes very faint and rightly appreciated only when viewed in the light of later developments.

7. *Gorboduc, Jocasta, Gismond of Salerne, Misfortunes of Arthur.*
8. *The Spanish Tragedy, Titus Andronicus, True Tragedie of Richard the Third, Richardus Tertius, Locrine, The True Chronicle History of King Leir.*

Elizabethan Oratory

For example, in the early Elizabethan interlude *Nice Wanton* (1560), there is in embryonic form the trial scene and forensic as developed later in Shakespeare. *Nice Wanton* is a short play. Throughout, the reader senses lack of development. Versification is crude; the situations are crudely handled. There is no division into acts and scenes; actors merely come on and go off the stage. The only approach to a distinctly worked-out scene is a trial scene. Judge Daniel enters and is followed by Iniquity, the Baily errand, who tries to bribe the judge on behalf of the prisoner, Ishmael. The judge is incensed by the attempt of Iniquity to bribe him and in a rage orders Iniquity to bring in the jury with their prisoner. When this is done, the judge makes his charge to the jury and calls for the verdict. The jury sentences Ishmael to be hanged the next morning at nine o'clock. When the judge has finished pronouncing the sentence, Ishmael makes a defense speech by pleading that Iniquity has been responsible for his being in court:

> *Ishmael.* Though I be judged to die, I require respite,
> For the King's advantage some things I can recite.

Iniquity attempts to prevent Ishmael's continuing but the judge allows him to proceed:

> *Judge.* Well, we will hear you say what you can,
> But see that ye wrongfully accuse no man.
> *Ishmael.* I will belie no man, but this I may say,
> Here standeth he that brought me to this way.

Iniquity interrupts and calls Ishmael a liar.

> *Ishmael.* His naughty company and play at dice
> Did me first to stealing entice:
> He was with me at robberies, I say it to his face;
> Yet can I say more in time and space.

In *Gorboduc* (1562), the plea of Porrex before the King,[9] made in the hope of obtaining a lightening of the punishment

---
9. Actus quartus, scena secunda.

for the death of Ferrex, is a speech worked out in the forensic manner that looks forward to the later Elizabethan forensic in Peele and Shakespeare; so, also, in the play *Jacob and Esau* (1568), Esau's defense of his selling his birthright. In *Gismond of Salerne* (1567-1568) the rhetorical Senecan speech of Lucretia, presenting her plea for a lessening of Tancred's severity towards his daughter, and Tancred's answer, presenting his brief for his sternness in not wanting his daughter to marry, represents admirably this chrysalis stage when the elements of the oration were developing within a showily-spun covering of Senecan rhetoric. Out of a long and busy period of experimentation and imitation, a period full of stunts and display in the use of the means and the opportunities which the classics placed in the hands of the Elizabethan dramatists, was to come the oration as we find it developed and used by Shakespeare.

By 1580, this period of imitation and experimentation had witnessed the growth of the native drama at court, the introduction of the classical drama into schools and hybridization resulting from the imitation of the classical drama, the development of the companies, the beginning of the theatres. With the plays of Lyly, Peele,[10] and the other immediate predecessors of Shakespeare, the native drama at court, under the influence of the classical drama of the school, entered the field of conscious art. Shakespeare's predecessors reveal a conscious effort to apply classical traditions of rhetoric and poetic to the native drama. We see signs, particularly in the work of Peele, Greene, and Marlowe, of conscious effort with appreciable success to distinguish and keep separate the functions of the two movements. Plot structure, the determinative element of classical poetic, begins to receive serious consideration, and the Elizabethan drama thus begins to function

---

10. The plays of Lyly and Peele, the first modern five-act plays ever known to have been performed before a public audience in an English theatre. See C. W. Stechert Wallace, *The Evolution of the English Drama Up to Shakespeare*, p. 181.

as pure poetic—imitation of action. The set speech, while still characterized often by the grandiloquent rhetoric of the earlier drama, begins more and more to suggest development of rhetoric as the "thought" part of dramatic action. Shakespeare thus fell heir to a growing sense for plot action as the essential and determinative principle of drama as an expression of the technique of poetic, and for persuasion as the essential and determinative principle of the oration as an expression of the technique of rhetoric.

There can be recalled some representative orations among the speeches of Shakespeare's immediate predecessors. In Greene's *James Fourth*,[11] just after Douglas and his Scots have surrendered to the English King, the Lawyer, the Merchant, and the Divine enter and discuss the condition of affairs in Scotland. The Divine charges the lawyers with being responsible in greatest measure for the corruptions of the times; the Lawyer, in his answer, presents a defense of his profession and charges the divines with being responsible for all the corruptions of the times.

Oration of the Divine

O Lawyer, thou haste curious eyes to prie
Into the secret maimes of their estate;
But if thy vaile of error were vnmaskt,
Thy selfe should see your sect do maime her most.
Are you not those that should maintaine the peace,
Yet onely are the patrones of our strife?
If your profession haue his ground and spring
First from the lawes of God, then countries right,
Not any wars inuerting natures power,
Why thriue you by contentions? Why deuise you
Clawses and subtile reasons to except?
Our state was first, before you grew so great,
A lanterne to the world for vnitie:
Now they that are befriended, and are rich
Oppresse the poore: come *Homer* without quoine,
He is not heard: What shall we terme this drift?

11. Actus Quintus (Scene IV).

To say the poore mans cause is good and just,
And yet the rich man gaines the best in lawe
It is your guise (the more the world laments)
To quoine *prouisoes* to beguile your lawes,
To make a gay pretext of due proceeding,
When you delay your common-pleas for yeares.
Mark what these dealings lately here haue wrought:
The craftie men haue purchaste great mens lands:
They powle, they pinch, their tennants are vndone:
If these complain, by you they are vndone:
You fleese them of their quoine, their children beg,
And many want, because you may bee rich:
This scarre is mightie, maister Lawyer.
Now war hath gotten head within this land,
Marke but the guise. The poore man that is wrongd
Is readie to rebell; hee spoyles, he pilles;
We need no foes to forrage that wee haue:
The lawe (say they) in peace consumed vs,
And now in warre we will consume the lawe.
Look to this mischiefe, Lawyers: conscience knowes
You liue amisse; amend it, least you end.

Oration of the Lawyer

Good Lord, that these diuines should see so farre
In others faults, without amending theirs?
Sir, sir, the generall defaults in state,
(If you would read before you did correct)
Are, by a hidden working from aboue,
By their successiue changes still remouvd.
Were not the lawe by contraries maintainde,
How could the trueth from falsehood be discernde?
Did we not taste the bitternesse of warre,
How could wee know the sweet effects of peace?
Did wee not feele the nipping winter frostes,
How should we know the sweetnesse of the spring?
Should all things still remaine in one estate,
Should not in greatest arts some scarres be found?
Were all vpright and changd, what world were this?
A *Chaos*, made of quiet, yet no world;
Because the parts thereof, did still accord:
This matter craues a variance, not a speech.
But sir Diuine, to you: looke on your maimes,

Elizabethan Oratory

> Diuisions, sects, your simonies, and bribes,
> Your cloaking with the great, for feare to fall;
> You shall perceive you are the cause of all.
> Did each man know there were a storme at hand,
> Who would not cloath him well, to shun the wet?
> Did Prince and Peere, the Lawyer and the least,
> Know what were sinne, without a partiall glose,
> Wee(d) need no long discouery then of crimes,
> For each would mend, aduisde by holy men:
> Thus (I) but slightly shadow out your sinnes;
> But if they were depainted out for life,
> Alasse, wee both had wounds inough to heale.

In the first part of *Tamburlaine* (I, ii) we find the conqueror delivering an oration to Theridamas,[12] envoy from Mycetes, King of Persia, with the aim in view of persuading Theridamas to desert the Persian monarch and swear allegiance to him:

> Tamburlaine, Zenocrate, Techelles, Usumcane, Agydas,
> Magnetes, Lords, and soldiers, laden with treasure.
> Enter Theridamas and others.

Ther. Where is this Scythan Tamburlaine?
Tamb. Whom seek'st thou, Persian?—Tamburlaine?
Ther. Tamburlaine!

> A Scythain Shepherd so embellished
> With nature's pride and richest furniture!
> His looks do menace Heaven and dare the gods:
> His fiery eyes are fixed upon the earth,
> As if he now devised some stratagem,
> Or meant to pierce Avernas' darksome vaults,
> To pull the triple-headed dog from hell.

Tamb. Noble and mild this Persian seems to be,
    If outward habit judge the inward man.

Tech. His deep affections make him passionate.
. . . .

Tamb. With what a majesty he rears his looks!
    In thee, thou valiant man of Persia,

---
12. Lines 152 ff.

I see the folly of thy emperor.
Art thou but captain of a thousand horse,
That by characters graven in thy brows,
And by thy martial face and stout aspect,
Deserv'st to have the leading of a host!
Forsake thy king, and do but join with me,
And we will triumph over all the world;
I hold the fates bound fast in iron chains,
And with my hands turn Fortune's wheel about:
And sooner shall the sun fall from his sphere
Than Tamburlaine be slain or overcome.
Draw forth thy sword, thou mighty man at arms,
Intending but to rage my charm'd skin,
And Jove himself will stretch his hand from heaven
To ward the blow and shield me safe from harm.
See how he rains down heaps of gold in showers,
As if he meant to give my soldiers pay!
And as a sure and grounded argument,
That I shall be the monarch of the East,
He sends this Soldan's daughter rich and brave,
To be my Queen and portly Emperess.
If thou wilt stay with me, renowned man,
And lead my thousand horse with my conduct,
Besides thy share of this Egyptian prize,
These thousand horse shall sweat with martial spoil,
Of conquered Kingdoms and of cities sacked;
Both we will walk upon the lofty cliffs,
And Christian merchants that with Russian stems
Plough up huge furrows in the Caspian sea,
Shall vail to us, as lords of all the lake,
Both we will reign as consuls of the earth,
And mighty kings shall be our senators.
Jove sometimes masked in a shepherd's weed,
And by those steps that he hath scaled the Heavens
May we become immortal like the gods.
Join with me now in this my mean estate,
(I call it mean because being yet obscure,
The nations far removed admire me not)
And when my name and honour shall be spread
As far as Boreas claps his brazen wings,
Or fair Booetes sends his cheerful light,

Then shalt thou be competitor with me,
And sit with Tamburlaine in all his majesty.

In Peele's *Arraignment of Paris*, we have as good an example of the forensic as can be found in the drama before Shakespeare. Paris, in consequence of his giving the golden ball to Venus, is brought before the Council of the Gods. Venus' plea that Paris be allowed an advocate is denied, and Paris is required to make his own defense. This he does in his oration before the Council:[13]

>Sacred and just, thou great and dreadful Jove,
>And you thrice reverend powers, whom love nor hate
>May wrest awry; if this to me a man,
>This fortune fatal be, that I must plead
>For the safe excusal of my guiltless thought,
>The honour more makes my mishap the less,
>That I a man must plead before the gods,
>Gracious forbears of the world's amiss,
>For her whose beauty how it hath entic'd
>This heavenly senate may with me aver.
>But sith nor that, nor this may do me boot,
>And for myself, myself must speaker be
>A mortal man amidst this heavenly presence;
>Let me not shape a long defense to them
>That been beholders of my guiltless thoughts.
>Then for the deed, that I may not deny,
>Wherein consists the full of mine offense,
>I did upon command; if then I err'd
>I did no more than to a man belong'd
>And if in verdict of their forms divine,
>My dazzled eye did swerve or surfeit more,
>On Venus' face, than any face of theirs,
>It was no partial fault, but fault of his
>Belike, whose eyesight not so perfect was,
>As might discern the brightness of the rest,
>And if it were permitted unto men,
>Ye Gods, to parle with your secret thoughts,
>There ben that sit upon that sacred seat,

13. Act IV, scene iv.

That would with Paris err in Venus' praise.
But let me cease to speak of error here:
Sith that my hand the organ of my heart,
Did give with good agreement of mine eye,
My tongue is void with process to maintain.

. . . .

First then, arraign'd of partiality,
Paris replies, unguilty of the fact:
His reason is, because he knew no more
Fair Venus' ceston than Dame Juno's mace.
Nor never saw wise Pallas' crystal shield.
Then, as I look'd, I liv'd and lik'd attonce,
And as it was referr'd from them to me,
To give the prize to her, whose beauty best
My fancy did commend, so did I praise
And judge as might my dazzled eye discern.

. . . .

Now (for I must add reason for my deed)
Why Venus rather pleas'd me of the three:
First in the entrails of my mortal ears,
The question standing upon beauty's blaze
The name of her that hight the queen of love,
Methought in beauty should not be excell'd:
Had it been destined to majesty,
(Yet will I not rob Venus of her grace)
Then stately Juno might have borne the ball.
Had it to wisdom been entituled,
My human wit had given it Pallas then.
But sith unto the fairest of the three
That power, that threw it for my father ill,
Did dedicate this ball: and safest durst
My shepherd's still adventure, as I thought,
To judge of form and beauty, rather than
Of Juno's state, or Pallas' worthiness,
That learn'd to ken the fairest of the flock,
And praised beauty but by nature's aim;
Behold to Venus Paris gave this fruit,
A daysman chosen there by full consent,
And heavenly powers should not repent their deeds.
Where it is said beyond desert of hers
I honored Venus with this golden prize;

Ye gods, alas! what can a mortal man
Discern betwixt the sacred gifts of heaven?
Or, if I may with reverence reason thus,
Suppose I gave and judg'd corruptly then,
For hope of that that best did please my thought,
This apple not for beauty's praise alone;
I might offend sith I was pardoned,
And tempted more than ever creature was,
With wealth, with beauty, and with chivalry,
And as preferr'd beauty before them all,
With the thing that hath enchanted heaven itself;
And for the one, contentment is my wealth;
The shell of salt will serve a shepherd swain,
A slender banquet in a homely scrip,
And water running from the silver spring,
For arms, they dredd no foes that sit so low.
A thorn can keep the wind from off my back,
A sheep cote thatch'd a shepherd's palace hight.
Of tragic muses shepherds con no skill,
Enough is them, if Cupid ben displeas'd,
To sing his praise on slender oaten pipe.
And thus, thrice reverend, have I told my tale,
And crave the torment of my quiet-less soul.
To be measured by my faultless thought,
If warlike Pallas or the queen of heaven
Sue to reverse my sentence by appeal,
Be it as please your majesties divine;
The wrong, the hurt not mine, if any be,
But hers whose beauty claim'd the prize of me.

The oration of Paris represents the stage of development which the oration had reached when Shakespeare came up to London in 1586 or 1587. By this time, the working out of an oration as an exercise in rhetorical structure had been established as a convention. Dramatists had recognized the essential nature of the oration in the Aristotelian sense. Artificiality in framework and adornment, in outline and diction, is characteristic of Peele's exercise throughout; but he had grasped the notion of the oration as being a carefully and logically constructed speech moving through a period of thought and aiming to influence action through appeal to reason. What the predecessors of Shakespeare do not exhibit is a sure grasp of plot development; and, consequently, they fail to make their orations integral parts of dramatic action, which Shakespeare succeeds so surely in doing.

However, at the very time that Shakespeare was making the oration truest to the classical ideal both in structure and dramatic integration, influences were at work that pointed to decline. On the one hand, the influence of the post-classical rhetoric still survived in the Senecan rhetoric of Marston, Chapman, and Tourneur. On the other hand, the neo-classical influence with its restrictions and refinements of theory shaped the drama of Jonson, and tended to make the oration mechanical and heavy in its movement.

There are after Shakespeare occasional reminders of Shakespearean rhetoric, particularly in the works of Massinger. But even in Massinger the oration tends to become artificial in striving for brilliant rhetorical effect. The classical tradition of rhetoric survives in the later Elizabethan drama but becomes, as it were, crystallized. To follow the development of the oration after Shakespeare is to discover a gradual loss of vitality and power as pure rhetoric suffered a divergence to poetry—sometimes extravagant poetry—on the one hand, and on the other, a weakening of rhetorical movement from mechanical periodic structure or lack of sustained effort.

There follow some examples of the oration in the period of the decline:

> Chapman's *Tragedy of Charles Duke of Byron*
> Act V, scene i
>
> Chancellor, Harley, Portier, Fleury, in scarlet gowns;
> La Fin, D'Escures, with other officers of state.
> Enter Vitry, Byron, with others and a guard.
>
> *Vi.* You see, My Lord, 't is in the golden chamber.
> *By.* The golden chamber where the greatest kings
> Have thought them honour'd to receive a place,

And I have had it: am I come to stand
In rank and habit here of men arraign'd,
Where I have sat assistant, and been honour'd
With glorious title of the chiefest virtuous,
Where the King's chief solicitor hath said
There was in France no man that ever lived
Whose parts were worth my imitation:
That but mine own worth I could imitate none:
And that I made myself inimitable
To all that could come after; whom this Court
Hath seen to sit upon the flower-de-luce
In recompense of my renowned service.
Must I be sat on now by petty judges?
These scarlet robes, that come to sit and fight
Against my life dismay my valour more,
Than all the bloody cassocks Spain hath brought
To field against it.

Vi. To the bar, my lord.
(He salutes and stands to the bar.)
Ha. Read the indictment.
Ch. Stay, I will invert,
For shortness' sake, the form of our proceedings
And out of all the points the process holds,
Collect five principal, with which we charge you.
First you conferr'd with one, called Picote
At Orleans born, and into Flanders fled,
To hold intelligence by him with the Archduke,
And for two voyages to that effect,
Bestow'd on him five hundred fifty crowns.
2. Next you held treaty with the Duke of Savoy,
Without the King's permission; offering him
All service and assistance 'gainst all men,
In hope to have in marriage his third daughter.
3. Thirdly, you held intelligence with the Duke,
At taking in of Bourg, and other forts;
Advising him, with all your prejudice,
'Gainst the King's army and his royal person.
4. Fourth is, that you would have brought the King
Before Saint Katherine's fort, to be there slain;
And to that end writ to the governor,
In which you gave him notes to know his highness.
5. Fifthly, You sent La Fin to treat with Savoy,

              And with the Count Fuentes, of more plots,
              Touching the ruin of the King and realm.
By.   All this, my lord, I answer, and deny.
              And first for Picote: he was my prisoner,
              And therefore I might well confer with him;
              But that our conference tended to the Archduke
              Is nothing so: I only did employ him
              To Captain La Fortune, for the reduction
              Severre to the service of the King,
              Who used such speedy diligence therein,
              That shortly 't was assured his Majesty.
              2. Next, For my treaty with the Duke of Savoy;
              Roucas, his secretary, having since
              Given me the understanding by La Force
              Of his dislike, I never dream'd of it.
              3. Thirdly, For my intelligence with the Duke,
              Advising him against his Highness' army:
              Had this been true I had not undertaken
              Th' assault of Bourg, against the King's opinion,
              Having assistance but by them about me;
              And, having won it for him, had not been
              Put out of such a government so easily.
              4. Fourthly, For my advice to kill the King:
              I would beseech his highness memory
              Not to let slip that I alone dissuaded
              His viewing of that fort; informing him
              It had good mark-men, and he could not go
              But in exceeding danger, which advice
              Diverted him; the rather since I said
              That if he had desire to see the place
              He should receive from me a plot of it;
              Offering to take it with five hundred men,
              And I myself would go to the assault.
              5. And lastly, For intelligences held
              With Savoy and Fuentes; I confess
              That being denied to keep the citadel,
              Which with incredible peril I had got,
              And seeing another honour'd with my spoils,
              I grew so desperate that I found my spirit
              Enraged to any act, and wish'd myself
              Cover'd with blood.
Ch.   With whose blood?

By.	With mine own;
	Wishing to live no longer, being denied,
	With such suspicion of me, and set will
	To rack my furious humour into blood.
	And for two months' space I did speak and write
	More than I ought, but have done ever well,
	And therefore your informers have been false,
	And, with intent to tyrannize, suborn'd.
Ch.	What if our witnesses come face to face,
	And justify much that we allege?
By.	They must be hirelings, then, and men corrupted.
Po.	What think you of La Fin?
By.	I hold La Fin
	An honour'd gentlemen, my friend and kinsman.
Ha.	If he then aggravate what we affirm
	With greater accusation to your grace,
	What will you say?
By.	I know it cannot be.
Ch.	Call in my Lord La Fin.
By.	Is he so near,
	And kept so close from me? Can all the world
	Make him a treacher?

Enter La Fin

Ch.	I suppose my lord,
	You have not stood within, without the ear
	Of what hath here been urged against the Duke;
	If you have heard it, and upon your knowledge
	Can witness all is true, upon your soul,
	Utter your knowledge.
La.	I have heard, my lord,
	All that hath pass'd here, and upon my soul,
	(Being charged so urgently in such a Court)
	Upon my knowledge I affirm all true;
	And so much more as, had the prisoner lived
	As many as his years, would make all forget.
By.	O all ye virtuous powers, in earth and heaven,
	That have not put on hellish flesh and blood,
	From whence these monstrous issues are produced,
	That cannot bear in execrable concord,
	And one prodigious subject, contraries;
	Nor as the isle that of the world admired,

Is sever'd from the world can cut yourselves
From the consent and sacred harmony
Of life, yet live; of honour, yet be honour'd
As this extravagant and errant rogue
From all your fair decorums and just laws
Finds power to do, and like a loathesome wen
Sticks to the face and nature and this Court;
Thicken this air, and turn your plaguy rage
Into a shape as dismal as his sin;
And with some equal horror tear him off
From sight and memory. Let not such a Court,
To whose fame all the kings of Christendom
Now laid their ears, so crack her royal trump,
As to sound through it, that her vaunted justice
Was got in such an incest. Is it justice
To tempt and witch a man to break the law,
And by that witch condemn him? Let me draw
Poison into me with this cursed air
If he bewitch'd me and transform'd me not;
He bit me by the ear, and made me drink
Enchanted waters; let me see an image
That utter'd these distinct words: Thou shalt die,
O wicked king; and if the devil gave him
Such power upon an image, upon me
How might he tyrannize? that by his vows
And oaths too Stygian had my nerves and will
In more awe than his own. What man is he
That is so high but he would higher be?
So roundly sighted, but he may be found
To have a blind side, which by craft pursued,
Confederacy, and simply trusted treason,
May wrest him past his angel and his reason?

Ch. Witchcraft can never taint an honest mind.
Ha. True gold will any trial stand untouch'd.
Po. For colours that will stain when they are tried,
The cloth itself is ever cast aside.
By. Sometimes the very gloss in anything
Will seem a stain; the fault not in the light,
Nor in the guilty object, but our sight.
My gloss, raised from the richness of my stuff,
Had too much splendour for the owly eye
Of politic and thankless royalty;

I did deserve too much; a pleurisy
Of that blood in me is the cause I die.
Virtue in great men must be small and slight,
For poor stars rule where she is exquisite.
'Tis tyrannous and impious policy
To put to death by fraud and treachery;
Sleight is then royal when it makes men live
And if it urge faults, urgeth to forgive.
He must be guiltless that condemns the guilty.
Like things do nourish like and not destroy them;
Minds must be found that judge affairs of weight,
And seeing hands, cut corrosives from our sight.
A lord intelligencer? hangman-like,
Thrust him from human fellowship to the dessert,
Blow him with curses; shall your justice call
Treachery her father? would you wish her weigh
My valour with the hiss of such a viper?
What have I done to shun the mortal shame
Of so unjust an opposition?
My envious stars cannot deny me this
That I may make my judges witnesses;
And that my wretched fortunes have reserved
For my last comfort; ye all know, my lords,
This body, gash'd with five and thirty wounds,
Whose life and death you have in your award,
Holds not a vein that hath not open'd been,
And which I would not open yet again
For you and yours; this hand that writ the lines
Alleged against me hath enacted still,
More good than there it only talked of ill.
I must confess my choler hath transferr'd
My tender spleen to all intemperate speech.
But reason ever did my deeds attend.
In worth of praise, and imitation,
Had I borne any will to let them loose,
I could have flesh'd them with bad services.
In England lately, and in Switzerland,
There are a hundred gentlemen by name
Can witness my demeanour in the first,
And in the last ambassage I adjure
Nor other testimonies than the Seigneurs
DeVic and Sillery, who amply know

In what sort and with what fidelity
I bore myself, to reconcile and knit
In one desire so many wills disjoin'd
And from the King's allegiance quite withdrawn.
My acts ask'd many men, though done by one;
And I were but one I hold my worth, though not my place:
Nor slight I judge my worth I be but one.
One man, of one sole expedition,
Reduced into th' Imperial Power of Rome
Armenia, Pontus, and Arabia,
Syria, Albania, and Iberia,
Conquer'd th' Hyrcanians, and to Caucasus
His arms extended; the Numidians
And Afric to the shores meridional
His power subjected; and that part of Spain
Which stood from those parts that Sertorious ruled,
Even to the Atlantic sea he conquered.
Th' Albanian kings he from the kingdoms chased,
And at the Caspian sea their dwellings placed;
Of all the earth's globe, by power and his advice,
The round-eyed ocean saw him victor thrice.
And what shall let me, but your cruel doom,
To add as much to France as he to Rome,
And to leave justice neither sword nor word
To use against my life; this senate knows
That what with one victorious hand I took
I gave to all your uses with another;
And this I took and propt the falling kingdom,
And gave it to the King; I have kept
Your laws of state from fire, and you yourselves
Fix'd in this high tribunal, from whose height
The vengeful Saturnals of the League
Had hurl'd ye headlong; do ye then return
This retribution? can the cruel King,
The Kingdom, laws, and you, all saved by me,
Destroy their saver? what, ay me! I did,
Adverse to this, this damn'd exchanger did,
That took into his will my motion;
And being bankrout both of wealth and worth,
Pursued with quarrels and with suits in law,
Fear'd by the kingdom, threaten'd by the King,
Would raise the loathed dunghill of his ruins

Elizabethan Oratory

Upon the monumental heap of mine;
Torn with possessed whirlwinds may he die,
And dogs bark at his murderous memory.

Ch. My lord, our liberal sufferance of your speech
Hath made it late, and for this session
We will dismiss you; take him back, my lord.
(Exit Vit. and Byron.)

Massinger's *Duke of Milan*
Act III, scene i

The Imperial Camp before Pavia.

Medina, Hernando, and Alphonso; Charles and attendants.
Enter Pescara with Sforza, strongly guarded.

Alph. He looks as if
He would outface his dangers.

Hern. I am cozened:
A suitor, in the devil's name!

Med. Hear him speak.

Sfor. I come not, emperor, to invade thy mercy,
By fawning on thy fortune; nor bring with me
Excuses, or denials. I profess,
And with a good man's confidence, even this instant
That I am in thy power, I was thine enemy;
Thy deadly and vowed enemy: one that wished
Confusion to thy person and estates;
And with my utmost powers, and deepest counsels,
Had they been truly followed, furthered it.
Nor will I now although my neck were under
The Hangman's axe, with one poor syllable
Confess, but that I honoured the French King,
More than myself, and all men.

Med. By saint Jacques,
This is no flattery.

Hern. There is fire and spirit in't;
But long-lived, I hope.

Sfor. Now give me leave,
My hate against thyself, and love to him
Freely acknowledged, to give the reasons
That make me so affected: in my wants
I ever found him faithful; had supplies

Of men and monies from him; and my hopes
Quite sunk, were, by his grace, buoyed up again;
He was indeed to me as my good angel
To guard me from all dangers. I dare speak
Nay, must and will, his praise now, in as high
And loud a key, as when he was thy equal.
The benefits he sowed in me, met not
Unthankful ground, but yielded him his own,
With fair increase, and I still glory in it.
And, though my fortunes, poor, compared to his,
And Milan, weighed with France, appear as nothing,
Are in thy fury burnt, let it be mentioned,
They served but as small tapers to attend
The solemn flame at this great funeral;
And with them I will gladly waste myself,
Rather than undergo the imputation
Of being base, or unthankful.

Alph. Nobly spoken!
Hern. I do begin, I know not why, to hate him
Less than I did.
Sfor. If that, then, to be grateful
For courtesies received, or not to leave
A friend in his necessities, be a crime
Amongst you Spaniards, which other nations
That like you, aimed at empire, loved and cherished
Where'er they found it, Sforza brings his head
To pay the forfeit. Nor come I as a slave,
Pinioned before thy feet, kneeling and howling,
For a forestalled remission; that were poor,
And would but shame thy victory; for conquest
Over base foes is a captivity,
And not a triumph. I ne'er feared to die,
More than I wished to live. When I had reached
My ends in being a duke, I wore these robes,
My crown upon my head, and to my side
This sword was girt; and witness truth that now
'Tis in another's power, when I shall part
With them and life together, I'm the same:
My veins then did swell with pride; nor now
Shrink they for fear. Know, sir, that Sforza stands
Prepared for either fortune.

Hern. As I live,
I do begin strangely to love this fellow;
And could part with three-quarters of my share in
The promised spoil, to save him.

Sfor. But, if example
Of my fidelity to the French, whose honours,
Titles, and glories, are now mixed with yours,
As brooks, devoured by rivers, lose their names,
Has power to invite you to make him a friend,
That hath given evident proof he knows to love,
And to be thankful: this my crown, now yours,
You may restore me, and in me instruct
These brave commanders, should your fortune change,
Which now I wish not, what they may expect
From noble enemies, for being faithful.
The charges of the war I will defray,
And what you may, not without hazard, force,
Bring freely to you: I'll prevent the cries
Of murdered infants, and of ravished maids,
Which in a city sacked, call on Heaven's justice,
And stop the course of glorious victories:
And, when I know the captains and the soldiers,
That are to be rewarded, I myself,
According to their quality and merits,
Will see them largely recompensed. I have said,
And now expect my sentence.

Jonson's *Sejanus*
Act I, scene ii
A State Room in the Palace
A Gallery discovered opening into the State Room.

Tib. (having read the letters.) Return the lords this voice,
We are their creature,
And it is fit a good and honest prince,
Whom they, out of their bounty, have instructed
With so dilate and absolute a power,
Should owe the office of it to their service,
And good of all and every citizen.
Nor shall it e'er repent us to have wished
The senate just, and favouring lords unto us,

Since their free loves do yield no less defence
To a prince's state, than his own innocence.
Say then, there can be nothing in their thought
Shall want to please us, that hath pleased them;
Our suffrage rather shall prevent, than stay
Behind their wills: 'tis empire to obey,
Where such, so great, so grave, so good determine.
Yet, for the suit of Spain, to erect a temple
In honour of our mother and our self
We must, with pardon of the senate, not
Assent thereto. Their lordships may object
Our not denying the same late request
Unto the Asian cities: we desire
That our defence for suffering that be known
In these brief reasons, with our after purpose.
Since deified Augustus hindered not
A temple to be built at Pergamum,
In honour of himself and sacred Rome;
We, that have all his deeds and words observed
Ever, in place of laws, the rather followed
That pleasing precedent, because with ours,
The senate's reverence, also, there was joined.
But as, t' have once received it, may deserve
The gain of pardon; so, to be adored
With the continued style, and note of gods,
Through all the provinces, were wild ambition,
And no less pride: yea, even Augustus' name
Would early vanish, should it be profaned
With such promiscuous flatteries. For our part,
We here protest it, and are covetous
Posterity should know it, we are mortal;
And can but deeds of men: 'twere glory enough
Could we be truly a prince. And, they shall add
Abounding grace unto our memory,
That shall report us worthy our forefathers,
Careful of your affairs, constant in dangers,
And not afraid of any private frown
For public good. These things shall be to us
Temples and statues, reared in your minds,
The fairest, and most during imagery:
For these of stone or brass, if they become
Odious in judgment of posterity,

Elizabethan Oratory

Are more contemned as dying sepulchres,
Than ta'en for living monuments. We then
Make here our suit, alike to gods and men;
The one, until the period of our race,
To inspire us with a free and quiet mind,
Discerning both divine and human laws;
The other, to vouchsafe us after death,
An honourable mention, and fair praise,
To accompany our actions and our name:
The rest of greatness princes may command,
And, therefore, may neglect; only a long,
A lasting, high, and happy memory
They should, without being satisfied, pursue:
"Contempt of fame begets contempt of virtue."

Ford's Perkin Warbeck
Act III, scene iv
Before the Castle of Norham.

Dur. Warlike King of Scotland,
Vouchsafe a few words from a man enforced
To lay his book aside, and clap on arms
Unsuitable to my age or my profession.
Courageous prince, consider on what grounds
You rend the face of peace, and break a league
With a confederate king that courts your amity,
For whom too? for a vagabond, a straggler,
Not noted in the world by birth or name,
An obscure peasant, by the rage of hell
Loosed from his chains to set great kings at strife.
What nobleman, what common man of note,
What ordinary subject hath come in,
Since first you footed on our territories,
To only feign a welcome? Children laugh at
Your proclamations and the wiser pity
So great a potentate's abuse by one
Who juggles merely with the fawns and youth
Of an instructed complement: such spoils,
Such slaughters as the rapine of your soldiers
Already have committed, is enough
To show your zeal in a conceited justice.
Yet, great king, wake not yet my master's vengeance

But shake that viper off which gnaws your entrails.
I and my fellow-subjects are resolved,
If you persist, to stand your utmost fury,
Till our last blood drop from us.

Jonson's *Poetaster*
Act V, scene i

An Apartment in the Palace.

Virg. Before you go together, worthy Romans,
We are to tender our opinion;
And give you those instructions, that may add
Unto your even judgment in the cause:
Which thus we do commence. First, you must know,
That where there is a true and perfect merit,
There can be no dejection; and the scorn
Of humble baseness, oftentimes, so works
In a high soul, upon the grosser spirit,
That to his bleared and offended sense,
There seems a hideous fault blazed in the object;
When only the disease is in his eyes.
Here hence it comes, our Horace now stands taxed
Of impudence, self-love, and arrogance,
By these, who share no merit in themselves;
And therefore think his portion is as small.
For they, from their own guilt, assure their souls,
If they should confidently praise their works,
In them it would appear inflation:
Which, in a full, and well digested man,
Cannot receive that foul abusive name,
But the fair title of erection.
And, for his true use of translating men,
It still hath been a work of as much palm,
In clearest judgments, as t' invent or make.
His sharpness,—that is most excusable;
As being forced out of a suff'ring virtue,
Oppressed with the license of the time;
And howsoever fools, or jerking pedants,
Players, or such like buffoon-barking wits,
May with their beggarly and barren trash
Tickle base vulgar ears, in their despite;

> This, like Jove's thunder, shall their pride control,
> The honest satire hath the happiest soul.
> Now, Romans, you have heard our thoughts; withdraw when you please.

As one reads these orations, one realizes that in the course of the decline of the drama the oration likewise suffered a decline. After 1600 the drama became more and more mechanical and conventional. Conventional themes and conventional treatment contributed to giving the drama but temporary and provincial appeal and succeeded in sapping it of spirit and interest through constant repetition. The oration likewise lost its vigor and spirit. An excessive refinement upon form, resulting in the monotony of mechanical arrangement; a reckless dissipation in development, resulting in an imposing display of grandiloquent rhetoric but a thickening and gumming of the processes of thought; and a difficulty in maintaining sustained effort are all evidences pointing to the decline of the oration as a vital convention of dramatic structure. To use in the case of the oration the biological analogy so often used in connection with the Elizabethan drama, the exuberance of youth and the vigor of maturity have been replaced by the impotence of old age.

In the later Elizabethan drama much is made of the trial scene and the forensic. The elaboration of setting which Shakespeare gives to the trial scene we find characteristic of dramatic integration of forensics in later Elizabethan drama. Special care is taken to give the trial scenes lifelikeness in the grouping of court personages; and the advocate and the advocate's speech come more and more into prominence. Massinger works out many trial scenes in his plays. Webster has taken great pains to make realistic the scene in the *White Devil* presenting the arraignment of Vittoria.

In the light of this review of the history of the oration in Elizabethan drama, the contribution that Shakespeare made to this history appears immediately. When one studies the oration in Shakespeare, one studies the oration at the center of Elizabethan drama, at the time when this drama reached its largest and richest expression of maturity. Professor Tucker Brooke, in his volume *The Tudor Drama*,[14] thus describes the growth of the Elizabethan drama:

> That strange literary product, the drama of the Tudor and Jacobean age, can best be likened, perhaps, by a rather homely comparison, to the seed pod of some leguminous plant. Starting from the slender promise of the stem, it grows with a fecundity beyond explanation, through imperfect or stunted products to the large girth and richness of the centre. Then, as if the life-giving power were gradually withdrawn, it becomes ever narrower and more restricted till it ends in sheer abortion. Those who attempt the study of such an organism from a cross-section through the middle—as is commonly the method in literature—are confounded by the number, the variety, the mutual unlikeness of the cells. It is better that one endeavor first to discover the few genital elements whose presence creates all the diverse manifestations of maturity and whose absence transforms maturity into decay.

When one thinks in terms of the oration in the Elizabethan Drama, the defense of Ishmael certainly makes one think of "starting from the slender promise of the stem." When one thinks of the oration developing as rhetorical composition in that period of "preparation and tentative endeavour,"[15] the multitude of speeches in early Elizabethan drama—speeches which when analyzed are found to have the primal elements common to all orations, however mechanical and experimental the development of these elements may be—reminds one of "it grows with a fecundity beyond explanation, through imperfect or stunted products." The oration in Shakespeare, as it reveals the full and rich development of the oration as an integral element of plot structure, is in terms of rhetoric in poetic "the large girth and richness of the centre." The orations of the dramatists of the decline

14. Pp. 438-439.
15. J. A. Symonds, *Shakespeare's Predecessors in the English Drama*, p. 3.

recall "as if the life-giving power were gradually withdrawn, it becomes ever narrower and more restricted till it ends in sheer abortion."

In Shakespeare, the oration in the Elizabethan drama attained the full and rich expression of maturity. This study has been an attempt to help indicate the elements that made possible that maturity. A steadiness in development, a restraint in the matter of expression, a spontaneity in the manner of expression, and an emphasis on a purpose which relates the oration to dramatic action are elements—the essential elements—that make possible the expression of rhetoric as a fine and, at the same time, practical art. The absence of these elements makes for immaturity on the one hand and decline on the other. One senses to a certain extent the immaturity in Biron's oration; one senses the decline in the allegiance speech of Wolsey unless the speech is felt to be in character; one senses a decline when Katherine's defense is compared with that of Hermione. But with these exceptions Shakespeare's orations reveal the maturity of rhetorical art.

CHAPTER VIII

Elizabethan Education

THE YEAR 1500 serves as an appropriate date about which to center the transition period in England from medieval to modern methods of education. It marks conveniently a point of focusing in intellectual development arising out of the revival of classical learning and issuing in the efforts to build on this learning the intellectual life of modern England. By 1500, the Revival of Learning had already passed its height in Italy but was still strongly felt there; in France, Germany, and England the movement was then just at its height. The purpose of this chapter is to relate the oration in Shakespeare to the education movements of sixteenth-century England.

Humanism had been introduced from Italy to Oxford in the closing years of the fifteenth century by Grocyn, Linacre, and Colet. The enthusiasm for the new learning was carried from Oxford to Cambridge. The early efforts of these humanists met considerable opposition at the hands of the clergy and the scholiasts of the universities, and the early efforts of English humanism made at first but little impression on the intellectual life of the country. But at Cambridge, the cause of humanism was given decided impetus and encouragement by Erasmus, who taught Greek in the university from 1510 to 1514, and who did more than anyone else "to substitute true classical culture for the poor Latin and the empty scholasticism of his time."[1] He wrote textbooks, educational treatises, and the two well-known works in satirical vein, *Praise of Folly* and the *Ciceronian;* in addition, his Latin-

---

1. E. P. Cubberley, *History of Education*, p. 274.

Greek edition of the New Testament definitely fixed the place of the New Testament in the humanistic schools.

With the encouragement of Erasmus, Colet made what was actually the establishment of humanism in English education. This he did through the secondary schools. Colet had been made Dean of St. Paul's and refounded (1510) the Cathedral School of St. Paul's. He devoted his wealth to establishing the school along humanistic lines, and Erasmus assisted him in securing teachers and writing textbooks for the school. William Lily was made the headmaster of the school. Like the introduction of genuine classical culture at the universities, this humanizing of the secondary schools met with opposition of the older generation of educationists, who could see nothing but heresy and heathenism in the new movement. But the influence of the new St. Paul's School spread throughout England. The older grammar schools—church, state, and private foundations—felt after a time the influence of Colet's school; and by the end of the century, practically all of them had been remodeled along humanistic lines. The new schools, founded after Colet's school, were almost entirely modeled upon St. Paul's.

This change in the system of education registered the reaction against medieval scholasticism. Men were ready to revive the practical education that was the aim of the best classical traditions, traditions that regarded education as preparation for a virile, cultured, useful life in the world. At the beginning of the sixteenth century some Englishmen had awakened to the possibilities of breaking the shackles of the cramping medieval education, with its consequent deadening effects not only on mind but spirit as well, and of being free to enjoy the ennobling inspiration that comes from the contemplation of high ideals and the perception of the beauties in the world of nature and the world of man. Mankind was shifting the emphasis in education from subjecting men to schematized discipline which exalted the letter at the expense of the spirit of learning to leading men to make their own both the letter and the spirit as a means of developing rich and wholesome culture in their lives. The ideal has, of course, never been realized; and, from the very beginning, it was clouded by the materialism and ecclesiastical contentions of the sixteenth century. But in England the reaction against medieval education was achieving some enduring results in the first half of the sixteenth century.

The basis of the new education was the study of the best Greek and Latin with a view to making these ancient languages one's own. The course of study was designed to give the student proficiency in speaking and writing the ancient languages and familiarity with the works of the best classical authors. Ascham, in his *Scholemaster*, quotes, as being particularly good, the scheme of study set down by Erasmus. This scheme includes Plato and Xenophon, for their philosophy; Aristotle, for his rhetoric; Livy and Sallust, for their history; Plautus and Terence, for their plays; Isocrates, Demosthenes, and Cicero, for their oratory. Plutarch was also included among the historical writers. Vergil, Lucan, Horace, Seneca, and Claudian were included among the poets studied. Cicero became the model for the study of prose style, and Quintilian for principles of pedagogy. Lily's Latin grammar was the standard Latin grammar, and Gaza's Greek grammar was the standard textbook in the study of Greek. The course of study at Eton in 1560 shows how thoroughly humanized the English grammar schools had become:

Lower or Usher's School

First Form

The *Disticha de Moribus* of Dionysius Cato
The *Exercitatio Linguae Latinae* of John Lewis Vives

Second Form

Terence
Lucian's *Dialogues* (in Latin)
Aesop's *Fables* (in Latin)

Third Form
Terence
Aesop's *Fables* (in Latin)
Selections by Sturmius from Cicero's *Epistles*.

Upper or Master's School
Fourth Form
Terence
Ovid's *Tristia*
Epigrams of Martial, Catullus, and Sir Thomas More.

Fifth Form
Ovid's *Metamorphoses*
Horace
Cicero's *Epistles*
Valerius Maximus
Lucius Florus
Justin
Epitome Troporum of Susenbrotus.

Sixth and Seventh Forms
Caesar's *Commentaries*
Cicero's *De Officiis* and *De Amicitia*
Vergil
Lucan
Greek Grammar

The younger boys had to decline and conjugate words, and their seniors had to repeat rules of grammar, for the illustration of which short phrases, called "Vulgaria," were composed and committed to memory. Some sort of Latin composition, however brief, was a necessary portion of the daily work of every Eton scholar. In the lower forms it was confined to the literal translation of an English sentence or passage, while in the Fifth Form it consisted of a theme on a subject set by the schoolmaster. The boys in the Sixth and Seventh Forms wrote verses.[2]

In the second half of the sixteenth century, the work of

2. Quoted in Cubberley's *Readings in History of Education*, pp. 222-223, from Maxwell-Lyte's *History of Eton College*, p. 149.

the various schools became more and more intensified and standardized. The following outlines, given by J. Howard Brown in *Elizabethan Schooldays* (pp. 97-99), suggest the work in the English Grammar School:

Sandwich

Usher's Forms

I. Accidence to rules of construction, nouns, verbs.
II. Rules of construction: Cato, making of Latin.
III. Latin catechism, dialogues of Costellion, Latin English and English Latin translation.

Master's Forms

IV. Terence, Cicero's Epistles (Ed. Sturm), Aphthomius.
V. Sallust, Cicero's *Offices*, Virgil's *Eclogues*, rules of versifying, disputing extempore.
VI. Cicero's orations, *Aeneid*, Horace (Epistles, and "certain of his chaste odes chosen."), making verses.

East Retford

Form

I. Inflection of verbs and nouns, easy epistles of Cicero.
II. Remainder of the Accidence, Syntax, *Colloquies* of Erasmus, harder epistles of Cicero, English-Latin translation, the Old Testament Scriptures, Sallust, Salern, Justinian's *Institutes*.
III. Virgil, Ovid, Cicero's *Epistles*, Erasmus: *De Copia*, English-Latin translation.
IV. Verse-making, writing epistles, Greek and Hebrew Grammar.

In the larger schools there was something like the following curriculum at Eton (1560):

I. Cato, Vives.
II. Terence, Lucian's *Dialogues*, Aesop's *Fables*.
III. Terence, Aesop, Cicero's *Epistles* (Sturm).
IV. Terence, Ovid *(Tristia)*, Martial *(Epigrams)*, Catullus, Sir Thomas More.

V. Ovid *(Metamorphoses)*, Horace, Cicero *(Epistles)*, Valerius Maximus, Lucius Florus, Justin, Susenbrotus (Epitome of Rhetoric in 1540).

VI. and

VII. Caesar *(Commentaries)*, Cicero *(De Officiis, de Amicitia)*, Virgil, Lucan, Greek grammar.

Brown goes on to outline the work done in the school at Plymouth by William Kemp. In the highest form there, the curriculum included the study of Greek, logic, rhetoric, Tully's *Offices* and *Orations*, Caesar's *Commentaries*, Virgil's *Aeneid*, Ovid's *Metamorphoses*, and Horace.

On the Continent, the grammar schools were even more thoroughly humanized, as the curriculum of the College de Guyenne and that of Sturm's Strassburg Latin School testify.[3] Each of these schools had ten classes, and the upper classes laid great stress on the study of rhetoric. The following sections are from the upper classes:

College de Guyenne

Fourth Class. Age twelve or thirteen

Pupils now study for first time an oration of Cicero, and study with it a manual of rhetoric, such as the *De Copia* of Erasmus.

Third Class. Age thirteen or fourteen

The *Epistolae Familiares* or *Ad Atticum* of Cicero, and one other oration.

Much emphasis on rhetoric, syntax, verse composition, and Latin composition in prose and verse.

Second Class. Age fourteen or fifteen

Cicero's orations, selected.

Much learning by heart; prose and verse compositions; and emphasis on rhetoric.

Latin declamation now first undertaken.

First Class. Age fifteen or sixteen

The art of oratory, from Cicero or Quintilian.

Speeches of Cicero, in illustration.

Composition in prose and verse, and declamation.[4]

3. See Cubberley's *Readings*, pp. 208-209, 211-213.
4. The declamation in the schools is of interest in connection with the rhetorical drama of the Renaissance, modeled upon Senecan drama.

Strassburg Latin School

Fifth Class. Age 12 to 13

Examples of eloquence for translation, and then re-translated into Latin.

Fourth Class. Age 13 to 14

Read sixth oration against Verres, second book of Cicero's *Letters to Friends*, part of *Adelphi* of Terence, and the epistles and satires of Horace in Latin.

Third Class. Age 14 to 15

Rhetoric to be begun.
The best efforts of Demosthenes to be carefully studied.
Select orations in Greek to be translated into Latin, and vice versa.

Second Class. Age 15 to 16

Literal interpretation of Greek poets and orators.
Connection between oratorical and poetic usage.
Striking passages to be copied into books for learning.
Rhetoric to be studied now from a text, and applied to orations of Demosthenes and Cicero.
Logic to be introduced in this class.
Read the second Philippic of Demosthenes, Cicero's pleas in behalf of Roscius Amerinus and Caius Rabirius.

First Class. Age 16 to 17

Logic and rhetoric to be extended, and applied to Cicero and Demosthenes.
Much translation and re-translation, writing in prose and poetry, and declamation.
Epistles of Saint Paul to be expounded, after the manner of the old rhetoricians.

These quotations suggest educational methods in sixteenth-century education.[5] In the second book of *The Scholemaster*, Ascham sets forth his method of "teaching the ready way to

---

5. It is of interest to note that these sixteenth-century grammar schools generally included physical activities retained from the medieval system of education. Physical sports and games including fencing, wrestling, dancing, running, and playing ball were given attention. The sixteenth-century humanism, then, aimed at a broad and thorough intellectual training combined with moral excellence and physical health—at a well-rounded education that would fit the pupil in every way to meet the demands of life.

the Latin tong." After taking up and discussing in turn double translation, paraphrasis, metaphrasis, and epitome, Ascham discusses quite at length "Imitatio," and says with reference to this part of instruction: "Imitation would bring forth more learning and breed up trewer judgment than any other exercise that can be used, but not for yong beginners, because they shall not be able to consider dulie thereof." Ascham's method in imitation is avowedly based on Cicero's views on imitation. Quintilian describes imitation as that in which "a great portion of art consists"; but like Cicero and Ascham, he recognizes that judgment should be exercised in the choice of authors to be imitated as well as in the choice of qualities to be imitated from any particular author.[6] Wilson says with reference to imitation:

> Now before we use, either to write, or speak eloquently, we must dedicate our myndes wholy, to followe the most wise and learned men and seeke to fashion as wel their speache and gesturing, as their witte or endyting. The which when we earnestly mynd to doe, we can not but in time appere somewhat like them. . . . By companying with the wise, a man shall learne wisedome.[7]

In the course of the sixteenth century, English education became more and more intensively organized along humanistic lines, and study and imitation of the classics became the *sine qua non* of Elizabethan education. The study of rhetoric was a principal element in Elizabethan education. At this time, rhetoric occupied second place in the list of the Seven Liberal Arts: in the early years of the Elizabethan period, it ranked after grammar;[8] toward the close of the century, it was accorded position above grammar and next after lit-

---

6. See *De Oratore*, I, xxxiv, II, xxii, II, lix; *Institutes*, X, ii.
7. *Arte of Rhetorique*, p. 5.
8. Grammar in the older medieval sense included Literature. By the end of the sixteenth century, "technical Grammar had been separated from Literature, and made a more elementary subject, while Rhetoric had developed into a critical study of literary art." See Cubberley's discussion and chart in his *History*, pp. 279-281.

erature. Cicero and Quintilian set the standards of Elizabethan theory of rhetoric. For practice, the orations of Cicero, Demosthenes, and Isocrates served as models. Drill in translation and double translation, in composition and declamation, and in imitation of the style of the ancient orators was intensified and extended from the days of Colet on through the sixteenth century and later.[9] Up to 1600, the cultural value of this process of drill was still uppermost in the minds of the majority of teachers; after 1600, however, the process lost much of its value as a means of securing a liberal education, through being regarded largely, on account of its disciplinary value, as an end in itself.

Elizabethan dramatists grew up under the influence of this humanistic education. Many of the earlier dramatists were scholarly men, men of the universities enthusiastic in the making of English education along humanistic lines and the developing of English drama along the lines of classical drama. As we have already noted, this drama was the postclassical drama, and the rhetoric in the drama the postclassical rhetoric. The immediate predecessors of Shakespeare, the younger generation of dramatists, evidently profited by the intensive study of classical rhetoric; and while the influence of the Senecan style persists in their plays, there are unmistakable evidences of a conscious effort to differentiate

9. Mair points out in Wilson's *Arte of Rhetorique* in a translation of Cicero's invective against Verres, "a passage which shows that a large part of the Euphuistic manner was derived from the imitation of Cicero practised by the teachers and students of rhetoric in the schools." See *Arte of Rhetorique*, p. 186, and Mair's introduction, p. xxvii. Mair also quotes from Prof. Foster Watson's *The English Grammar Schools to 1660:* "Unless the school and university training in rhetoric is borne in mind, an important factor in accounting for the wealth of imagery and expression in the English literature of the sixteenth and seventeenth centuries is overlooked." Mair also refers to Cox's *Arte or Crafte of Rhetorique*, Sherry's *Treatise of the Figures of Grammar and Rhetoric, profitable for all that be studious of eloquence*, Richard Mulcaster's *Grammar and Rhetoric*, Brindsley's *Ludus Litterarius*, or *Grammar Schoole* (1616), and Hoole's *New Discovery of the old art of teaching schoole* (1659).

rhetoric and poetic by emphasizing rhetoric as the art of persuasion through logical appeal to reason. The university men among the immediate predecessors of Shakespeare had already sensed the distinction given to rhetoric by Aristotle. Shakespeare thus built upon what they had already done.

Shakespeare brought to London the background of Elizabethan secondary education. *Love's Labour's Lost* is full of reminiscences of Elizabethan educational methods and educational practices, much of it being studied burlesque.[10] In Act I, scene i, Constable Dull enters with a letter, and Costard comes with him. From this point there is much burlesque of the methods of teaching rhetoric and of the exercises prescribed in textbooks on rhetoric, specifically Wilson.[11] Here are two passages from this scene:

10. Coleridge in his note on *Love's Labour's Lost* expresses the belief that it represented his earliest dramatic work and sees in it reminiscences of his recent school days in Stratford (T. M. Raysor, *Coleridge's Shakespearean Criticism*, I, 92). The following is of special interest in connection with this study:

"Hence the comic matter chosen in the first instance is a ridiculous imitation or apery of this constant striving after logical precision, and subtle opposition of thoughts, together with a making the most of every conception or image, by expressing it under the least expected property belonging to it, . . .

"The same kind of intellectual action is exhibited in a more serious and elevated strain in many other parts of this play. Biron's speech at the end of the fourth act is an excellent specimen of it. It is logic clothed in rhetoric; but observe how Shakespeare, in his two-fold being of poet and philosopher, avails himself of it to convey profound truths in the most lively images—the whole remaining faithful to the character supposed to utter the lines, and the expressions themselves constituting a further development of that character.

"However, it is not unimportant to notice how strong a presumption the diction and allusions of this play afford, that, though Shakespeare's acquirements in the dead languages might not be such as we suppose in a learned education, his habits had, nevertheless, been scholastic, and those of a student." Raysor, I, 94-96.

11. The changes that developed in sixteenth-century education were accompanied by a constant demand for new textbooks; and there were many rhetorics written to supply the demand for progress in the teaching of rhetoric; but the books of Wilson and Cox seem to have remained standard throughout the century. See *Education of Shakespeare* by G. A. Plimpton, for textbooks of Shakespeare's day.

Cost. In manner and form following, sir; all those three: I was seen with her in the manor-house, sitting with her upon the form, and taken following her into the park; which, put together, is in manner and form following. Now, sir, for the manner,—it is the manner of a man to speak to a woman; for the form,—in some form.

King: (Reads) So it is, besieged with sable-coloured melancholy, I did commend the black oppressing humour to the most wholesome physic of thy health-giving air; and, as I am a gentleman, betook myself to walk. The time when? About the sixth hour; when beasts most graze, birds best peck, and men sit down to that nourishment which is called supper; so much for the time when. Now for the ground which; which I mean, I walk'd upon: it is ycleped thy park. Then for the place where; where, I mean, I did encounter that obscene and most preposterous event, that draweth from my snow-white pen the ebon-coloured ink which here thou viewest, beholdest, surveyest, or seest; but to the place where: it standeth north-northeast and by east from the west corner of thy curious-knotted garden.

Again, Act I, scene ii contains much in the way of wit contests, much question and answer; here, for example, are two reminiscences of textbook and teaching methods:

Arm. I will have that subject newly writ o'er, that I may example my digression by some mighty precedent.

Arm. I do affect the very ground, which is base, where her shoe, which is baser, guided by her foot, which is basest, doth tread.

There is perhaps burlesque in the discussion of "L'envoy" in Act III, scene i:

Arm. No, page; it is an epilogue or discourse to make plain
Some obscure precedence that hath tofore been sain.
I will example it:
    The fox, the ape, and the humble bee,
    Were still at odds, being but three. etc.

In Act IV, scene i, Armado's letter recalls not only textbook methods but also the professional letter-writing—the dic-

Elizabethan Education

tamen—which was an important part of medieval rhetoric. The letter is quoted not only as a clear case of burlesque, but also as a clear evidence of familiarity with the formal written exercises and recitation methods characteristic of Elizabethan education:

Boyet (Reads) By heaven, that thou art fair, is most infallible; true, that thou art beauteous; truth itself, that thou art lovely. More fairer than fair, beautiful than beauteous, truer than truth itself, have commiseration on thy heroical vassal! The magnanimous and most illustrate King Cophetua set eye upon the pernicious and indubitate beggar Zenelophon; and he it was that might rightly say, *veni, vidi, vici;* which to annothanize in the vulgar! . . . videlicet, He came, saw, and overcame; he came, one; saw, two; overcame, three. Who came? The King. Why did he come? To see. Why did he see? To overcome. To whom came he? To the beggar. What saw he? The beggar. Who overcame he? The beggar. The conclusion is victory; on whose side? The King's. The captive is enriched; on whose side? The beggar's. The catastrophe is a nuptial; on whose side? The king's; no, on both in one, or one in both. I am the King, for so stands the comparison; thou the beggar, for so witnesseth thy lowliness. Shall I command thy love? I may. Shall I enforce thy love? I could. Shall I entreat thy love? I will. What shalt thou exchange for rags? robes; for tittles? titles; for thyself? me. Thus expecting thy reply, I profane my lips on thy foot, my eyes on thy picture, and my heart on thy every part. Thine, in the dearest design of industry.
        Don Adriano de Armado.

Act IV, scene ii is full of burlesque. The stilted style of Holofernes, with his latinized English and scraps of Latin from sixteenth-century textbooks, is a travesty of the linguistic extravagances of the day. Dull tests the learnedness of the "book-men" with his question:

What was a month old at Cain's birth, that's not five weeks old as yet?

Holofernes recalls the examples of speeches in Wilson's rhetoric when he asks,

Sir Nathaniel, will you hear an extemporal epitaph on the death of the deer?

And he recalls materials of rhetoric in:

This is a gift that I have, simple, simple; a foolish extravagant spirit; full of forms, figures, shapes, objects, ideas, apprehensions, motions, revolutions. These are begot in the ventricle of memory, nourished in the womb of pia mater, and delivered upon the mellowing of occasion.

And again in:

I will look again on the intellect of the letter, for the nomination of the party writing to the person written unto.[12]

Other reminiscences of Elizabethan education in *Love's Labour's Lost* include:

V, i

Arm. (To Hol.) Monsieur, are you not lettered?
Moth. Yes, yes; he teaches boys the hornbook.

V, ii

Kath. Fair as a text B in a copy-book.

V, ii

Ros. But shall we dance, if they desire us to 't?
Prin. No, to the death, we will not move a foot;
Nor to their penn'd speech render we no grace,
But while 'tis spoke each turn away her face.
Boyet. Why, that contempt will kill the speaker's heart
And quite divorce his memory from his part.

. . . .

Enter the Boy, Moth, with a speech.

The last two references recall the custom of writing out declamations for delivery.

The matter of Shakespeare's thinking specifically of Wilson's *Arte of Rhetorique* is of great interest. We have already referred in Chapter IV to the book as containing prob-

---

12. Compare Wilson's "Intellection, called by the Grecians, *Synecdoche*, is a Trope, when we gather or judge the whole by the part, or the part by the whole." *Arte of Rhetorique*, p. 174.

Elizabethan Education 211

able source material for Biron's oration and the oration of Ulysses. Mair points out that the character of Dogberry might be derived from Wilson:[13]

> An other good fellowe of the country; being an Officer and Maior of a towne, and desirous to speake like a fine learned man having just occasion to rebuke a runnegate fellowe, said after this wise in great heate. Thou yngrane an vacation Knaue, if I take thee anymore within the circumcision of my dampnation, I will so corrupt thee, that all other vacation knaves shall take illsample by thee.[14]

Compare this with the character of Dogberry as drawn by Shakespeare, and with Dogberry's

> I leave an arrant knave with your worship; which I beseech your worship to correct yourself, for the example of others.[15]

Mair also points out the similarity of several speeches of Falstaff to some of those in Wilson's book.[16] A comparison of Wilson's speech "to prove by conjectures the knowledge of a notable and most hainous offence committed by a Souldier" with Falstaff's speech derogatory to Justice Shallow suggests, to a certain extent, a similarity of idea and treatment.[17] Falstaff's speech in *1 Henry IV*, V, i, while not recalling any of the speeches of Wilson, suggests Wilson's method of "examining the circumstances," the end of the speech. Falstaff's

> Honour hath no skill in surgery, then? No. What is honour? A word. What is in that word honour? What is that honour? Air; a trim reckoning! Who hath it? He that died o' Wednesday. Doth he feel it? No. Doth he hear it? No. 'Tis insensible then? Yea, to the dead. But will it not live with the living? No. Why? Detraction will not suffer it.

recalls the series of the questions and answers appended by Wilson to his Example of commending King David:[18]

13. Mair's Introduction to Wilson. 14. *Arte of Rhetorique*, p. 164.
15. *Much Ado*, V, ii.
16. Reference to Professor Raleigh in Mair's Introduction.
17. *2 Henry IV*, III, ii. Consider also Falstaff's speeches: *1 Henry IV*, II, iv, V, i, V, iv; *2 Henry IV*, IV, iii.
18. *Arte of Rhetorique*, pp. 18-20.

i. Who did the deede? David. ii. What was done? He slew Goliah. iii. Where was it done? About the vale of Terebinthus. iiii. What help had he to it? He had no help of any man but himself went alone, etc. v. Wherefor did he it? For the love of his country, etc. vi. How did he it? He put a stone in his Sling, etc. vii. What time did he it? When Saull reigned first King over the Israelites, etc.

Don Armado's letter, quoted above, also recalls Wilson's series of questions and answers.

That Shakespeare knew Wilson's book appears highly probable. The first edition bears the date 1553. Up to the time of the Spanish Armada it enjoyed popularity as a textbook and went through frequent reprints. It is very likely, then, that Shakespeare became acquainted with the book at the Stratford Grammar School. About the time that Shakespeare came to London, the popularity of Wilson's book began to wane, a fact of interest in that the possible references to Wilson which we note in Shakespeare's early plays are introduced for comic effect.[19]

Other reminders of school practices include:

Comedy of Errors, I, ii

Dro. E. She is so hot because the meat is cold;
    The meat is cold because you come not home;
    You come not home because you have no stomach;
    You have no stomach having broke your fast;

Two Gentlemen of Verona, II, i

Speed. To sigh like a school-boy that had lost his ABC;
    . . . .

Val. As you enjoin'd me, I have writ your letter
    Unto the secret nameless friend of yours;
    Which I was much unwilling to proceed in
    But for my duty to your ladyship.

Sil. I thank you, gentle servant. 'Tis very clerkly done.

---

19. See Mair's Introduction.

Elizabethan Education

Taming of the Shrew, I, i

Tra. Glad that you thus continue your resolve
To suck the sweets of sweet philosophy.
Only, good master, while we do admire
This virtue and this moral discipline,
Let's be no stoics nor no stocks, I pray,
Or so devote to Aristotle's checks
As Ovid be an outcast quite abjur'd.
Balk logic with acquaintance that you have,
And practise rhetoric in your common talk.
Music and poesy use to quicken you.
The mathematics and the metaphysics,
Fall to them as you find your stomach serves you;
No profit grows where is no pleasure ta'en.
In brief, sir, study what you most affect.

Attention should be called in passing to the schoolmaster scenes in *Taming of the Shrew*, and the humorous "school-in-the-street" scene in *Merry Wives of Windsor* (IV, i).

In Act III, scene ii of *As You Like It*, there is some good burlesque on the schoolbook catechizing, from line 325 on. Again, in *King John*, I, i, we are reminded of the same practice:

Philip. And when my knightly stomach is suffic'd,
Why then I suck my teeth and catechise
My picked man of countries. "My dear sir,"
Thus, leaning on my elbow, I begin,
"I shall beseech you"—that is question now;
And then comes answer like an Absey book.
"O sir," says answer, "at your best command;
At your employment; at your service, sir."
"No sir," says question, "I, sweet sir, at yours."
And so, ere answer knows what question would,
Saving in dialogue of compliment,
And talking of the Alps and Apennines,
The Pyrenean and the river Po,
It draws toward supper in conclusion so.

Two other passages that recall the Elizabethan educational system are:

Richard Third, I, i

Clar. Yea, Richard, when I know, for I protest
As yet I do not; but as I can learn,
He hearkens after prophecies and dreams,
And from the cross-row plucks the letter G,
And says a wizard told him that by G
His issue disinherited should be;
And, for my name of George begins with G
It follows in his thought that I am he.

Titus Andronicus, IV, ii

Dem. What's here? A scroll; and written round about.
Let's see:
(Reads) "Integer vitae, scelerisque purus,
Non eget Mauri jaculis, nec arcu."
Chi. O, 'tis a verse in Horace; I know it well
I read it in the grammar long ago.
Aer. Ay, just; a verse in Horace; right, you have it.

The oration is a reminder of Elizabethan educational methods. In fact, it is interesting to think of Shakespeare's orations and the orations of other Elizabethan dramatists as reflecting the drill in writing and delivering orations during schooldays, drill which was based upon the study of the orations of the great ancient orators.[20] Several interesting facts cluster about this matter of drill in rhetoric in the Elizabethan schools. The invention of printing and the manufacture and general use of paper had worked great transformations in the methods of teaching. The textbook method superseded the

20. In Chapter I, p. 11 of his *Shakespeare's Books*, H. R. D. Anders points out, in the review of the curriculum of the English grammar schools, that some of Cicero's orations were included in the work of the sixth year. In *Titus Andronicus* IV, i, 12-14, as Anders notes, the author of the play shows familiarity with Cicero's *De Oratore* when he makes Titus say of Lavinia:
 Oh, boy, Cornelia never with more care
 Read to her sons than she hath read to thee
 Sweet poetry and Tully's Orator.

older medieval "lecture" method of reading by the teacher; the written theme took the place of the medieval disputation.[21] Both of these changes made possible great gains in accuracy, orderliness, and polish in expression, reflecting clear, steady, and careful thinking. This emphasis on rhetoric as the painstaking expression of logical thinking revived and made to function in education the Aristotelian ideal; the drill in writing and delivering orations in the schools gave us ultimately the oration in Shakespeare. We find in the Shakespeare oration the greatest testimony to the thoroughness with which Elizabethan education became informed with the spirit of the classics.

Our study of Shakespeare's orations against the background of Elizabethan education supports the conviction that Shakespeare must have profited in generous measure from his secondary-school education and that, when he got his schooling, Stratford Grammar School furnished a thorough foundation in the study of the classics. Shakespeare must have had more Latin and, no doubt, more Greek than some of his contemporaries have given him credit for.[22] From what we know of Shakespeare's personality as it impressed his contemporaries, we can readily understand this: he does not seem to have been the kind of man to impress one with his learning. Somehow his greatness seems all the more satisfying when one thinks of his bringing to London, along with a native genius for the dramatic in literature and in life, a background

---

21. J. Howard Brown in *Elizabethan Schooldays* has an interesting paragraph on theme-writing in the Elizabethan Grammar School. I quote his sentence on the parts of the theme: "The several parts of the theme were carefully distinguished for the scholar's benefit, and had to be duly observed: exordium, 'to gain the approbation of the hearers and their attention'; narratio, 'That the auditors may fully understand the matter'; confirmatio, proofs, arguments, and reason, illustrated by quotations; confutatio, 'To consider what may be objected against it, and how to answer them'; conclusio, 'a short recapitulation.' "

22. See J. Churton Collins, "Shakespeare as a Classical Scholar" and "Sophocles and Shakespeare as Theological and Ethical Teachers," in *Studies in Shakespeare*.

of classical training which fitted him for making of the Elizabethan drama a drama greater than the classic writers themselves had ever dreamed of. This background enabled him to comprehend and appreciate the achievements of his predecessors and to lose no time and waste no effort in going over ground that his predecessors had already cleared. He certainly went straight forward in the development of the oration in the drama as a vital element of plot structure. He set his hand at once to transform the oration in the drama from a mere mechanical exercise in rhetorical composition betraying characteristics of practice exercises in the schools into a speech of character and purpose in which the mechanics of rhetoric are made but contributory to the natural and effective expression of one main, leading idea. He soon freed the oration of the academic manner which is sensed in Biron's oration and the oration of Pandulph; and, except for these orations, he succeeded in keeping the oration a speech free of the practicing of the schools. Biron's oration alone might be regarded as burlesque; elsewhere, the oration must be recognized as a speech of serious purpose and a work of conscious art.

In this appreciation, then, of what Shakespeare made of the oration in the drama, much credit must be given to classical training in Elizabethan schools. This does not imply, in the slightest degree, failure to recognize the native ability which Shakespeare possessed as a dramatist; his orations make us realize this all the more. But we can also understand how his making the most of the educational opportunities offered him at Stratford led out his inherent ability and furnished the background upon which he drew to write his dramas.

CHAPTER IX

Literary Criticism

"All beginnings are hard," so the saying goes, and literary criticism in England met difficulties at the very outset that prevented it from making much headway in the direction of the establishment of a satisfactory body of literary principles. The Puritan opposition to poetry made those who undertook essays on poetic feel called upon to begin by defending poetry;[1] and, in the case of Lodge and Sidney, the essays were avowedly polemics in defense of the art. The controversy arising out of the question as to the relative merits of rhyme and quantitative verse as the basis of the new English prosody centered attention in large measure on metrics; and, in the case of Campion and Daniel, the essays brought the controversy to a focus.[2] Webbe and Puttenham and Sidney, to a limited extent, undertook to review and evaluate the progress of poetry in England, thus combining discussion of theory with the history of practice; and Sidney, Bacon, and Jonson established unmistakably the viewpoint in England of the best classical traditions of poetic and rhetoric. Wilson had established earlier the viewpoint of the best classical traditions of rhetoric.[3] But even at the end of the Elizabethan

---

1. Lodge's *Defence*, Sidney's *Apology*, Webbe's *A Discourse of English Poetry*, Puttenham's *Arte of English Poesie*.
2. Campion's *Observations on the Art of English Poesie;* Daniel's *Defense of Rime*. See also Webbe and Puttenham, and Gascoigne's *Notes*.
3. Wilson's theory of rhetoric was derived from Cicero and Quintilian. His rhetoric, like other Elizabethan rhetorics and works on logic, shows little if any influence of Aristotle's *Rhetoric*, and then only by way of reference. The only approximation to Aristotle's theory seems to be in Abraham Fraunce's *The Lawiers Lojike;* his *Arcadian Rhetorike* is concerned with elocution and delivery. For a discussion of Aristotle's *Rhetoric*

[217]

period there had been no organized body of theory of poetic established, Jonson's *Discoveries* or *Timber*, as it is sometimes called, being the nearest approach.

Shakespeare had Wilson's *Arte of Rhetorique* as a basis for theory of rhetoric. He had no similar work in English as a basis for theory of poetic. But the study of his use of rhetoric in poetic leads to the belief that he may have been familiar with Aristotle's *Poetics*. In fact, it seems the natural thing to suppose that he came to know it through contact with dramatists who had attended the universities, if he had not known it before. As has been demonstrated, his earliest plays reveal a grasp of Aristotle's principle of organic plot development; his earliest orations reveal a grasp of Aristotle's principle of the "thought" element as an integral part of that plot development. As has already been pointed out, too, the poetic of Shakespeare's plays is a liberalizing and extension of the Aristotelian poetic; his rhetoric in poetic is a revival of the Aristotelian conception of rhetoric in poetic. If Shakespeare had written a critical work of poetic, the basis of it would have been Aristotle's *Poetics*. The question naturally arises: Did he know the *Poetics*, and how may he have come to know it?

A short review of the history of the *Poetics* will be valuable here. From the time of Augustus to the Renaissance, the *Poetics* of Aristotle was in eclipse. Aristotle was not popular with the Romans of the Empire. As Herrick in his introduction to *The Poetics of Aristotle in England* says, "His Poetics and Rhetoric were too philosophical for the practical men of the Empire and too practical for the finedrawn theories of the professional philosophers."[4] Boethius was apparently the last of the Romans to study Aristotle in the Greek; but Boethius was interested in the philosopher,

---

in England to 1600, see L. S. Hultzen's Cornell doctoral dissertation, 1932, of which an abstract has been published.
4. P. 4. See also Cicero, *Treatise on Topics*, I.

not the critic.⁵ In 1483, an original Greek text of the *Poetics* turned up in Italy; Politian owned a manuscript of the work,⁶ and in 1498 appeared the Italian version of Giorgio Valla.⁷

During the early Middle Ages, the works of Aristotle had passed, in the hands of Moslem scholars, from the East into Spain. But they had undergone frequent translation—from Greek into Syriac, Arabic, Castilian, Latin; and consequently the Latin translations of the twelfth century were not very accurate. The taking of Constantinople by the Venetians and Crusaders in 1203-1204 gave to Western Europe in time the original Greek versions, which were translated directly into Latin.⁸ But these Latin translations were poor, and it was difficult to obtain them as well as the Greek copies.⁹

The *Poetics*, however, was still neglected. Even Roger Bacon, by whom it is first mentioned in England, paid little attention to it. As Herrick says, "The learned friar was not specially interested in either rhetoric or poetry, and like medieval scholars, he regarded them as parts of logic and moral philosophy."¹⁰ And in the list of Aristotle's works in use in medieval universities by 1300, the *Rhetoric* and the *Poetics* were prescribed as merely optional texts at the University of Paris.¹¹ The translation of Aristotle by William of Brabant, made under the direction of Thomas Aquinas, included the *Rhetoric* but not the *Poetics*.¹²

Chaucer may have seen a medieval Latin version of the *Poetics*. At any rate, he knew the common medieval tradition

---

5. Herrick's Introduction, p. 2. See also, Boethius, *Commentaries*, ed. Meiser.
6. Lane Cooper, *The Poetics of Aristotle, Its Meaning and Influence*, p. 100. Noted by Herrick, Chap. I, p. 13.
7. For a full list of the editions of the *Poetics*, see L. Cooper and Alfred Gudeman, *Bibliography of the Poetics of Aristotle*.
8. Cubberley gives a good concise account in his *History of Education*, pp. 180-186. See also *Readings*, pp. 127-138.
9. Herrick, *Poetics of Aristotle in England*, Chap. I, p. 8.
10. Herrick, Chap. I, p. 10.
11. Cubberley, *Readings*, p. 136.   12. Herrick, Chap. I, p. 11.

of what tragedy is—a tradition which is reminiscent of the Aristotelian theory of Reversal and Recognition.[13] In *Boethius*, Book II, Prose II, Chaucer translates:

> What other thing biwailen the cryinges of tragedies, but only the dedes of fortune, that with an unwar stroke overtorneth realmes of grete nobley—*Glose*, Tragedie is to seyn, a ditee of a prosperitee for a tyme, that endeth in wrecchednesse.[14]

In Troilus and Criseyde, Pandarus tells Troilus:

> For of fortunes sharp adversitee
> The worst kinde of infortune is this,
> A man to have ben in prosperitee,
> And it remembren when it passed is.[15]

In the Prologue to the "Monk's Tale," the monk says:

> Tragedie is to seyn a certeyn storie,
> As olde bokes maken us memorie,
> Of him that stood in greet prosperitee
> And is y-fallen out of heigh degree
> Into miserie, and endeth wrecchedly.[16]

It may be that the English scholars, Linacre and Latimer, had a part in producing the Great Aldine *Aristotle* in 1495-1498,[17] but this edition omitted the *Poetics*. In 1508 appeared the *Aldine Editio princeps* of the *Poetics* along with the *Rhetoric* in *Rhetores Graeci*.[18] Erasmus had a part in editing the first complete Greek text of Aristotle printed at Basel in 1531.[19] From this time on, the *Poetics* was known at both Oxford and Cambridge, and in the generation of Cheke and Ascham was of interest as a subject for academic

---

13. See *Poetics*, ix, x, xi. See also Cooper, *The Poetics of Aristotle*, p. 92.
14. Noted by Herrick, Chap. I, p. 12.   15. Book III, 1625-1628.
16. 85-89 (B. 3163-3167). Pointed out by Herrick, Chap. I, p. 12.
17. See Herrick, Chap. I, p. 13, and also P. S. Allen, "Linacre and Latimer in Italy," *English Historical Review*, XVIII (1903), 514-17.
18. See Herrick, Chap. I, p. 13, and Cooper and Gudeman, *Bibliography*.
19. Herrick, Chap. I, p. 14. Herrick, Chap. I, pp. 14-34, gives an excellent discussion of the *Poetics* in Renaissance England of the sixteenth century.

discussion. But in the generation of Harvey and the other younger university men, the *Poetics* was generally neglected in favor of Plato and Cicero, the enthusiastic idealist and the impressive orator. Sidney's *Apology*, however, marked the beginning of dramatic criticism in England in the tradition of Aristotle. Sidney's criticism, it is true, was derived through Italian commentators; and, as Herrick puts it, was a "typical Renaissance blend of Aristotle and Horace, with a good measure of Plato thrown in."[20]

But Sidney could easily have known the *Poetics* first-hand; beyond question, he established the Aristotelian point of view in English dramatic criticism in his *Apology*. Herrick thus excellently indicates the main course that literary criticism was to pursue from Sidney on:

For nearly two centuries English criticism was to remain classical and Aristotelian. We must bear in mind, however, that from the first these English interpretations of Aristotle's theories were hopelessly adulterated with Horatian maxims and continental scholarship, first with Italian, then with Dutch, and finally, and most influential of all, with French. We may agree with Robinson's Ben Jonson, and regard it as unfortunate that Shakespeare, for one, could not have studied the *Poetics* at first hand, without the accretions and inflammations from men of less insight than either Aristotle or Shakespeare.[21]

And now, what of Shakespeare? Critics in general have been quite hesitant to admit that Shakespeare may have known the *Poetics*—some of them that he even knew it second-hand from others.[22] Herrick refrains from attempting to

---

20. Chap. I, p. 24.
21. Herrick, Chap. I, p. 34. His chapters II, III, IV follow in detail the story of the *Poetics* in England during the seventeenth and eighteenth centuries. I cannot, however, from my present study, agree entirely with Robinson and Herrick as to Shakespeare's inevitable ignorance of the *Poetics*. (See Edwin Arlington Robinson's "Ben Jonson Entertains a Man From Stratford.")
22. For discussion of Shakespeare's knowledge of the classics, see J. Churton Collins, *Studies in Shakespeare*, Essay I, "Shakespeare as a Classical Scholar," and Essay II, "Sophocles and Shakespeare as Theological and Ethical Teachers." In I, Collins discusses at length echoes of Greek

deduce Shakespeare's principle of dramatic composition, but points out that he was "alive to current dramatic theories,

tragedy in Shakespeare, especially Sophocles. Of particular interest for this study are the following points: Comparisons—the soliloquy of Ajax in *Ajax*, 646-92, and the speech of Jocasta in *Phoenissae*, 528-85, with orations of Agamemnon, Nestor, and Ulysses in *Troilus and Cressida*, I, iii.—pp. 61-62. "The development of the author (Shakespeare) . . . is at least difficult to explain as merely the natural result of maturer powers. If this was the case, we must assume that instinct led Shakespeare to the Greek conception of the scope and functions of tragedy, and that by a certain natural affinity he caught also the accent and tone as well as some of the most striking characteristics of Greek Tragedy."—pp. 86-87. "That with most scrupulous care Shakespeare has, with the exception of his immature works, notably *Richard III*, observed these canons (Aristotle's) will be evident to anyone who will consider the protagonists of his mature tragedies."—p. 86. "Differences (between Greek and Shakespearean tragedy) lie mainly in the fact that what is presented in the one is presented in elaborate miniature, and that what is presented in the other is presented in broad bold fresco; in other words, that simplicity and concentration are the notes of the one, comprehensiveness and discursiveness the notes of the other. Much has been made of the Unities. In reading the *Agamemnon* and the *Eumenides*, the *Antigone*, the *Trachiniae*, the *Suppliants* of Euripides, and at least half a dozen other plays, Shakespeare would most certainly not have discerned the existence of the Unity of time. In the *Eumenides* and in the *Ajax* he would have seen the unity of Place equally disregarded. With regard to the unity of Action it is practically observed as faithfully in his tragedies as it is in those of Sophocles. Where it is apparently violated, as in his so-called double plots, this is simply to be attributed to the colossal scale on which the action is presented and developed. Occasionally, as in *Richard III*, *Macbeth*, and the *Tempest*, where the plot is as simple and concentrated as that of a typical Greek drama, it is exactly observed."—p. 90. For more extended reading on this extensive and controversial subject of Shakespeare's classical learning, see William Theobald, *The Classical Element in the Shakespeare Plays*—from the viewpoint of a Baconian; William Francis C. Wigston, *A New Study of Shakespeare*—an inquiry into the connection of the plays and poems with the origins of the classical drama, and the Platonic philosophy through the Mysteries; Paul Stapfer, *Shakespeare and Classical Antiquity*, trans. Emily Carey—Greek and Latin antiquity, as presented in Shakespeare's plays; Richard Farmer, *An Essay on the Learning of Shakespeare*—thinks him Nature's poet, and ridicules those who think him learned in the classics; Peter Whalley, *An Enquiry into the Learning of Shakespeare, with remarks on several passages of his plays* —the opposite extreme of belief in Shakespeare's wide acquaintance with the classics. This line of study leads ultimately to the controversy over the identity of the author of the Shakespeare plays. My study makes no venture into this field. The arguments of the Baconians and Oxfordians have been of interest however in connection with the results of my investigation; in particular, the following: Delia Bacon, *The Philosophy of the*

particularly after the year 1598, when he became acquainted with Ben Jonson."²³

Herrick points out further Shakespeare's apologies for his violations of the "rules" of the current dramatic theories,²⁴ and the striking parallel to be found between Aristotle's criticism of excessive gesture and Hamlet's advice on acting and his insistence on restraint.²⁵ He also thinks that there may be a reminiscence of Aristotle's *Poetics* in *Richard II*, Act 5:

> Tell thou the lamentable tale of me,
> And send the hearers weeping to their beds,
> For why, the senseless brands will sympathize
> The heavy accent of thy moving tongue
> And in compassion weep the fire out.

This study has already committed itself to an impression of Shakespeare's principles of dramatic composition, which are felt conclusively to be essentially Aristotelian; so faithful is he to the dramatic theories of Aristotle, that the natural conclusion must be that he may very likely have known Aristotle's *Poetics* first-hand, at least in Latin. At any rate, being either consciously or unconsciously Aristotelian, he apologized for violations of the "rules" of neo-Aristotelian criticism and practice which were current in his day.²⁶

It is reassuring to find others sharing this natural appreciation of Shakespeare's dramatic practice. But it took two

---

Plays of Shakespeare Unfolded, Book I, Part II, pp. 63-172, "The Baconian Rhetoric, or the Method of Progression," particularly pp. 87-91 on the definition and function of rhetoric; Percy Allen, *The Case for Edward de Vere, 17th Earl of Oxford, as "Shakespeare"*; Percy Allen, *The Life Story of Edward de Vere as "William Shakespeare."*

23. P. 33.
24. P. 32: Chorus in *Henry V*, Act II; Chorus in *Henry V*, Act V; Chorus, *Winter's Tale*, Act IV.   25. P. 33, note.
26. In the *Eumenides* of Aeschylus, months or years elapse between the opening of the play and the next scene; and the *Trachiniae* of Sophocles and the *Supplices* of Euripides violate the "rule." These lapses of time in Greek drama are noted by Butcher in *Aristotle's Theory of Poetry and Fine Art*, p. 291. See also Baldwin, *ARP*, pp. 158-166, especially p. 162. Jonson violates the unities: note the apology in Preface to *Sejanus* (noted by Herrick, Chap. II, p. 40).

centuries for this kind of appreciation to establish itself in England. The neo-classical critics of the seventeenth and eighteenth centuries naturally found themselves in a difficult situation when trying to criticize Shakespeare. They had either to attempt to riddle his matchless dramas as Rymer tried to do,[27] in order to make out a case for their neo-classical criticism, or admit they were unable to undertake the job, as Rowe wisely did:

> But as Shakespeare lived under a kind of mere light of nature, and had never been made acquainted with the regularity of those written precepts, so it would be hard to judge him by a law he knew nothing of.[28]

As has just been indicated, there are passages in Shakespeare which lead to the belief that he knew something of the new-Aristotelian "law" indeed; but he fashioned his dramas according to the "regularity" of Aristotelian criticism, which his "mere light of nature" enabled him to comprehend and follow where his contemporaries failed.

But bit by bit, here and there, in this period dominated by neo-classical criticism, the natural appreciation of Shakespeare seems to break through. It had to come in spite of an inhibiting attitude of apology and hesitancy in admitting the genius of Shakespeare in the face of "rules" which even the critics recognized were unreasonably severe when it came to practice.[29] But the inhibition was accompanied by a growing

27. See the translation of Rapin's *Reflexions sur la poétique d'Aristote* (1674); *Tragedies of the Last Age; Short View of Tragedy.* Discussed by Herrick, Chap. II, pp. 57-63.
28. *Some Account of the Life of Mr. William Shakespeare*, p. xxvi. Noted by Herrick, Chap. III, p. 96.
29. I have already referred to Jonson, and Corneille also recognized the difficulty of observing the "rules." See *Œuvres de Corneille avec les Commentaires de Voltaire*, Tome X—the three lectures on drama, especially the third, "Des Trois Unités." I quote two significant passages from this lecture: "La règle de l'unité de jour a son fondement sur ce mot d'Aristote que la tragédie doit renfermer la durée de son action dans un tour du soleil, ou tâcher de ne lé passer pas de beaucoup." p. 105. As Butcher notes (*Aristotle's Theory of Poetry and Fine Art*, p. 293) Corneille and d'Aubignac translate πειρᾶται (endeavours) by *doit* (must); and Butcher

feeling that Aristotle—certainly the Aristotle of the neo-classicists—had not said the last word in the *Poetics* on the subject of dramatic composition, particularly in the matter of comedy. And the greatest critics recognized and admitted the genius of Shakespeare, but recognized it as genius either ignorant of or indifferent to the "rules." To Milton, he was

> Sweetest Shakespeare, Fancy's child
> Warbles his native wood-notes wild.

And when Milton states his theories of poetic in his prose[30] and exemplifies them, as to drama, in his *Samson Agonistes*, we understand easily that the Elizabethan drama, including Shakespeare, he regarded as immature and crude from the standpoint of fine art.[31]

Dryden, in *An Essay of Dramatic Poetry*, gives us interesting glimpses of the struggle that went on whenever a neo-classicist undertook to write literary criticism about Shakespeare. First, from Crites:

I must remember you, that all the rules by which we practice the drama at this day (either such as relate to the justness and symmetry of the plot; or the episodical ornaments, such as descrip-

---

points out (p. 297) that Corneille admitted he found no such precept in Aristotle as the unity of place: "Quant à l'unité de lieu, je n'en trouve aucun précept ni dans Aristote, ni dans Horace."—p. 110. Dryden also admitted that few modern plays would endure trial if judged by the "rules" (*Dramatic Poesy*, ed. Ker, p. 41).

30. Milton in his "Tractate on Education" says: "To which (logic and rhetoric) poetry would be made subsequent or indeed rather precedent, as being less subtile and fine, but more simple, sensuous, and passionate. I mean not here the prosody of verse, which they could not but have hit on before among the rudiments of grammar; but that sublime art which in Aristotle's *Poetics*, in Horace, and the Italian commentaries of Castelvetro, Tasso, Mazzoni, and others, teaches what the laws are of a true epic poem; what of dramatic; what of a lyric; what decorum is; which is the grand masterpiece to observe. This would make them soon perceive what despicable creatures our common rhymers and play-writers be; and shew them what religious, what glorious and magnificent use may be made of poetry both in divine and human things." Myers edition, pp. 89-90. See also Preface to *Samson Agonistes*.

31. For a discussion of Milton's poetic, see Ida Langdon, *Milton's Theory of Poetry and Fine Art*.

tions, narrations, and other beauties, which are not essential to the play) were delivered to us from the observations which Aristotle made of these poets, who either lived before him or were his contemporaries. We have added nothing of our own, except we have the confidence to say, our own, better; of which none boast in this our age, but such as understand not theirs. Of that book which Aristotle has left us, περι τῆς ποιητικῆς, Horace his *Art of Poetry* is an excellent comment, and, I believe, restores to us that Second Book of his concerning comedy, which is wanting in him.

Out of these two have been extracted the famous "rules" which the French call *Des Trois Unités,* or the three unities, which ought to be observed in every regular play, namely, of time, place, and action.[32]

This rule of time, how well it has been observed by the ancients most of their plays will witness. You see them in their tragedies (wherein to follow this rule is certainly most difficult).[33]

Then from Eugenius:

I deny not what you urge of arts and sciences, that they have flourished in some ages more than others; but your instance in philosophy makes for me; for if natural causes be more known now than in the time of Aristotle, because more studied, it follows that poesy and other arts may, with the same pains, arrive still nearer to perfection; and, that granted, it will rest for you to prove that they wrought more perfect images of human life, than we; which seeing in your discourse you have avoided to make good, it shall now be my task to show you some part of their defects, and some few excellencies of the moderns.[34]

But, in the first place, give me leave to tell you, that the unity of place, however it might be practiced by them, was never any

32. Ker's edition, p. 38. And then Dryden devoted a paragraph to the usual neo-classical interpretation of the ancient observation as to the matter of dramatic time—very restrictive interpretation indeed, and calculated to squeeze dramatic action to the limit so far as time goes.

33. Ker's edition, p. 39. And then begins in the next paragraph the discussion of the Unity of Place. But what Dryden discusses is, of course, the cramping French dictum about dramatic place. His discussion of the unity of action Dryden begins rather unpromisingly: "As for the third Unity, which is that of Action, the Ancients meant no other by it than what the logicians do by their *finis,* the end or scope of any action." But he fortunately gets away from this misleading beginning to give a sensible discussion of the unity of action, as Corneille also gives.

34. Ker's edition, p. 44.

of their rules; we neither find it in Aristotle, Horace, or any who have written of it, till in our own age the French poets first made it a precept of the stage.³⁵

Then from Neander:

> To begin then with Shakspere. He was the man Who of all modern and perhaps ancient poets, had the largest and most comprehensive soul. All the images of nature were still present to him, and he drew them not laboriously, but luckily; when he describes anything, you more than see it, you feel it too. Those who accuse him to have wanted learning, give him the greater commendation. He was naturally learned; he needed not the spectacles of books to read nature; he looked inwards, and found her there.³⁶
>
> If I would compare him (Jonson) with Shakspere, I must acknowledge him the more correct poet, but Shakspere the greater wit. Shakspere was the Homer or father of our dramatic poets; Jonson was the Virgil, the pattern of elaborate writing. I admire him, but I love Shakspere.³⁷

More striking still is the struggle when the traditionally ponderous Dr. Johnson waxes evangelical in his Preface to the Edition of Shakespeare. In his effort to stand by the "rules" of the neo-classicists and at the same time emphasize the genius of Shakespeare, Dr. Johnson inevitably gives expression to many conflicting sentiments. After spending many pages in eulogy of Shakespeare as a dramatist, he launches into what we at first fear is going to be a very militant discussion of Shakespeare's faults; but while he admits that Shakespeare has been guilty of violations of neo-classical laws, he more than makes out a case in defense of Shakespeare. We point out some of the strikingly conflicting statements in the course of the preface. After writing (p. ix),³⁸

---

35. Ker's edition, p. 48. And then Dryden points out violations by the ancients: Terence and Euripides.
36. Ker's edition, pp. 79-80. This comes after Neander's ringing defense of the English stage.
37. Ker's edition, pp. 82-83.
38. The 1765 edition has been used.

"Real power is shown by the progress of his fable and the tenour of his dialogue," Dr. Johnson cites as a fault that his plots are loosely and aimlessly constructed; and then later writes (p. xxiv), "His plan has commonly what Aristotle requires, a beginning, a middle, and an end; one event is concatenated with another and the conclusion follows by easy consequence." Again, after citing as a fault, Shakespeare's disregard for the unities of time and place, Dr. Johnson not only defends Shakespeare's violations of these unities but also later ventures the opinion that the unities of time and place will finally be ruled out. And then he goes on to take the position (p. xxix), "Whether Shakespeare knew the unities and rejected them by design or deviated from them by happy ignorance, it is, I think, impossible to decide and useless to inquire."

Among the minor critics who were, without fully realizing it perhaps, the forerunners of the great critics of the Romantic period to follow, we find an ever-growing dissension from the authority of Aristotle as a last word in dramatic criticism, and impatience with the restrictions of the neo-Aristotelians. Fielding, recognizing the difference between Aristotle and the neo-classical commentators, took a crack at them in *Tom Thumb*.[39] Henry Pemberton, in his *Observations on Poetry*, took issue with Aristotle to the extent of contending that the drama is the only form of art that is imitative; that character, not plot, is the main consideration in drama; and that epic is a higher form of poetic art than tragedy.[40] Sir Richard Blackmore recognized Aristotle's claim to genius, but refused to consider him the last word in poetic.[41] Hurd, Aristotelian as to drama, represented the growing tendency to harmonize

39. Noted by Herrick, Chap. IV, p. 113.
40. Noted by Herrick, Chap. III, p. 98. See sections 1, 2, and 3 on epic and dramatic poetry, pp. 4-45. This on Shakespeare is of value: "Who with the greatest imperfections and even absurdities in the plans of his fable, has executed his characters in a manner scarce to be rivalled." p. 8.
41. Herrick, Chap. III, p. 98.

classical theory and romantic practice.[42] John Upton, in *Critical Observations of Shakespeare*, admits, as Dr. Johnson does, that Shakespeare disregards the unities of time and place, but believes that he obeys the unity of action.[43]

From 1750 on, Shakespearean criticism assumed more and more emphatically the position which it has maintained to the present time. Lessing pioneered in emancipating German criticism from the restraints of neo-classicism. At the end of the eighty-first section of the *Hamburgische Dramaturgie*, he gives this challenging statement as to his position with respect to the French dramatists and Shakespeare, and their relation to Aristotle:

Verschiedene französische Tragödien sind sehr feine, sehr unterrichtende Werke, die ich alles Lobes wert halte: nur dass sie keine Tragödien sind. Die Verfasser derselben konnten nicht anders, alles, als sehr gute Köpfe sein; sie verdienen, zum Teil, unter den Dichtern keinen geringen Rang; nur dass sie keine tragische Dichter sind; nur dass ihr Corneille und Racine, ihr Crebillon und Voltaire von dem wenig oder gar nichts haben, was den Sophokles zum Sophokles, den Euripides zum Euripides, den Shakespear zum Shakespear macht. Diese sind selten mit den wesentlichen Forderungen des Aristoteles im Widerspruch; aber jene desto "öfterer."[44]

42. *Letters on Chivalry and Romance* (*Works*, Vol. IV). See particularly this about Shakespeare at the end of Letter 7 (pp. 294-295): "I shall add nothing to what I before observed of Shakespear because the sublimity (the divinity, let it be if nothing else will serve) of his genius kept no certain rout, but rambled at hazard into all the regions of human life and manners. So that we can hardly say what he preferred, or what he rejected on full deliberation. Yet one thing is clear, that even he is greater when he uses Gothic manners and machinery than when he employs classical, which brings us again to the same point, that the former have, by their nature and genius, the advantages of the latter in producing the sublime." See also, in Vol. II: "On the Idea of Universal Poetry" (Aristotelian in the main); "Provinces of the Drama" (Aristotelian—action the main element in tragedy; character, in comedy—the section on comedy intended to supply the lack of discussion in Aristotle); "Discourse on Poetical Imitation" (Aristotelian); "Marks of Imitation" (means of detecting one author's indebtedness to another or to other works).

43. Book I, Sect. 5, pp. 26-27. Noted by Herrick, Chap. III, pp. 110-111.

44. Lessing's *Hamburgische Dramaturgie*, abridged and edited by Charles

Schlegel, after expressing his amusement at the efforts to claim Aristotle as authority to sanction the three unities of the neo-classicists, commits himself to the belief that Shakespeare was Aristotelian in the matter of dramatic composition. In the ninth lecture of the *Vorlesungen über Dramatische Kunst und Literatur*, he says:

> Diese war eine sehr günstige Aeusserung für die Compositionen Shakespeares und anderer romantischer Dramatiker, die einen umfassenderen Kreis von Leben, Characteren und Begebenheiten als die einfache griechische Tragödie in ein einziges Gemählde zusammengestellt haben, falls sie ihm nur die nöthige Einheit zu geben und die klare Übersicht zu erhalten gewusst, welches beiden wir allerdings von ihnen behaupten.[45]
>
> Diese Einheit finde ich in den tragischen Compositionen Shakespeares eben so vollkommen als in denen des Aeschylus und Sophokles; ich vermisse sie dagegen in manchen von der zergliedernden Kritik als korrekt gepriesenen Tragödien.[46]

And with Lessing and Schlegel stood the other great German romantic critics, Herder and Schiller and Goethe.[47] In

---

Harris, p. 228. This is Harris's translation: "Several French tragedies are very fine, very instructive works, which I consider worthy of all praise; only they are not tragedies. Their authors were certainly clever persons, they deserve, in part, no low rank among poets, only they are not tragic poets; only their Corneille, and Racine, their Crebillon and Voltaire, have very little or nothing at all of that which makes Sophocles Sophocles, Euripides Euripides, Shakespeare Shakespeare. The latter are seldom in opposition to the essential demands of Aristotle, but the former so much the oftener." Introduction, pp. xxvi-xxvii.

45. A. W. von Schlegel, *Vorlesungen über Dramatische Kunst und Literatur*, ed. Giovanni Vittorio Amoretti, Band II, pp. 8-9. Translation by John Black: "This opinion would be highly favourable for the compositions of Shakespeare and other romantic poets, who have included a much more extensive circle of life, character, and events in one picture, than is to be found in the simple Greek tragedy, if we could only show that they have given it the necessary unity and such a magnitude as can be clearly taken in at a view, and this we can have no hesitation in affirming to have been actually done by them." I, 329.

46. Schlegel, *Vorlesungen*, Band II, p. 14. Translation by Black: "I find this unity in the tragical compositions of Shakespeare in as great perfection as in those of Aeschylus and Sophocles; while on the contrary, I do not find it in many of those tragedies extolled as correct by the critics of the dissecting school." I, 337.

47. For discussions of the criticism of Goethe, Schiller, and Herder, see:

England, Coleridge, following the lead of the German critics, established for Shakespeare's own countrymen the triumph of the romanticists over the neo-classicists. In Chapter XXIII of *Biographia Literaria,* Coleridge says:

> It was Lessing who first introduced the name and the works of Shakespeare to the admiration of the Germans; and I should not perhaps go too far, if I add, that it was Lessing who first proved to all thinking men, even to Shakespeare's own countrymen, the true nature of his apparent irregularities. These, he demonstrated, were deviations only from the *accidents* of the Greek tragedy; and from such accidents as hung a heavy weight on the wings of the Greek poets, and narrowed their flight within the limits of what we may call the *heroic opera.* He proved, that, in all the essentials of art, no less than in the truth of nature, the plays of Shakespeare were incomparably more coincident with the principles of Aristotle, than the productions of Corneille and Racine, notwithstanding the boasted regularity of the latter.[48]

Since Coleridge's day, Shakespearean scholarship, in England and America, has gone far in appreciation of Shakespeare's dramatic art. The study of texts and the study of his times, the study of Elizabethan drama before and after Shakespeare, and the study of Shakespearean drama as a

---

R. H. Hutton, "Goethe and His Influence," *Essays in Literary Criticism;* Herman Ulrici, *Shakespeare's Dramatic Art and Its Relation to Calderon and Goethe,* trans. A. J. W. Morrison; Paul Emerson Titsworth, "The Attitude of Goethe and Schiller Toward French Classic Drama," *JEGP,* XI (Oct., 1912), 509-564; Hertha Isaacsen, *Der Junge Herder und Shakespeare.* See also Goethe's essays on epic and dramatic poetry; Schiller's "Über die Tragische Kunst"; and Herder's "Shakespear" in *Von Deutscher Art und Kunst,* ed. Edna Purdie.

48. P. 304 of "Everyman" edition. Noted by Raysor in his Introduction (p. xxvi) to the edition of Coleridge's *Shakespearean Criticism.* Raysor goes on to say: "Coleridge's tribute seems to indicate that he had forgotten or never known the English critics who had emphasized the art of Shakespeare and that he had perhaps combined his memories of Lessing and Schlegel. The "weight on the wings of the Greek poets" sounds much more like Schlegel than Lessing; and Lessing rather suggested than "demonstrated" or "proved" the views of Shakespeare which Coleridge justly attributes to him. Coleridge seems to imply, moreover, that he, like Lessing, reconciled the admiration of Shakespeare with Aristotelian principles. This is not the case, for Coleridge rather follows Schlegel in treating Shakespearean and Greek drama as two equally admirable but opposite types."

part of this Elizabethan drama have clarified and enhanced the achievements of Shakespeare, and have been indispensable to a right appreciation of his dramatic art. Recently there has been a revival of interest in Aristotle's *Poetics*; studies by Butcher, Bywater, Lane Cooper, and Marvin Herrick have opened new avenues of approach to Shakespeare. All through the nineteenth and into the twentieth century, critics have been impressed with the unity of action to be found in Shakespeare's plays—in other words, plot structure. And Butcher in his *Aristotle's Theory of Poetry and Fine Art,* makes some interesting observations:

If unity of action is preserved, the other unities will take care of themselves.

Years may elapse between successive acts without the unity being destroyed as we see from *The Winter's Tale.*[49]

Shakespeare deals freely, and as he will, with place and time; yet he is generally nearer to the doctrine of the *Poetics* than those who fancied they wrote in strict accordance with the rules of the treatise.[50]

Lane Cooper has gone one step farther. He has also undertaken an interpretation of Aristotle's poetic in *The Poetics of Aristotle, Its Meaning and Influence,* from which come some pertinent observations about Shakespeare:

It is a question how much Shakespeare knew about the "rules" till near the end of his career; but he could not have been produced without the Italian dramatists and critics, his forerunners, who studied Aristotle, and diffused the knowledge of classical drama that was in the air.[51]

Sidney, ushering in the great age of Elizabethan poetry, must have been read by Shakespeare's friends and contemporaries often with the Italian critics, and sometimes with the *Poetics* itself; Jonson, however, is mainly dependent upon the interpretation of Heinsius. Shakespeare did not escape the current talk about the unities.[52]

49. P. 299.
50. P. 300. Compare Butcher's views with what has been said in Chapter VI.
51. Chap. IX, p. 118. 52. Chap. XII, p. 133.

Literary Criticism

In truth, Shakespeare, though more Roman than Greek in his dramatic origins, is nearer than the formalists to Aristotle and the spirit of Greek tragedy. His friend Ben Jonson, translator of the *Ars Poetica* of Horace, is in tragedy far more like Seneca. Jonson hardly assimilated much from the *Poetics* before 1611. Some time thereafter he paraphrased bits of Heinsius, in his *Discoveries*; here, not in the English critics between Sidney and Jonson, the *Poetics* begins to be understood, and we wonder what Shakespeare might have learnt from it, could he have known it as he did Ovid, or Seneca, and Plautus.[53]

In addition, Lane Cooper has given us *Aristotle On Comedy*. Using, as a suggestive guide, the interesting tenth-century manuscript *(Tractatus Coislianus)*[54] outlining a theory of comedy, Lane Cooper works out an Aristotelian treatise on comedy by applying to comedy the principles of the *Poetics* for tragedy. This will probably prove to be one of the most valuable contributions to Shakespearean scholarship.

With this background of literary criticism, our impressions of Shakespeare's rhetoric in poetic become surer and more distinct. As to Shakespeare's first-hand knowledge of the *Poetics*, at present the impressions derived from a study of the oration in his plays will be relied upon.[55] This study

53. Chap. XII, p. 134.
54. Very reasonably, I think, regarded as Aristotelian.
55. The reference to Aristotle by Hector in *Troilus and Cressida*, ed. W. J. Rolfe, II, ii, is of interest:

>Paris and Troilus, you have both said well,
>And on the cause and question now in hand
>Have gloz'd, but superficially; not much
>Unlike young men, whom Aristotle thought
>Unfit to hear moral philosophy.

Rolfe has this note: "Aside from the anachronism common enough in Shakespeare, there is a mistake which Bacon has also made in the *Advancement of Learning*, iii: 'Is not the opinion of Aristotle worthy that young men are not fit auditors of moral philosophy because they are not settled from the boiling heat of their affections, nor attempered with time and experience?' As Mr. Ellis has pointed out, it is not of moral but of political philosophy that Aristotle speaks. It is possible that Shakespeare may have taken the allusion from Bacon's book, which was published in 1605. Judge Holmes (authorship of Shakespeare) of course tries to make the coincidence tell in favour of the Baconian theory. It is curious that Virgilio Malvezzi, in his *Discorsi sopra Cornelio Tacito*, 1622, makes the

makes us believe that he more than likely knew it first-hand in Latin; maybe, later in life, in Greek. At any rate, his plays reveal an application of the principles of the *Poetics*, not only in tragedy, but in comedy and history play as well.

Shakespeare has left us merely his plays from which we may judge of him as a critic of poetic. But he has left us in addition to the rhetoric in his plays, several passages which seem easily capable of being interpreted as suggestive of his criticism of rhetoric. *Love's Labour's Lost* establishes unmistakably Shakespeare's attitude as a critic of rhetoric. This play is full of evidences that Shakespeare perceived the weakness of the rhetorical drama as drama, and the inferiority of mere word-display as rhetoric. The following passages are suggestive of criticism of rhetoric:

I, i, 165-180

King. A man in all the world's new fashion planted,
That hath a mint of phrases in his brain;
One who the music of his own vain tongue
Doth ravish like enchanting harmony;
A man of complements, whom right and wrong
Have chose as umpire of their mutiny.
This child of fancy, that Armado hight,
For interim to our studies shall relate,
In high-born words, the worth of many a knight
From tawny Spain, lost in the world's debate.
How you delight, my lords, I know not, I;
But I protest, I love to hear him lie,
And I will use him for my minstrelsy.
Bir. Armado is a most illustrious wight,
A man of fire-new words, fashion's own knight.
Long. Costard, the swain, and he shall be our sport;

---

same mistake: 'e non e discordante da questa mia opinione Aristotele, il qua dice, che i giovani non sono buoni ascultatori delle Morali.' Other instances of it have been pointed out." Rowe suggested the revision: "whom graver sages thought." This revision is noted by Ronald B. McKerrow in "The Treatment of Shakespeare's Text by His Earlier Editors, 1709-1768," *Proceedings of the British Academy: Annual Shakespeare Lecture,* 1933.

II, i, 13-19

Prin. Good Lord Boyet, my beauty, though but mean,
Needs not the painted flourish of your praise.
Beauty is bought by judgement of the eye,
Not utt'red by base sale of chapmen's tongues.
I am less proud to hear you tell my worth
Than you much willing to be counted wise
In spending your wit in the praise of mine.

II, i, 69-76

Ros. His eye begets occasion for his wit,
For every object that the one doth catch
The other turns to a mirth-moving jest,
Which his fair tongue, conceit's expositor,
Delivers in such apt and gracious words
That aged ears play truant at his tales,
And younger hearings are quite ravished,
So sweet and voluble is his discourse.

II, i, 225-230

Prin. Good wits will be jangling; but, gentles, agree.
This civil war of wits were much better used
On Navarre and his book-men; for here 'tis abused.

Boyet. If my observation, which very seldom lies,
By the heart's still rhetoric disclosed with eyes,
Deceive me not now, Navarre is infected.

III, i, 62-66

Moth. You are too swift, sir, to say so.
Is that lead slow which is fir'd from a gun?

Arm. Sweet smoke of rhetoric!
He reputes me a cannon; and the bullet that's he;
I shoot thee at the swain.

IV, ii, 152-155

Nath. Sir, you have done this in the fear of God,
very religiously; and as a certain father saith,—

Hol. Sir, tell not me of the father;
I do fear colourable colours.

IV, iii, 60-62

Long. (reads the sonnet)
    "Did not the heavenly rhetoric of thine eye,
    'Gainst whom the world cannot hold argument,
    Persuade my heart to this false perjury?"

V, ii, 315-320

Bir. This fellow pecks up wit as pigeons pease,
    And utters it again when God doth please.
    He is wit's pedler, and retails his wares
    At wakes and wassails, meetings, markets, fairs:
    And we that sell by gross, the Lord doth know,
    Have not the grace to grace it with such show.

V, ii, 402-413

Bir. O, never will I trust to speeches penn'd
    Nor to the motion of a school-boy's tongue,
    Nor never come in vizard to my friend,
    Nor woo in rhyme like a blind harper's song.
    Taffeta phrases, silken terms precise,
    Three-piled hyperboles, spruce affectation,
    Figures pedantical; these summer flies
    Have blown me full of maggot ostentation,
    I do forswear them, and I here protest,
    By this white glove,—how white the hand, God knows!—
    Henceforth my wooing mind shall be express'd
    In russet yeas and honest kersey noes;

This last passage from Biron might well be taken as expressive of Shakespeare's own promise to break with the prevailing rhetorical drama of his day and with the sophistic rhetoric which was universally popular in Elizabethan literature.

In Act I, scene i, line 123 of *Comedy of Errors*, the Duke tells Aegeon:

    Do me the favour to dilate at full.

This is reminiscent of the "dilation at the full" of sophistic rhetoric.[56] Dilation at the full is the more characteristic way

---

56. See Baldwin, *Medieval Rhetoric and Poetic*, p. 17.

of describing sophistic amplification. Shakespeare must have chuckled, when he wrote this line. The criticism is outspoken and given at some length in *Midsummer Night's Dream* (V, i, 93-105):

The. Where I have come, great clerks have purposed
To greet me with premeditated welcomes;
Where I have seen them shiver and look pale,
Make periods in the midst of sentences,
Throttle their practis'd accent in their fears.
And in conclusion dumbly have broke off,
Not paying me a welcome. Trust me, sweet,
Out of this silence yet I pick'd a welcome;
And in the modesty of fearful duty
I read as much as from the rattling tongue
Of saucy and audacious eloquence.
Love, therefore, and tongue-ti'd simplicity
In least speak most, to my capacity.

Again in *Merchant of Venice* (III, ii, 73-80):

Bass. So may the outward shows be least themselves;
The world is still deceiv'd with ornament.
In law, what plea so tainted and corrupt
But, being season'd with a gracious voice,
Obscures the show of evil? In religion,
What damned error but some sober brow
Will bless it and approve it with a text,
Hiding the grossness with fair ornament?

Troilus brings to mind sophistic rhetoric—and in a letter too—when he blurts out (V, iii, 108-109):

Words, words, mere words, no matter from the heart;
The effect doth operate another way.

Claudio's words recall to mind the finer classical tradition when he says (*Measure for Measure*, I, ii, 182-191):

This day my sister should the cloister enter
And there receive her approbation.
Acquaint her with the danger of my state;
Implore her, in my voice, that she make friends

> To the strict deputy; bid herself assay him.
> I have great hope in that; for in her youth
> There is a prone and speechless dialect,
> Such as move men; beside she hath prosperous art
> When she will play with reason and discourse,
> And well she can persuade.

Paulina makes us think of both types of rhetoric (*Winter's Tale*, II, ii, 33-35, 38-39, 41-42):

> If I prove honey-mouth'd, let my tongue blister
> And never to my red-look'd anger be
> The trumpet any more.
>
> I'll show 't the King and undertake to be
> Her advocate to the loud'st.
>
> The silence often of pure innocence
> Persuades when speaking fails.

In *1 Henry IV* (II, iv, 422 ff.), Falstaff recalls the histrionic actor and his Senecan rhetoric:

> Give me a cup of sack to make my eyes look red,
> that it may be thought I have wept; for I must
> speak in passion, and I will do it in King
> Cambyses' vein.

1 Henry VI furnishes the following passages suggestive of criticism:

I, i, 76-77

1 Mess. A third thinks, without expense at all,
By guileful fair words peace may be obtain'd.

III, iii, 17-20

Puc. Then thus it must be; this doth Joan devise;
By fair persuasions mix'd with sug'red words
We will entice the Duke of Burgundy
To leave the Talbot and to follow us.

III, i, 1-7

Win. Com'st thou with deep premeditated lines,
With written pamphlets studiously devis'd,
Humphrey of Gloucester? If thou canst accuse,

> Or aught intend'st to lay unto my charge,
> Do it without invention, suddenly;
> As I with sudden and extemporal speech
> Purpose to answer that thou canst object.

From *2 Henry VI* come the following:

> I, i, 104-106; 156-157

Car. Nephew, what means this passionate discourse,
　　　This peroration with such circumstance?
　　　. . . . .
　　　Look to it, Lords! Let not his smoothing words
　　　Bewitch your hearts.

> V, i, 191

Queen. A subtle traitor needs no sophister.

3 Henry VI offers the following:

> III, i, 33-34, 48-50

K. Henry. For Warwick is a subtle orator,
　　　And Lewis a prince soon won with moving words.

　　　Whiles Warwick tells his title, smooths the wrong,
　　　Inferreth arguments of mighty strength,
　　　And in conclusion wins the King from her.

Richard III furnishes another reminder of the histrionic actor (III, v, 1-11):

Glou. Come, cousin, canst thou quake, and change thy colour,
　　　Murder thy breath in middle of a word,
　　　And then again begin, and stop again,
　　　As if thou were distraught and mad with terror?

Buck. Tut, I can counterfeit the deep tragedian;
　　　Speak and look back, and pry on every side,
　　　Tremble and start at wagging of a straw,
　　　Intending deep suspicion. Ghastly looks
　　　Are at my service, like enforced smiles;
　　　And both are ready in their offices,
　　　At any time, to grace my stratagems.

Another passage suggestive of criticism comes in Act IV, scene iv, lines 124-131 of *Richard III*:

Q. Eliz. My words are dull; O, quicken them with thine!
Q. Marg. Thy woes will make them sharp, and pierce like
       mine.   (exit)
Duch. Why should calamity be full of words?
Q. Eliz. Windy attorneys to their client woes,
       Airy succeeders of intestate joys,
       Poor breathing orators of miseries,
       Let them have scope! though what they will impart
       Help nothing else, yet do they ease the heart.

Julius Caesar contains the following criticism (III, i, 39-43):

Caes.   Be not fond
       To think that Caesar bears such rebel blood
       That will be thaw'd from the true quality
       With that which melteth fools; I mean, sweet words,
       Low-crooked curtsies and base Spaniel-fawning.

Shakespeare puts into the mouth of Lartius (*Coriolanus*, I, iv, 58-61) a brief and pointed description of Marcius that recalls the histrionic actor and Senecan rhetoric:

                 With thy grim looks and
       The thunder-like percussion of thy sounds,
       Thou mad'st thine enemies shake, as if the world
       Were feverous and did tremble.

As conclusion, part of the extended criticism in *Hamlet* is quoted:

II, ii

Ham. We'll have a speech straight.
   Come, give us a taste of your quality; come, a passionate
   speech.
1 Play. What speech, my lord?
Ham. I heard thee speak me a speech once, but it was never
   acted; or, if it was, not above once. For the play, I remember, pleas'd not the million; 't was caviare to the general; but it was—as I receiv'd it, and others, whose judgement in

such matters cried in the top of mine—an excellent play, well digested in the scenes, set down with as much modesty as cunning. I remember one said, there were no sallets in the lines to make the matter savoury, nor no matter in the phrase that might indict the author of affectation; but call'd it an honest method, as wholesome as sweet, and by very much more handsome than fine. One speech in it I chiefly lov'd; 't was Aeneas' tale to Dido, and thereabout of it especially where he speaks of Priam's slaughter. If it live in your memory, begin at this line: let me see, let me see.

III, ii

Ham. Speak the speech, I pray you, as I pronounc'd it to you, trippingly on the tongue; but if you mouth it, as many of your players do, I had as lief the town-crier spoke my lines. Nor do not saw the air too much with your hand thus, but use all gently; for in the very torrent, tempest, and, as I may say, the whirlwind of passion, you must acquire and beget a temperance that may give it smoothness. O, it offends me to the soul to see a robustious periwig-pated fellow tear a passion to tatters, to very rags, to split the ears of the groundlings, who for the most part are capable of nothing but inexplicable dumb-shows and noise. I could have such a fellow whipp'd for o'erdoing Termagant. It out-herods Herod. Pray you, avoid it.

1 Play. I warrant your honour.

Ham. Be not too tame neither, but let your own discretion be your tutor. Suit the action to the word, the word to the action; with this special observance, that you o'erstep not the modesty of nature. For anything so overdone is from the purpose of playing, whose end, both at the first and now, was and is, to hold, as't were, the mirror up to nature; to show virtue her own feature, scorn her own image, and the very age and body of the time his form and pressure. Now this overdone, or come tardy off, though it make the unskilful laugh, cannot but make the judicious grieve; the censure of the which one must, in your allowance, o'erweigh a whole theatre of others. O, there be players that I have seen play, and heard others praise, and that highly, not to speak it profanely, that neither having the accent of Christians nor the gait of Christian, pagan, nor man, have so strutted and bellowed that I have thought some of Nature's journeymen had made men and not made them well, they imitated humanity so abominably.

1 Play. I hope we have reform'd that indifferently with us, sir.

Ham. O, reform it altogether, and let those that play your clowns speak no more than is set down for them; for there be of them that will themselves laugh to set on some quantity of barren spectators to laugh too, though in the mean time some necessary question of the play be then to be considered. That's villanous, and shows a most pitiful ambition in the Fool that uses it. Go make you ready.

These passages reveal a disapproving—at times satirical—attitude to the traditional sophistic rhetoric, an attitude which is in keeping with what has been shown that Shakespeare made of emotional rhetoric in his plays—a natural expression of individual character and not just conventional word display. Moreover, they include lines that reveal a grasp of the Aristotelian conception of the rhetoric of oratory to which the Shakespeare oration rings true.

In this connection it is interesting to note passages in which Shakespeare uses the terms orator, oratory, and oration.

Comedy of Errors, III, ii, 10

Luc. Be not thy tongue thy own shame's *orator:*

Merchant of Venice, III, ii, 177-185

Bass. Madam, you have bereft me of all words,
Only my blood speaks to you in my veins;
And there is such confusion in my powers,
As, after some *oration* fairly spoke
By a beloved prince, there doth appear
Among the buzzing pleased multitude;
Where every something being blent together,
Turns to a wild of nothing, save of joy
Express'd and not express'd.

As You Like It, IV, i, 72-77

Ros. Nay, you were better speak first; and when you were gravell'd for lack of matter, you might take occasion to kiss. Very

good *orators*, when they are out, they will spit; and for lovers
lacking—God warn us!—matter, the cleanliest shift is to kiss.

Troilus and Cressida, I, iii, 165-166

Ulyss. Now play me Nestor: hem, and stroke thy beard,
As he being drest to some *oration*.

1 Henry VI, II, ii, 44-50

Bur. Is it even so? Nay, then, I see our wars
Will turn unto a peaceful comic sport
When ladies crave to be encount'red with.
You may not, my lord, despise her gentle suit.
Tal. Ne'er trust me then; for when a world of men
Could not prevail with all their *oratory*.
Yet hath a woman's kindness over-rul'd.

IV, i, 174-175

War. My lord of York, I promise you, the King
Prettily, methought, did play the *orator*.

2 Henry VI, III, ii, 273-274

Suf. But you, my lord, were glad to be employ'd
To show how quaint an *orator* you are:

3 Henry VI, I, ii, 2

Edw. No, I can better play the *orator*.

I, iv, 110

Q. Mar. Nay, stay; let's hear the *orisons* he makes.

II, ii, 43-44

K. Henry. Full well hath Clifford play'd the orator,
Inferring arguments of mighty force.

III, ii, 188

Glou. I'll play the *orator* as well as Nestor,

Richard III, III, i, 37-39

Card. My Lord of Buckingham, if my weak *oratory*,
Can from his mother win the Duke of York,
Anon expect him here;

III, vii, 20

Buck. And when my *oratory* drew toward end

IV, iv, 126-131

Duch. Why should calamity be full of words?
Q. Eliz. Windy attorneys to their client woes,
Airy succeeders of intestate joys,
Poor breathing *orators* of miseries,
Let them have scope! though what they will impart
Help nothing else, yet do they ease the heart.

Titus Andronicus, III, i, 26

Tit. My tears are now prevailing *orators*.

IV, iii, 91-97 ff.

Clo. Why, I am going with my pigeons to the tribunal plebs, to take up a matter of brawl betwixt my uncle and one of the emperial's men.
Marc. Why, sir, that is as fit as can be to serve for your *oration;* and let him deliver the pigeons to the Emperor from you.

V, iii, 89-92

Marc. Nor can I utter all our bitter grief,
But floods of tears will drown my *oratory*
And break my utterance, even in the time
When it should move you to attend me most.

Julius Caesar, III, i, 292-294

Ant. There shall I try,
In my oration, how the people take
The cruel issue of these bloody men;

These passages reveal a conception of the oration as oral discourse—a speech of public utterance. As to purpose, they regard the oration as a speech of public utterance spoken with the aim in view of persuading or of giving expression to some emotion. In some instance, the satirical vein is unmistakable in the matter of style and mannerism.

Finally, two passages are quoted which recall terms associated with rhetoric:

Twelfth Night, V, i, 360-363

Oli.   This practice hath most shrewdly pass'd upon thee;
But when we know the grounds and authors of it,
Thou shalt be both the plaintiff and the judge
Of thine own *cause*.

1 Henry IV, I, iii, 201-210

Hot.   By heaven, methinks it were an easy leap,
To pluck bright Honour from the pale-fac'd moon,
Or dive in to the bottom of the deep,
Where fathom-line could never touch the ground,
And pluck up drowned Honour by the locks;
So he that doth redeem her thence might wear
Without corrival all her dignities.
But out upon this half-fac'd fellowship!
Wor.   He apprehends a *world of figures* here,
But not the form of what he should attend.

Shakespeare's critical attitude toward rhetoric reveals, as in the case of Aristotle, the mind of the philosopher. Like Aristotle, Shakespeare perceived that unity of ideas, purposeful progress, sincerity in expression, and totality or convincingness of impression make for the best in art as they make for the best in life. This perception determined the character of his orations. When we read a Shakespeare oration, we sense the philosophic attitude of mind—the mind that sees the end at the beginning, sees the parts in their relation to one another and to the whole, and sees it all clearly and logically worked through to the end. This attitude of mind perceives the best in rhetoric as it perceives the best in life.

In the modern world, Shakespeare reveals at its best the incarnation of the philosophic mind. It is no accident that in rhetoric, poetic, and even in philosophy we find ourselves interpreting Shakespeare in terms of Aristotle: the philosophic mind at its best views art and life in the same terms in all ages. This study is concerned with that mind as revealed in Shakespeare's orations; they have been catalogued, referred to source material, analyzed structurally, approached as an integral part of dramatic composition, and discussed in relation to Elizabethan oratory and against the background of Elizabethan education. By such means is there gained a valid appreciation of the mind of the artist; this chapter has been an attempt at appreciation of the mind of the critic as well.

CHAPTER X

Shakespeare and Rhetoric in Poetic

LIKE CHAUCER, Shakespeare left no critical work setting forth his theories of his art; he left merely his "book." But like Chaucer, too, Shakespeare made statements in his works that express a critical viewpoint as to rhetoric. Both Chaucer and Shakespeare perceived that the display of sophistic rhetoric for its own sake made at best for but inferior art; and, as their own art matured, their styles grew too in the control of rhetorical expression. Shakespeare's style matured, it would seem, much more rapidly than Chaucer's. In fact, the critical viewpoint established early in his career in *Love's Labour's Lost*, he applied immediately, and he soon became master of the rhetoric in his plays.

The first step in the direction of this mastery of rhetoric in the drama was the substitution of climactic plot movement for the episodic movement characteristic of the earlier Elizabethan drama. As has been observed, there are signs pointing in this direction in his first history plays, and in *Titus Andronicus* the climactic plot movement is quite successfully worked out but still covered up with much Seneca-like rhetoric. In the early comedies and *Romeo and Juliet*, he achieved success in climactic plot structure free of the Seneca-like rhetoric, carrying over to comedy the technique set down by Aristotle for tragedy.

Along with placing the emphasis on plot as the main element of his poetic, he set about making the interplay of character and circumstance the essence of plot action. Thus his plot action became essentially dramatic rather than narrative.

Moreover, in centering the dramatic action about a crisis, he secured unity of action through leading to it from an initial action and away from it to a denouement. Having secured unity of action, he let the matters of time and place take care of themselves, and instead of losing in dramatic effect thereby, he gained immeasurably.

The third step was the individualizing of character along with the psychological study of character. In his development of dramatic character, he emphasized emotional reaction in its relation to state of mind and habit of thinking or mental attitude. In this way he developed greatly in explanation of character and critical circumstance. And while keeping always foremost emphasis on plot action as determined by what characters did or did not do, he recognized the possibilities of plot action determined by characters through the expression of thought.

With this Aristotelian basis for his poetic, Shakespeare worked out his rhetoric in poetic. His emotional rhetoric he kept from running into the detached showiness and extravagance of traditional sophistic by making it integral in character—the natural expression of emotional thinking. His rhetoric of oratory he kept from being the mere declamation or academic exercise of traditional sophistic by making it integral in plot development—the logical expression of intellectual thinking designed in the interest of persuasion which would influence action. His rhetoric in poetic is thus also Aristotelian.

But Shakespeare extended both Aristotelian poetic and rhetoric in poetic. He applied Aristotelian poetic to the history play, and gave the essentially episodic movement of chronicle history as much climactic movement as he could. He applied to comedy the technique of Aristotle's plot movement for tragedy and lifted comedy to a place of dignity as a form of dramatic art. He extended Aristotle's rhetoric in poetic by developing the purely narrative and occasional speech as an oration in the drama.

The oration in the drama he perfected as an artistic convention of plot development. He received it from his predecessors a more or less studied academic exercise ineffectively integrated in a drama that was struggling to free itself from the influence of the Senecan episodic plot development; he passed it on as a speech in keeping with the best traditions of classical rhetoric and one vitally integrated in a drama which realized to the fullest all the implications of the best traditions of classical poetic. When he began to write the oration into the drama, he found both rhetoric and poetic closing a stage of experimentation in the direction of a recovery of the classical traditions of these arts. He fell heir to a growing sense for plot action as the essential and determinative principle of drama as an expression of the technique of poetic, and for persuasion as the essential and determinative principle of the oration as an expression of the technique of rhetoric. His own first efforts in the use of these techniques were experimental. But early in his career as dramatist he caught clearly the classical conceptions of the two movements and clearly distinguished the two movements in the development of his art. He transformed dramatic structure from a mere stringing together of incidents and speeches into a development of a well-defined plot in which incidents and speeches are made to contribute to the working out, step by step, of an ultimate conclusion—from a mechanical arrangement into an organic development. In this plot development Shakespeare made the oration function as the natural outgrowth of a situation and contribute to the direction of subsequent action. He revealed the spontaneity and effectiveness that could be attained by the oration as an integral part of dramatic technique. He perfected the revival of the ancient rhetoric in poetic.

Bibliography

Editions of Shakespeare's Plays:
  Arden Shakespeare. Ed. W. J. Craig. 16 vols. London, 1899.
  Cambridge Shakespeare. Ed. William A. Neilson. Boston, 1906. Used in text of this book for play references.
  College Shakespeare. Ed. William John Tucker. New York, 1932.
  Collier Edition. Ed. John Payne Collier. 3 vols. New York, 1855.
  Larger Temple Shakespeare. Ed. Israel Gollancz. 12 vols. London, 1899.
  Shakespeare, The Works in One Volume. Oxford, 1934.
  Stratford Shakespeare. Ed. Charles Knight. 6 vols. New York, 1870.
  Variorum Edition. Ed. H. H. Furness. 21 vols. Philadelphia and London, 1871.
Adams, John Quincey. *Lectures on Rhetoric and Oratory.* 2 vols. Cambridge, Mass., 1810.
Adams, Joseph Quincey. *Chief Pre-Shakespearean Dramas.* Boston, 1924.
———. *A Life of William Shakespeare.* Boston, 1925.
———. *Shakespearean Playhouses.* Boston, 1917.
Albright, V. E. *Shakespearean Stage.* New York, 1909.
Alexander, Peter. *Shakespeare's Henry VI and Richard III.* Cambridge, 1929.
Alexander, Sir William. *Works.* 3 vols. Glasgow, 1870.
Allen, Percy. *The Case for Edward De Vere 17th Earl of Oxford as "Shakespeare."* London, 1930.
———. *The Life Story of Edward De Vere as William Shakespeare.* London, 1932.
Anders, H. R. D. *Shakespeare's Books.* Berlin, 1904.
Aristotle. *Ethics and Politics.* Trans. John Gillies. London, 1913.

Bibliography

———. *The Poetics of Aristotle.* Ed. S. H. Butcher. London and New York, 1902.
———. *Rhetoric.* Trans. Daniel Michael Crimmin. London, 1818.
———. *The Rhetoric of Aristotle, with a Commentary by E. M. Cope.* Ed. J. E. Sandys. 3 vols. Cambridge, 1877.
Arnold, Morris LeRoy. *The Soliloquies of Shakespeare.* New York, 1911.
Ascham, Roger. *The Scholemaster.* "Arber Reprints." Westminster, 1897.
Bacon, Delia. *The Philosophy of the Plays of Shakespeare Unfolded.* Preface by Nathaniel Hawthorne. Boston, 1857.
Bacon, Francis. *Works.* Ed. James Spedding. 7 vols. London, 1857.
Bagehot, Walter. *Shakespeare the Man.* New York, 1901.
Bailey, John. *Shakespeare.* London and New York, 1930.
Baker, G. P. *The Development of Shakespeare as a Dramatic Artist.* New York, 1907.
Baldwin, Charles S. *Ancient Rhetoric and Poetic.* New York, 1924.
———. *Medieval Rhetoric and Poetic.* New York, 1928.
Baldwin, T. W. *The Organization and Personnel of the Shakespearean Company.* Princeton, 1929.
Beaumont, Francis, and Fletcher, John. *Works.* Variorum ed. 4 vols. London, 1904.
———. *Works.* Ed. Henry Weber. 14 vols. Edinburgh, 1812.
Best Plays of the Old Dramatists. "Mermaid Series." London and New York, 1896.
Blair, Hugh. *Lectures on Rhetoric and Belles Lettres.* 6th ed. 3 vols. London, 1796.
Boas, F. S. *Shakespeare and His Predecessors.* New York, 1899.
Boethius, Anicius Manlius Severinus. *Consolation of Philosophy.* Trans. George Colville, 1556. Ed. Ernest Belfort Box. London, 1897.
———. *De Consolatione Philosophiae.* Libri V. Instruxit Theodorus Obbarius. Jenae, 1843.
———. *King Alfred's Version of the Consolations of Boethius.* Done in Modern English by Walter John Sedgefield. Oxford, 1900.
Boileau, Nicolas. "L'Art poétique." *Œuvres.* Strasbourg, New York, n.d.

———. *Œuvres en vers.* 2 vols. Amsterdam, 1721.
Bornecque, Henri. *Les déclamations et les déclamateurs d'après Senèque le père.* Université de Lille, 1902.
———. *Senèque le rhétor, controverses et suasoires.* 2 vols. Paris, 1902.
Boswell-Stone, W. G. *Shakespeare's Holinshed.* New York and London, 1896.
Bradley, A. C. *Shakespearean Tragedy.* London, 1929.
Brandes, George. *William Shakespeare, A Critical Study.* New York, 1927.
Brooke, Arthur. *Romeus and Juliet.* Ed. J. J. Munro. "Shakespeare Classics." New York and London, 1908.
Brooke, C. F. Tucker. *The Shakespeare Apocrypha.* Oxford, 1918.
———. *Tudor Drama.* Boston, 1911.
Brown, J. Howard. *Elizabethan Schooldays.* Oxford, 1933.
Butcher, S. H. *Aristotle's Theory of Poetry and Fine Art.* 4th ed. New York and London, 1927.
Butler, Pierce. *Materials for the Life of Shakespeare.* Chapel Hill, 1930.
Campion, Thomas. *Observations on the Art of English Poesie.* Ed. A. H. Bullen. London, 1903.
Chambers, E. K. *The Elizabethan Stage.* 4 vols. Oxford, 1923.
———. *Shakespeare, A Survey.* New York, 1926.
———. *William Shakespeare.* 2 vols. Oxford, 1930.
Chambrun, Clara (Longworth). *Shakespeare, Actor-Poet.* New York and London, 1927.
Chapman, George. *Dramatic Works.* 3 vols. London, 1873.
———. "Homer's *Illiad* and *Odyssey.*" *Works.* Ed. Richard Herne Shepherd. London, 1903.
———. *Works.* 3 vols. London, 1874-1875.
Cicero. *De Oratore.* Trans. John Selby Watson. New York, 1860.
———. *Pro Milone, with a translation of Asconius' Introduction. . . .* Ed. Rev. John Smyth Purton. Cambridge, 1891.
Clark, Cumberland. *A Study of Shakespeare's Henry VIII.* London, 1931.
Clark, D. L. *Rhetoric and Poetry in the Renaissance.* New York, 1922.
Coleridge, Samuel Taylor. *Biographia Literaria.* Ed. J. C. Metcalf. New York, 1926.

Coleridge's Shakespearean Criticism. Ed. T. M. Raysor. 2 vols. London, 1930.
Collier, J. P. *English Dramatic Poetry and Annals of the Stage.* 3 vols. London, 1879.
———. *Memoirs of the Principal Actors in the Plays of Shakespeare.* London, 1846.
Collins, J. Churton. *Studies in Shakespeare.* Westminster, 1904.
Cooper, Lane. *Aristotle on Comedy.* New York, 1922.
———. *The Poetics of Aristotle, Its Meaning and Influence.* Boston, 1923.
Cooper, Lane, and Guderman, Alfred. *Bibliography of Poetics.* New Haven and London, 1928.
Corneille, Pierre. *Œuvres de Corneille avec les Commentaires de Voltaire.* Vol. X. Paris, 1817.
Croll, Morris W. "Attic Prose in the Seventeenth Century." *Studies in Philology,* XVIII (April, 1921).
———. "The Cadence of English Oratorical Prose." *Studies in Philology,* XVI (1919), 1-55.
Cubberley, E. P. *The History of Education.* Boston, 1920.
———. *Readings in the History of Education.* Boston, 1920.
Cunliffe, J. W. *Early English Classical Tragedies.* Oxford, 1912.
———. *The Influence of Seneca on Elizabethan Tragedy.* London and New York, 1893.
Daniel, Samuel. *Works.* Ed. Alexander B. Grosart. 5 vols. London, 1885.
Deane, Cecil V. *Dramatic Theory and the Rhymed Heroic Play.* Oxford, 1931.
DeQuincey, Thomas. *Essays on Philosophical Writers and Other Men of Letters.* 2 vols. Boston, 1854.
Deutsche National-Litteratur. Herausgegeben von Joseph Kurschner. Berlin, 1882-1899.
Dodsley, Robert. *Old English Plays.* Ed. W. Carew Hazlitt. London, 1874.
Dowden, Edward. *Shakespeare's Mind and Art.* New York, 1881.
Drinkwater, John. *Shakespeare.* London, 1933.
Dryden, John. *Selected Works.* Ed. W. P. Ker. 2 vols. Oxford, 1900.
Ebisch, Walther, and Schucking, Levin L. *A Shakespeare Bibliography.* Oxford, 1931.

Einstein, Lewis. *The Italian Renaissance in England.* New York, 1902.
Elson, Arthur. *A Critical History of Opera.* Boston, 1901.
Elson, L. C. *Shakespeare in Music.* London, 1901.
Elyot, Sir Thomas. *The Book named the Governour.* Ed. Arthur Turbeville Eliot. Newcastle-upon-Tyne, 1834.
Famous Victories. Ed. A. F. Hopkinson. London, 1896.
Farmer, Richard. *An Essay on the Learning of Shakespeare.* 3rd ed. London, 1789.
Feuillerat, Albert. *Lyly, Contribution à l'Histoire de la Renaissance en Angleterre.* Cambridge, 1910.
Ford, John. *Works.* Ed. William Gifford. 2 vols. London, 1827.
Fox, John. *Book of Martyrs.* Revised and corrected as *The New and Complete Book of Martyrs.* Ed. Paul Wright. 2 vols. New York, 1794.
Gascoigne, George. *Works.* Ed. J. W. Cunliffe. 2 vols. Cambridge, 1910.
Gaw, Allison. *The Origin and Development of 1 Henry VI, in Relation to Shakespeare, Marlowe, Peele, and Greene.* Los Angeles, 1926.
Gayley. *Representative English Comedies.* 3 vols. New York, 1903.
Gervinus, G. G. *Shakespeare Commentaries.* Trans. F. E. Bunnett. London and New York, 1892.
Goddard, Joseph. *The Rise and Development of the Opera.* New York and London, 1912.
Gordon, George. *Airy Nothings or What You Will.* New York, 1917.
Gosson, Stephen. *School of Abuse.* Reprint for Shakespeare Society. London, 1841.
Gossip From a Muniment Room, Being Passages from the lives of Anne and Mary Fitton, 1574-1618. Ed. Lady Newdigate-Newdegate. London, 1898.
Green, Clarence C. *The Neo-Classic Theory of Tragedy in England during the Eighteenth Century.* Cambridge, Mass., 1934.
Greene, Robert. *Life and Complete Works.* Ed. Alexander B. Grosart. 12 vols. London, 1881-1883.
———. *Pandosto.* Ed. P. G. Thomas. "Shakespeare Classics." New York and London, 1907.

Bibliography

Grove, Sir George. *Dictionary of Music and Musicians.* London and New York, 1879-1890.
Halliwell-Phillips, J. Q. *Shakespeare's Tours.* Brighton, 1887.
Harrison, Benjamin S. "Medieval Rhetoric in the Book of the Duchesse," *Publications of the Modern Language Association,* XLIX (June, 1934), 428-442.
Haskins, C. H. *The Renaissance of the Twelfth Century.* Cambridge, Mass., 1927.
Hazlitt, William. *Characters of Shakespeare's Plays.* London, 1848.
——. *Criticism and Dramatic Essays on the English Stage.* Ed. by his son. London, 1851.
——. *Lectures on Dramatic Literature of the Age of Elizabeth.* London, 1840.
——. *Lectures on the English Comic Writers.* London, 1819.
Helmholtz, Mrs. Anna Augusta. "The Indebtedness of S. T. Coleridge to August Wilhelm von Schlegel." *Bulletin of the University of Wisconsin,* No. 63, III (1907), 273-370.
Herder, Johann Gottfried von. "Shakespear." *Von Deutscher Art und Kunst.* Ed. Edna Purdie. Oxford, 1924.
Herrick, Marvin. *The Poetics of Aristotle in England.* New Haven, 1930.
Holinshed, Raphael. *Shakespeare's Holinshed.* Ed. W. G. Boswell-Stone. London, 1896.
——. *Holinshed's Chronicles of England, Scotland, and Ireland.* . . . Ed. Sir Henry Ellis. 6 vols. London, 1807-08.
Horace. *Ars Poetica.* Ed. Edward Blakeney. London, 1928.
Hudson, H. N. *Shakespeare's Life, Art and Characters.* 2 vols. Boston, 1902.
Hultzen, L. S. *Aristotle's Rhetoric in England to 1600.* Thesis abstract, Cornell University. Ithaca, N. Y., 1932.
Hurd, Richard. *Works.* 8 vols. London, 1811.
Hutton, Richard Holt. "Goethe and his Influence." *Essays in Literary Criticism.* Philadelphia, 1876.
Isaacsen, Hertha. *Der Junge Herder und Shakespeare.* "Germanische Studien." Berlin, 1930.
Isocrates. *Orations.* Trans. J. H. Freese. London and New York, 1894.
Jameson, Anna. *Shakespeare's Heroines.* London, 1876.
Jebb, Sir R. C. *The Attic Orators.* London, 1876.

Johnson, Samuel. *Preface to Edition of Shakespeare's Plays.* London, 1765.
Jonson, Ben. *Works.* Ed. William Gifford. London, 1816.
Ker, W. P. *Epic and Romance.* London and New York, 1897.
Kilbourne, F. W. *Alterations and Adaptations of Shakespeare.* Boston, 1906.
King, Lucille. "Text Sources of the Folio and Quarto Henry VI," *Publications of the Modern Language Association,* LI (Sept., 1936) 702-718.
———. "The Use of Halle's Chronicles in the Folio and Quarto Texts of Henry VI," *Philological Quarterly,* XIII (1934), 321-332.
King Leir (Chronicle play). Ed. Sidney Lee. "Shakespeare Classics." New York and London, 1909.
Knowlton, E. C. "Nature and Shakespeare," *Publications of the Modern Language Association,* LI (Sept., 1936), 719-744.
Kyd, Thomas. *Works.* Ed. F. S. Boas. Oxford, 1901.
Lamb, Charles. *The Art of the Stage.* Commentary by Percy Fitzgerald. London, 1885.
———. *The Dramatic Essays of Charles Lamb.* Ed. Brander Matthews. New York, 1891.
———. *Specimens of English Dramatic Poets.* London, 1890.
Langdon, Ida. *Milton's Theory of Poetry and Fine Art.* "Cornell Studies in English." New Haven, 1924.
Lee, Guy Carleton. *Orators of the Early and Medieval Church.* New York and London, 1900.
Lee, Sir Sidney. *Life of William Shakespeare.* New York, 1909.
Lessing, Gotthold. *Hamburgische Dramaturgie.* Trans. and ed. Charles Harris. New York, 1901.
Lessing's Hamburgische Dramaturgie. Ed. Charles Harris. New York, 1901.
Lodge, Thomas. *A Defence of Poetry, Music, and Stage Plays.* ... London (for Shakespeare Society), 1853.
———. *Rosalynde.* Ed. W. W. Greg. "Shakespeare Classics." New York and London, 1907.
Lyly, John. *Euphues the Anatomy of Wit and Euphues and His England.* "Arber Reprints." Westminster, 1900.
———. *Works.* Ed. R. Warwick Bond. 3 vols. Oxford, 1902.
McKerrow, Ronald B. "A Note on the 'Bad Quartos' of 2 and 3 Henry VI," *Review of English Studies,* XIII (Jan., 1937), 64-72.

———. "The Treatment of Shakespeare's Text by His Earlier Editors, 1709-1768." *Proceedings of the British Academy: Annual Shakespeare Lecture, 1933.* Vol. XIX. London, 1933.
Malone Society Reprints. Gen. ed. W. W. Greg. London, Oxford, 1907-1934.
Manly, John M. *Specimens of the Pre-Shakespearean Drama.* 2 vols. Boston, 1897.
Marlowe, Christopher. *Works.* Ed. A. H. Bullen. London, 1885.
Marston, John. *Works.* Ed. A. H. Bullen. London, 1887.
Massinger, Philip. *Works.* Ed. William Gifford. London, 1805.
Melton, Wightman Fletcher. *The Rhetoric of John Donne's Verse.* Baltimore, 1906.
Middleton, Thomas. *Works.* Ed. Alexander Dyce. London, 1840.
Milton, John. *Selected Prose Writings.* Ed. Ernest Myers. London, 1884.
Montaigne, Michel Eyquem de. *The Essays of Montaigne.* Trans. George B. Ives. 4 vols. Cambridge, Mass., 1925.
———. *The Essays of Michael Montaigne.* Trans. from French ed. of Peter Coste. 7th ed. 3 vols. London, 1759.
Moulton, R. G. *Shakespeare as a Dramatic Artist.* Oxford, 1897.
Neilson, W. A. and Thorndike, A. H. *Facts About Shakespeare.* New York, 1913.
Odell, G. C. D. *Shakespeare from Betterton to Irving.* 2 vols. New York, 1920.
Orations from Homer to William McKinley. Ed. Mayo W. Hazeltine. 25 vols. New York, 1902.
Painter, William. *Palace of Pleasure.* Ed. Joseph Jacobs. 3 vols. London, 1890.
Patterson, W. M. *The Rhythm of Prose.* New York, 1916.
Peele, George. *Works.* Ed. Alexander Dyce. London, 1829.
Pemberton, Henry. *Observations on Poetry.* London, 1738.
Plautus, *The Comedies of.* Trans. Henry Thomas Riley. 2 vols. London, 1894. See also *T. Maccii Plauti Comediae.*
Plimpton, G. A. *Education of Shakespeare.* London and New York, 1933.
Plutarch's Lives, North's Translation. Ed. C. F. Tucker Brooke. 2 vols. "Shakespeare Classics." New York and London, 1909.

Pollard, A. W. "The Foundation of Shakespeare's Text." *Proceedings of the British Academy: Annual Shakespeare Lecture*, X (1923), 379-394.
Puttenham, George. *The Arte of English Poesie.* "Arber Reprints." London, 1869.
Quintilian. *Institutes of Oratory.* Trans. John S. Watson. London, 1899.
Rand, Edward Kennard. *Founders of the Middle Ages.* Cambridge, Mass., 1928.
Rowe, Nicholas. *Works, with Some Account of the Life and Works of Mr. William Shakespeare.* London, 1714.
Rymer, Thomas. *A Short View of Tragedy.* London, 1693.
———. *Tragedies of the Last Age.* London, 1692.
Saintsbury, George. *The Flourishing of Romance and the Rise of Allegory.* New York, 1897.
———. *A History of Criticism.* 3 vols. London, 1904.
———. *A History of Elizabethan Literature.* London and New York, 1887.
———. *A History of English Prose Rhythm.* London, 1912.
Sampley, Arthur M. "Plot Structure in Peele's Plays," *Publications of the Modern Language Association,* LI (Sept., 1936), 688-701.
Schelling, Felix E. *Elizabethan Drama.* Boston, 1908.
Schlegel, A. W. *Vorlesungen über Dramatische Kunst und Litteratur.* 2 vols. Leipzig, 1846.
———. *Lectures on Dramatic Art and Literature.* Trans. John Black. London, 1815.
Schucking, Levin L. *Character Problems in Shakespeare's Plays.* London, 1922.
Seneca. *Tragedies.* Text with trans. by Watson Bradshaw. London, 1902.
Shakespere Allusion Book. Ed. Clement M. Inglesby (1874), John Munro (1909). Preface by Sir Edmund Chambers. 2 vols. London, 1932.
Shakespeare Classics. Ed. Israel Gollancz. 9 vols. New York and London, 1907-1909.
Shakespeare Quarto Facsimiles. General ed. F. J. Furnivall. 43 vols. London, 1889.
Shakespeare's Library. Ed. W. C. Hazlitt. 2 parts, 6 vols. London, 1875.

Shakespeare's Ovid, Arthur Golding's Translation of the Metamorphoses. Ed. W. H. D. Rouse. London, 1904.
Shakespeare's Plutarch. Ed. C. F. Tucker Brooke. "Shakespeare Classics." London, 1909.
Shakespeare Studies. Ed. Brander Matthews and A. H. Thorndike. New York, 1916.
Shurter, Edward D. *Rhetoric of Oratory.* New York, 1916.
Sidney, Sir Philip. *Works.* Ed. Albert Feuillerat. Cambridge, 1912-1926.
Simpson, Percy. *Shakespearean Punctuation.* Oxford, 1911.
———. *Proof-Reading in the Sixteenth, Seventeenth, and Eighteenth Centuries.* London, 1925.
Smith, Charles G. *Spenser's Theory of Friendship.* Baltimore, 1935.
Sources and Analogues in Midsummer Night's Dream. Comp. Frank Sidgwick. "Shakespeare Classics." London, 1908.
Spingarn, J. E. *Critical Essays of the Seventeenth Century.* 2 vols. Oxford, 1908.
———. *A History of Literary Criticism in the Renaissance.* New York, 1899.
Spurgeon, Caroline. *Shakespeare's Imagery.* New York and London, 1935.
Stapfer, Paul. *Shakespeare and Classical Antiquity.* Trans. Emily J. Carey. London, 1880.
Stephenson, Henry Thew. *The Elizabethan People.* New York, 1910.
Strong, John R. *Note upon the "Dark Lady" Series of Shakespeare's Sonnets.* New York and London, 1921.
Sykes, H. Douglas. *Sidelights on Shakespeare.* Stratford on Avon, 1919.
Symonds, John A. *Shakespeare's Predecessors in the English Drama.* London and New York, 1900.
T. Maccii Plauti Comediae. Recensuit et Enarravit Ioannes Ludovicus Ussing. Havniae, 1875.
Taming of a Shrew, The. Ed. F. S. Boas. "Shakespeare Classics." London, 1908.
Taylor, Henry Osborn. *The Medieval Mind.* 2 vols. New York, 1930.
Taylor, Thomas. *The Herbert-Fitton Theory of Shakespeare's Sonnets.* London, 1890.

Teager, Florence E. "Chaucer's Eagle and the Rhetorical Colors." *Publications of the Modern Language Association*, XLVII (June, 1936), 410-418.
Theobald, William. *The Classical Element in the Shakespeare Plays*. London, 1909.
Thorndike, Ashley H. *English Comedy*. New York, 1929.
―――. *Influence of Beaumont and Fletcher on Shakespeare*. Worcester, 1901.
―――. *Shakespeare's Theater*. New York, 1916.
―――. *Tragedy*. Boston, 1908.
Titsworth, Paul Everson. "The Attitude of Goethe and Schiller toward French Classic Drama." *Journal of English and Germanic Philology*, II (October, 1912), 509-564.
Tucker, William John. *College Shakespeare*. New York, 1932.
Tupper, Frederick, Jr. "The Shakespearean Mob," *Publications of the Modern Language Association*, XX (1912), 486-526.
Ulrici, Herman. *Shakespeare's Dramatic Art and Its Relation to Calderon and Goethe*. Trans. A. J. W. Morrison. 2 vols. London, 1896-1900.
Upton, John. *Critical Observations on Shakespeare*. London, 1748.
Von Deutscher Art und Kunst. Ed. Edna Purdie. Oxford, 1924.
Wagner, Richard. *Oper und Drama*. Leipzig, 1852. Trans. Edwin Evans. 2 vols. New York and London. 1913.
Wallace, C. W. Stechert. *Evolution of the English Drama up to Shakespeare*. Berlin, 1912.
Ward, A. W. *A History of English Dramatic Literature*. 3 vols. London and New York, 1899.
Webbe, William. *Discourse of English Poetrie*. "Arber Reprint." London, 1870.
Webster, John. *Works*. Ed. Alexander Dyce. 4 vols. London, 1830.
Whalley, Peter. *An Enquiry into the Learning of Shakespeare, with remarks on several passages of his plays*. London, 1748.
Wigston, William Francis C. *A New Study of Shakespeare*. London, 1884.
Wilson, Thomas. *Arte of Rhetorique*. Ed. G. H. Mair. Oxford, 1909.
―――. *Discourse upon Usurye*. Ed. R. H. Tawney. New York, 1925.

Index

Aaron, speech of, 51
Actes and Monuments, 100-101
Actors, and sophistic rhetoric in Shakespeare's plays, 48-50
Aegenetikos, analysis of, 123-124
Aegeon, speech of, 129, 132, 137
Aeneid, 7, 203
Aeschylus, tragedies of, 6; plot action in plays of, 11
Alcibiades, speech of, 33, 85, 131, 133, 137
Aldine Editio princeps, 220
All's Well That Ends Well, emotional rhetoric in, 43, 55
Andrews, Bishop, 168
Andromache, speech of, 7
Antony and Cleopatra, sophistic rhetoric in, 43; psychological analysis in, 60-61; absence of orations in, 72
Antony, speeches of, 8, 132, 133; role of, 60-61; analysis of oration of, 138-139
Apology for Poetry, 22, 221
Aquinas, Thomas, 219
Aran en Titus and *Titus Andronicus*, 77
Aristotle, *Poetics* of, 3 ff.; *Rhetoric* of, quoted, 63; on the parts of an oration, 116-119; on rhetoric in poetic, 148; and dramatic action, 156-157; and poetic of Shakespearean drama, 163; history of *Poetics* of, 218 ff.; poetic of, and Shakespeare, 248 ff.; 34, 39, 43, 65, 147, 150, 152, 153, 156, 157, 163, 181, 200, 207, 245
Aristotle, Great Aldine, 220

Aristotle on Comedy, 233
Aristotle's Theory of Poetry and Fine Art, 232
Armado, letter of, 208-209, 212
Arraignment of Paris, 33, 179-182
Arte of Rhetorique. See Wilson, Thomas
Ascham, Roger, and the *Scholemaster*, 200, 204-205, 220; mentioned, 21
As You Like It, speeches in compared with those in *Twelfth Night*, 42; extended rhetorical speaking in, 55; reference to school in, 213; reference to orators in, 242-243

Bacon, Francis, 168, 217
Bacon, Roger, 219
Baldwin, Charles Sears, vii
Bandello, Matteo, and *Much Ado About Nothing*, 79
Bassanio, speech of, 237
Beaumont, Francis, 170
Bellay, Du, Joachim, 21
Belleforest, and *Hystorie of Hamblet*, 80
Bestrafte Brudermord oder Prinz Hamlet aus Daennemark, Der, and *Hamlet*, 80-81
Biographia Literaria, 231
Biron, speeches of, 77, 112, 135, 234, 236
Blackmore, Sir Richard, 228
Boccaccio, *Decameron* of, and *Cymbeline*, 82; 110
Boethius, 13, 218-219
Brabant, William of, 219

[261]

Brooke, Arthur, *Romeus and Juliet*, 79
Brooke, Tucker, and *The Tudor Drama*, 196
Brown, J. Howard, and *Elizabethan Schooldays*, 202
Browne, Sir Thomas, 168
Brutus, role of, 57
Burbage, Richard, 49
Butcher, S. H., and *Aristotle's Theory of Poetry and Fine Art*, 232
Byron, speech of in *Tragedy of Charles Duke of Byron*, 182 ff.
Bywater, Ingram, 232

Caesar, Julius, *Commentaries* of, 203
Campion, Thomas, 217
Canterbury, conclusion in oration of, 135; introduction, 134
Carlisle, speech of, quoted, 144
Cassandra, speech of, 80
Cassius, role of, 57-58
Castelvetro, 21
Cavalli, Francesco, and development of the opera, 45-46
Chapman, George, 83; and *Tragedy of Charles Duke of Byron*, 33, 182-189
Chaucer, Geoffrey, and Aristotle's *Poetics*, 18, 219-220; and Shakespeare, 247
Cheke, Sir John, 220
Chief Justice, speech of, 97, 144
Chronicles, Holinshed's and Halle's, and *1 Henry VI*, 89; and *2 Henry VI*, 90-91; and *3 Henry VI*, 91-93; and *Richard III*, 93-94; and *King John*, 94-95; and *Richard II*, 95-96; and *1 Henry IV*, 96-97; and *2 Henry IV*, 97; and *Henry V*, 97-99; and *Henry VIII*, 99-101
Chronology, of Shakespeare's plays and the orations, 164-165
Church, and drama, 169
Cicero, and sophistic rhetoric, 9; and Renaissance criticism, 23; on classification of orations, 63-64; on arrangement of orations, 117-119; as orator, 126-128; *Offices* and *Orations*, 203; mentioned, 65, 147, 200, 205, 206, 221
Ciceronian, 198
Cinthio, and Renaissance, 20; his *Hecatommithi* and Shakespeare's *Othello*, 81
Clark, Donald L., vii
Classics, Shakespeare's knowledge of, 221 ff., note 22
Claudian, 200
Claudio, speech of, 237
Cleopatra, role of, 61
Coleridge, Samuel Taylor, and *Biographia Literaria*, 231
Colet, John, and humanism, 198, 199, 206
Comedy of Errors, sophistic rhetoric in, 41; speeches of Adriana and Luciana in, 54; and Plautus' *Menaechmi*, 77; structure of orations in, 105; and forensic orations, 113; dramatic integration of, 153; chronology of, 164; quoted, 212; references to rhetoric in, 236-237; references to oratory in, 242
Comedy, and Renaissance critics, 21; use of rhetoric in, 54
Commentaries, of Julius Caesar, 203
Conrad, Joseph, his *Nostromo* quoted, 37-39
Constance, role of, 52
Conclusions, of Shakespeare's orations, 132-135
Cooper, Lane, and *Aristotle on Comedy*, 233; and *The Poetics of Aristotle*, 232-233; mentioned, vii
Coriolanus, speeches of, 8, 32, 61, 108, 131, 133, 134, 138, 146-147
Coriolanus, oration of Coriolanus in, 32; sophistic rhetoric in, 43; forensic achievements in, 108-109; psychological analysis in,

Index

61; number of orations in, 72; and Plutarch's *Coriolanus*, 86; deliberative orations in, 115-116; introduction in oration of Coriolanus in, 134; conclusion in oration of Volumnia in, 135; quality of orations in, 136; analysis of oration of, 138; dramatic integration of, 154, 155; reference to rhetoric in, 240
Costard, speech of, 208
Court scenes, as setting of Shakespeare's plays, 161-162
Cranmer, speech of, 100-101
Crites, and Dryden, 225-226
Critical Observations of Shakespeare, 229
Criticism, medieval, 15-18; Renaissance, 18-23
Croll, Morris W., 167, 168
Cymbeline, sophistic rhetoric in, 43-44; construction of, 56

Da capo, 46, 47, 48
Damon and Pithias, 32
Daniel, Samuel, 217
Daniello, 20
Dante, and *De Vulgari Eloquio*, 15-16, 17; and the *Divina Commedia*, 18; and *Paradise*, 84, note 31
David and Bethsabe, 33
Decameron. See Boccaccio
Declamation, definition of, 26-28
Deighton, K., and *Troilus and Cressida*, 83
Deliberative orations, table of, 70, 115-116; outline of, 115-116
Demonstrative orations, table of, 68-69; outline of, 113-114
Demosthenes, orations of, 6, 122, 200, 206; and Isocrates, 122
Desdemona, role of, 58-59
Discoveries, 218
Divina Commedia, 18
Dogberry, role of, 211
Donne, Dr., 168
Dryden, John, and *An Essay of Dramatic Poetry*, 225-227; mentioned, 48

Duke of Milan, example of orations in, 189-191; 33

Education, English, humanization of, 198 ff.
Edwards, Richard, and *Damon and Pithias*, 32
Elizabeth, Queen, and public speaking, 167
Elizabethan Schooldays, 202
Elizabethans, drama of, and rhetoric in poetic, 24-25; interminable speechmaking in, 44-45; rhetoric of compared with that of Shakespeare, 61-62; and Greek and Roman rhetoricians, 121; oratory of, 166 ff.; set speeches of, 166 ff.; and public speaking, 166-167; and Asian style, 168-169; and Euphuism, 168; and preaching, 168; and morality play, 169; and classical tradition, 169-170; and Italian models, 170; culmination of, 170; decadence of, 170-171; frequency of speech-making in, 171-172; history of oration in, 172 ff.; and emergence of native type, 170, 174-175; decline in, 182 ff.; and education, 198 ff.; and humanistic education, 206 ff.
Elizabethans, education of, and Shakespeare, 207 ff.
Eloquence, of Shakespeare's orations, 140-147
Elyot, Sir Thomas, *Governour* of, and *2 Henry IV*, 97
Enobarbus, role of, 60
Erasmus, 20, 77, 198-199, 220
Eton, course of study at, 200-201
Eugenius, and Dryden, 226-227
Euphues and His England, 98
Euphuism, style of, 168
Euripides, tragedies of, 6; plot action in plays of, 11
Everyman, 36

Facts about Shakespeare, 65
Famous Victories of Henry Fifth, 88

Falstaff, speeches of, 211, 238
Fielding, Henry, 228
First Part of the Contention, 86, 90, 101
"First Sophistic," 8
Fletcher, John, 100, 170
Ford, John, and *Perkin Warbeck*, 32, 193-194; 171
Forensic orations, table of, 67; outline of, 113-114
Foxe, John, *Actes and Monuments*, 100-101
Francastoro, 21
Francis, Friar, 79
Franklin's Tale, 18

Galilei, Vincenzio, and development of the opera, 45
Gascoigne, George, 21
Gaza, Theodorus, 200
Gismond of Salerne, 28, 174
Gloucester, conclusion in oration of, 135; speech of, 137
Gluck, Christoph Willibald, and development of the opera, 46-47, 48
Goethe, 230
Gorboduc, 28, 32, 173-174
Gorgias, and sophistic rhetoric, 9
Gosson, Stephen, and *School of Abuse*, 22
Governour, and *2 Henry IV*, 97
Grand Opera, and rhetorical drama, 45-48
Greene, Robert, and *James IV*, 35, 175-177; his *Pandosto* and *The Winter's Tale*, 82; mentioned, 168, 170, 174
Grocyn, 198

Halle. See *Chronicles*
Hamburgische Dramaturgie, quoted, 229
Hamlet, and oration to Danes, 80
Hamlet, use of soliloquy in, 28; emotional rhetoric in, 43; sophistic rhetoric in, 44; psychological analysis in, 58; number of orations in, 72; structure of orations in, 107; setting of king's speech in, 161; references to rhetoric in, 240-242
Harris, L. M., vii
Harvey, Gabriel, 221
Hasse, J. A., 47
Hecatommithi, *Moor of Venice*, and *Othello*, 81
Hench, Atcheson Laughlin, viii
1 Henry IV, Henry's conference with the Prince in, 29; rhetorical conversation in, 29; and the *Chronicles*, 96-97; structure of orations in, 106; and introduction in speech of Worcester, 134; and Falstaff's speech on "honour," 211; references to rhetoric in, 238; reference to rhetorical terms in, 245
2 Henry IV, and *Famous Victories of Henry V*, 97; and *Governour*, 97; and the *Chronicles*, 97; structure of orations in, 106; setting of orations in, 159
Henry V, declamatory rhetoric in, 41-42; sophistic rhetoric in, 54; and the *Chronicles*, 97-99; structure of orations in, 106; quality of speeches in, 112; and demonstrative oration, 114; deliberative orations in, 115; and introduction in speech of Canterbury, 134; conclusion in oration of Canterbury in, 135; conclusion in oration of Henry in, 135; and Shakespeare's grasp of rhetorical structure, 136; dramatic integration of, 155
Henry V, speeches of, 97-99, 144-145
1 Henry VI, speech of messenger in, 35; declamation in, 40; traditional use of declamatory rhetoric in, 51; speech of Henry in, 89; orations in, 89; orations in, and problem of authorship of play, 104-105; introduction in speech of La Pucelle, 134; conclusion in speech of La Pucelle in, 135; consistency in plot development

of, 150; and Sophoclean tragedy, 156; setting of orations in, 158; chronology of, 164; references to rhetoric in, 238-239; references to oratory in, 243
2 *Henry VI*, rhetoric in, 40, 51; orations in, 90; and *First Part of the Contention*, 86, 90, 101; and *The True Tragedie*, 86, 90, 101; and the *Chronicles*, 90-91; structure of orations in, 105; conclusion in oration of Gloucester in, 135; consistency in plot development of, 151-152; references to rhetoric in, 239; references to orator in, 243
3 *Henry VI*, Margaret's speech in, 35; rhetorical dialogue in, 40; sophistic rhetoric in, 44; artificial rhetoric in, 51; and *First Part of the Contention*, 86; orations in, 90; and the *Chronicles*, 91-93; structure of orations in, 105; conclusions in orations of, 135; plot development of, 149, 150-152; reference to orators in, 243; mentioned, 40, 55, 101
Henry VIII, speeches of, 130-131, 132; analysis of oration of, 139
Henry VIII, Katherine's speech in, 32; Wolsey's speech in, 35; sophistic rhetoric in, 43, 44; 61; and the *Chronicles*, 99-101; structure of orations in, 109-110; and the demonstrative orations, 115; and the deliberative oration, 116; and the introduction in the speech of Gloucester, 134; setting of orations in, 159-161
Herder, von, Johann Gottfried, 230
Hermione, speeches of, 33, 110, 131-132, 133, 137, 143-144, 162
Herrick, Marvin, vii, 218, 219, 221, 223, 232
Heywood, John, and the interlude, 169
History plays, number of orations in, 72
Homer, epics of, 6; plot action of, 11; and the *Iliad*, 7, 11, 82-83

Horace, 12, 13, 20, 200
Humanism, introduction of, in England, 198 ff.
Hurd, Richard, 228-229
Hystorie of Hamblet and *Hamlet*, 80-81

Iachimo, oration of, 110
Imperio Gnaei Pompeii Oratio, De, analysis of, 127-128
Imagery, art of, and ancient poetic, 11-12
Institutes of Oratory, 119
Integration, dramatic, in Shakespeare's plays, 148 ff.
Introductions, in Shakespearean orations, 129-132, 133-134
Iphigenie en Aulide, 47
Isabella, speeches of, 33, 79-80, 134, 137, 142-143
Isocrates, orations of, 9, 121-126, 136, 200, 206
Italians, drama of, 20-21, 169-170

Jacob and Esau, 174
James IV, oration of divine in, 35, 175-176; oration of lawyer in, 176-177
Jocasta, 28
Johnson, Dr. Samuel, 48, 227-228
Jonson, Ben, and *Sejanus*, 191-193; and *Poetaster*, 194-195; and *Discoveries*, 218; mentioned, 21, 48, 170, 182, 217, 223
Julius Caesar, funeral orations in, 35; declamation in, 43; psychological analysis in, 57-58; structure of orations in, 106-107; quality of orations in, 112; Antony's speech in, 136; dramatic integration of, 154; setting of orations in, 161; references to rhetoric in, 240; reference to orations in, 244

Kate, speech of, 29
Katherine, speeches of, 32, 99-100, 110

Kemp, William, 203
King John, sophistic rhetoric in, 40, 52-53; speeches of Constance in, 52; and *The Troublesome Raigne of John*, 94-95; structure of orations in, 105; the deliberative oration in, 115; and introduction in speech of Citizen, 134, 136; unity of plot of, 152; dramatic action of, 156; and speech of Philip, 213
King Lear, role of, 59
King Lear, emotional rhetoric in, 43; psychological analysis in, 59; absence of orations in, 72
Knox, John, 168
Kyd, Thomas, and *Ur-Hamlet* tragedy, 81; mentioned, 170

Lady Macbeth, role of, 59-60
La Pucelle, speeches of, 104-105, 135, 145, 151
Latimer, Hugh, 168, 200
Laurence, Friar, speech of, 79
Lessing, Gotthold, and *Hamburgische Dramaturgie*, 229
Life of Alcibiades, 85
Life of Brutus, 82
Life of Julius Caesar, 82
Lily, William, 199, 200
Linacre, Thomas, 198, 220
Livy, 200
Lodge, Thomas, and *Wounds of Civil War*, 35; mentioned, 168, 170, 217
Love's Labour's Lost, sophistic rhetoric in, 41; Biron's speeches in, 54; and *Arte of Rhetorique*, 77; conclusion in speech of Biron in, dramatic integration of, 152-153; chronology of, 164; and Elizabethan educational methods, 207 ff.; speech of king in, 208; reference to rhetoric in, 234-236; critical viewpoint in, 247
Lucan, Marcus Annaeus, 200
Lully, Jean-Baptiste, 46, 47
Lyly, John, and *Euphues and His England*, 98; and Elizabethan prose, 167; mentioned, 168, 170, 174
Lysias, speech of, 122

Macbeth, role of, 59-60
Macbeth, emotional rhetoric in, 43; psychological analysis in, 59-60; absence of orations in, 72
Mair, G. H., and *Arte of Rhetorique*, 83; mentioned, 211
Margaret, speeches of, 51-52, 93, 145-146
Marlowe, Christopher, and *Tamburlaine*, 32; and poetic of Elizabethan drama, 155-156; mentioned, 40, 170, 174
Marston, John, 182
Massinger, Philip, and *Duke of Milan*, 33, 189-191; and *Roman Actor*, 33; mentioned, 171, 182, 195
Measure for Measure, speech of Isabella in, 33, 74; sophistic rhetoric in, 43; number of orations in, 72; setting of orations in, 74; structure of orations in, 106; forensic achievements in, 108; introduction in speech of, references to rhetoric in, 237-238
Menaechmi, 77
Merchant of Venice, speeches of suitors in, 42; structure of orations in, 106, 107; quality of orations in, 112; and the forensic oration, 113; dramatic integration of, 153-154; setting of speeches in, 161; references to rhetoric in, 237; references to orations in, 242
Merry Wives of Windsor, 213
Metamorphoses, of Ovid, 203
Metastasio, P. T., 47
Metcalf, J. C., viii
Midsummer Night's Dream, speeches of compared with those in *Richard III*, 42; emotional rhetoric in, 54; "passionate words" in 55; references to rhetoric in, 237

Milton, John, 225
Minturno, and the new poetic, 21; and *De Poeta*, 22
Misfortunes of Arthur, 28
Mob, and the oration, 162-163
"Monk's Tale," 220
Moor of Venice, and Cinthio's *Hecatommithi*, 81
Much Ado About Nothing, emotional rhetoric in, 42; sophistic rhetoric in, 55; and Bandello, 79; structure of orations in, 106; speech of friar in, 136; dramatic integration of, 154

Neander and Dryden, 227
Neilson, W. A., on chronology of Shakespeare's plays, 164; and *Facts about Shakespeare*, 65 (with A. H. Thorndike)
Nice Wanton, 173
Nostromo, 37-39

Observations on Poetry, 228
Odyssey, 7, 11
Offices and Orations, 203
Oration, definition of, 29-36; classes of, 31 ff.; expository, 65; classification of, 63 ff., 66-71; structure of, 103 ff.; deliberative, 31-32, 64, 74, 112; demonstrative, 34-35, 65, 72, 74, 112, 114-115; epideictic, 34-35, 33-36, 64, 65; forensic, 32-33, 65, 74, 112, 113-114; judicial, 32-33, 64, 65, 112; occasional, 34-35, 65, 72, 74, 112
Orator, Silvayn's, and Shylock, 78-79
Oratore, De, of Cicero, 117-119
Oratory, pulpit, 35-36
Orfeo, 46
Othello, speeches in, 8, 31; and declamation, 43; psychological analysis in, 58; number of orations in, 72; forensic achievements in, 108; and the forensic oration, 113; speech of, quoted, 129-130, 132; oration of Othello in, 33, 137; dramatic integration of, 154; setting of speeches in, 161. See Cinthio; *Hecatommithi*
Ovid, 12, 203

Painter, William, and *Palace of Pleasure*, 79
Palace of Pleasure, 79
Palestrina, and church music, 45
Pandarus, speech of, 220
Pandosto, 82
Pandulph, speech of, 95
Panegyrikos, analysis of, 124-125
Paradise, 84, note 31
Paradise Lost, 7
Paris, speech of, 179-182
Patay, battle of, 89
Patrizzi, Francesco, 21
Paulina, speech of, 135, 238
Peele, George, and *Arraignment of Paris*, 33, 179-182; and *David and Bethsabe*, 33; mentioned, 170, 174
Pemberton, Henry, and *Observations on Poetry*, 228
Pericles, role of, 56
Pericles, rhetoric in, 43, 44, 55; as rhetorical drama, 55-56
Perkin Warbeck, orations in, 32, 193-194
Philip, speeches of, 52, 213
Piramo et Tisbe, 46
Plato, 9, 200, 221
Plautine Comedy, 170
Plautus, and *Comedy of Errors*, 77; and Elizabethan education, 200
Plutarch, his *Julius Caesar* and Shakespeare's *Julius Caesar*, 82; and *Life of Alcibiades*, 85; and *Timon of Athens*, 85; and Coriolanus, 86; and Elizabethan education, 200
Poeta, De, 22
Poetaster, examples of orations in, 194-195
Poetic, medieval, 13-14
Poetics, of Aristotle, 3 ff.; and Renaissance criticism, 21; history

of, 218 ff.; and Shakespeare, 221 ff.; revival of interest in, 232
Poetics of Aristotle, Its Meaning and Influence, The, 232
Poetics, of Vida, and Renaissance criticism, 20
Poetry, defended by Renaissance critics, 22
Politian, 219
Praise of Folly, 198
Pro Milone Oratio, analysis of, 126-127
Promos and Cassandra, and *Measure for Measure*, 80
Protagoras, and sophistic rhetoric, 9
Prospero, speech of, 110-111
Puttenham, George, 21, 217

Quintilian, and sophistic rhetoric, 9; on classification of orations, 64; and deliberative oration, 65; on structure of the oration, 119-121; and *Institutes of Oratory*, 119; mentioned, 147, 200, 205, 206

Raigne of King Edward the Third, 35
Renaissance, and literary criticism, 18 ff.
Rhetoric, medieval, 14-15
Rhetoric, of Aristotle, quoted, 63
Rhetorical conversation, definition of, 28-29
Richard, role of, 53; conclusion in oration of, 135
Richard II, sophistic rhetoric in, 41, 53; speech of Gaunt in, 53; and the *Chronicles*, 95-96; structure of orations in, 105-106; setting of orations in, 158-159; and Aristotle's *Poetics*, 223
Richard III, and orations before the soldiers, 35; rhetoric in, 40, 42, 44, 51-52, 55; and the *Chronicles*, 93-94; structure of orations in, 105; and the demonstrative oration, 114; conclusion in oration of Richmond in, 135; conclusion in oration of Richard in, 135; plot of, 152; and Sophoclean tragedy, 156; quoted, 214; references to rhetoric in, 239-240; references to oratory in, 243-244
Richmond, conclusion in oration of, 135; structure of oration of, 135
Romance, and Renaissance critics, 21
Roman Actor, 33
Romans, rhetoric of, 9-10
Romeo and Juliet, lyric speeches in, 42-43; declamatory rhetoric in, 56-57; Friar's speech in, 136; chronology of, 164; plot of, 247
Romeus and Juliet, 79
Ronsard, Pierre de, 21

Saint Augustine, 15
St. Paul's School, 199
Savonarola, and *De Scientiis*, 22
Sallust, 200
Samson Agonistes, 225
Scaliger, 21
Scarlatti, Alessandro, and opera, 46; and drama, 47
Schiller, 230
Schlegel, A. W., and *Vorlesungen über Dramatische Kunst und Literatur*, 230
Scholemaster, 200, 204-205
Schoene Phoenicia, Die, 79
School of Abuse, 22
Scientiis, De, 22
"Sea Dreams," 37
"Second Sophistic," 10
Sejanus, examples of orations in, 191-193
Seneca, 10, 12, 41, 47, 51, 58, 73, 105, 149, 150, 156, 170, 174, 182, 200
Setting, of orations in Shakespeare's plays, 157-162
Sforza, speech of, 189 ff.
Shirley, James, 171

Index 269

Shylock, speech of, 135-136, 137, 141
Sidney, Sir Philip, and the new poetic, 21; and the *Apology for Poetry*, 22, 221; and Elizabethan prose, 168; and progress of poetry in England, 217
Soliloquy, definition of, 28
Sophists, rhetoric of, 9
Sophistic Rhetoric, development of, 8 ff.
Sophocles, tragedies of, 6; speech of Oedipus in, 7; plot action in plays of, 11
Sources, of Shakespeare's orations, 75-102; table of, 76, 87-88
Sturm, Johannes, course of study in school of, 203-204
Style, imagery of, 11-12; emphasis on after Aristotle, 12-13

Talbot, speech of, 40, 51
Tamburlaine, and deliberative oration, 32; quoted, 177-179
Taming of the Shrew, Kate's speech in, 29; sophistic rhetoric in, 55; quoted, 213
Tamora, speech of, 74-75; role of, 149-150
Tennyson, Alfred, 37
Terence, 200
Thorndike, A. H., vii. See Neilson
Timon of Athens, speech of Alcibiades in, 33; sophistic rhetoric in, 43, 44; number of orations in, 72; and *Life of Alcibiades*, 85; forensic achievements in, 108
Tito Andronico and *Titus Andronicus*, 77-78
Titus Andronicus, role of, 40, 41; speech of, 51
Titus Andronicus, sophistic rhetoric in, 40-41, 44, 54, 55; use of traditional lament in, 51; speech of Tamora in, 74-75, 149, 150; structure of orations in, 105; plot development of, 149-150; and Sophoclean tragedy, 156; chronology of, 164; quoted, 214; reference to orators in, 244; plot of, 247
Tom Thumb, 228
Tourneur, Cyril, 182
Tractatus Coislianus, 233
Tragedies, number of orations in Shakespearean, 72; psychological studies in Shakespearean, 57
Tragedy of Charles Duke of Byron, orations in, 182-189
Tragedy, Sophoclean, 156
Trissino, G. G., and Renaissance criticism, 20
Troilus and Cressida, rhetoric in, 28, 43, 55; number of orations in, 72; and the *Iliad*, 82-83; structure of orations in, 107; and the demonstrative oration, 115; references to rhetoric in, 237
Troublesome Raigne of John, The, 94-95
True Tragedie, The, 86, 90, 101
Tudor Drama, The, quotation from, 196
"Tullie," Wilson on, 129
Twelfth Night, speeches in compared with those in *As You Like It*, 42; rhetoric in, 54, 55; references to rhetorical terms in, 245
Two Gentlemen of Verona, sophistic rhetoric in, 41; speeches of lovers in, 54; quoted, 212

Ulysses, speech of, 130, 132, 141-142; psychological and philosophical approach in oration of, 136; analysis of oration of, 139
Upton, John, and *Critical Observations of Shakespeare*, 229
Ur-Hamlet, 81

Valla, Giorgio, 219
Vergil, 20, 200, 203
Vida, *Poetics* of, and Renaissance criticism, 20
Volumnia, conclusion in speech of, 135
Vulgari Eloquio, De, 15-16

Webbe, William, 217
Webster, John and the *White Devil*, 195
Whetstone, George, and *Promos and Cassandra*, 80
White Devil, 195
Wilson, James Southall, viii
Wilson, Thomas, and the *Arte of Rhetorique*, 21, 30, 64-65, 77, 83-84, 128-129, 147, 205, 207, 209, 210-213, 218
Winter's Tale, The, speeches of Hermione in, 31, 44, 110, 162; speech of Leontes in, 44; sophistic rhetoric in, 44; construction of, 56; and Pandosto, 82; quality of orations in, 112; and the forensic oration, 113-114; conclusion in oration of, 135; dramatic integration of, 154-155; setting of speeches in, 161; references to rhetoric in, 238
Women, Shakespeare's portrayal of, 50
Worcester, speech of, 96-97, 134
Wounds of Civil War, 35

Xenophon, 200

www.ingramcontent.com/pod-product-compliance
Lightning Source LLC
Chambersburg PA
CBHW021120300426
44113CB00006B/229